A Hemisphere
to Itself

A Hemisphere to Itself

A History of US–Latin American Relations

Frank Niess

with assistance from
Béatrice Mandeau
Gudrun Fienemann

Translated by Harry Drost

Zed Books Ltd
London and New Jersey

A Hemisphere to Itself was first published in German
under the title *Der Koloss im Norden* (The Colossus in
the North) by Pahl-Rugenstein Verlag GmbH Köln in 1986.
First published in English by Zed Books Ltd, 57 Caledonian
Road, London N1 9BU, UK and 171 First Avenue, Atlantic
Highlands, New Jersey 07716, in 1990.

Copyright © Pahl-Rugenstein Verlag, 1984, 1986.
Translation copyright © Harry Drost, 1990.

Cover designed by Sophie Buchet.
Typography by Keith Addison.
Printed and bound in the United Kingdom
by Biddles Ltd, Guildford and King's Lynn.

British Library Cataloguing in Publication Data

Niess, Frank
    A hemisphere to itself : a history of US–Latin American relations.
    1. United States. Latin America. Foreign relations, history
    I. Title II. Mandeau, Béatrice III. Fienemann, Gudrun IV.
    [Koloss im Norden. *English*].
    327.098

    ISBN 0-86232-866-7
    ISBN 0-86232-867-5 Pbk

Library of Congress Cataloging-in-Publication Data

Niess, Frank, 1942–
        (Koloss im Norden. English)
        A hemisphere to itself : a history of US–Latin American relations
    / Frank Niess ; translated by Harry Drost.
            p.   cm.
        Translation of : Der Koloss im Norden.
        Includes bibliographical references.
        ISBN 0–86232–866–7. — ISBN 0–86232–867–5 (pbk.)
        1. Latin America—Relations—United States. 2. United States—
    Relations—Latin America. I. Title.
    F1418.N4813   1990
    303.48'27308—dc20   89–18272
                                                           CIP

This book is dedicated to
Pablo Neruda, José Martí, Victor Jara
and all those who have suffered under
the Colossus of the North.

Contents

Tables

Maps

Preface

What contemporary historians and political analysts formally and euphemistically call the 'asymmetry of power' between the United States and Latin America has been described more graphically by earlier generations. The Cuban poet and freedom fighter José Martí referred to the United States as *el coloso del norte*, the Colossus of the North, to highlight the political burden and the economic pressures with which the United States encumbers Latin America.

Over the years much has been written, particularly by Americans, about the turbulent relationship between the unequal neighbours. Most studies, however, devote little or no attention to an analysis of the relationship as a variation of the conflict between the industrialized North and the developing South. This book starts from that premise.

As part of my research I visited the Library of Congress in Washington on various occasions to peruse its ample source materials on the never-ending quarrels between the United States and Latin America. After some time a librarian took an interest in my work and asked me about the scope of the book. When I told him, he exclaimed, 'That must be a horror story!' And indeed it is. Over the last 200 years the Americans have resorted to all available means, no matter how reprehensible, to further their economic and political interests in the south. They engaged in ideological tutelage, violations of international law, diplomatic intrigues, covert intelligence work, economic reprisals and direct military intervention. Relations as among equals have been the exception, not the rule, in this horror story.

Because of this 'asymmetry of power', this book must also be one-sided. The exposition cannot be value-free, because the subject matter is not; it is partial because in the reciprocal relationship between the two Americas almost invariably only one side profited, while the other suffered. I have deliberately analysed this relationship primarily from the US perspective, because the structures of dependence, underdevelopment and oppression are brought to light more clearly in this way.

This study relies on scientific research and methods. But to make it accessible to the widest possible audience, it has not been written in an academic style. Nor does it claim to be comprehensive. The experts will point to huge omissions in the eight chapters that follow, but giving equal treatment to all the incidents and developments mentioned only in passing would require not one book but many. This study aims no more and no less than to provide an initial overview of the history of US Latin American policy since the days of Monroe.

I would like to thank the librarians and other staff at the Library of Congress in Washington, the Library of the Organization of American States in Washington, the Dag Hammarskjöld Library of the United Nations in New York, the library of the Lateinamerika Institut in Berlin, the library of the Centro de Información y Documentación Tercer Mondo (CIDOB-TM) in Barcelona, the university library at Heidelberg, and the library of the German-American Institute in Heidelberg.

I would also like to thank Chris and Martin Kronauer and Christoph Niess for their many helpful comments and suggestions. And above all I would like to thank Béatrice Mandeau and Gudrun Fienemann for their invaluable assistance and moral support in the preparation of this book.

Frank Niess

Acronyms and Abbreviations

ADELA	Atlantic Community Development Group for Latin America
AEI	American Enterprise Institute
AID	Agency for International Development
AIFLD	American Institute for Free Labor Development
ALALC/LAFTA	Latin American Free Trade Association
ARDE	Revolutionary Democratic Alliance
CBI	Caribbean Basin Initiative
CECLA	Special Commission for Latin American Coordination
CEPAL/ECLA	Economic Commission for Latin America
CIAP	Inter-American Committee for the Alliance of Progress
CIAS	Council for Inter-American Security
CIDOB-TM	Centro de Información y Documentación Tercer Mondo
CODELCO	Chilean Copper Corporation
CONDECA	Central American Defense Council
CSIS	Center for Strategic and International Studies
FDN	Nicaraguan Democratic Forces
FEAC	Inter-American Financial and Economic Advisory Committee
FMLN	Farabundo Martí National Liberation Front
FSLN	Sandinista National Liberation Front
GATT	General Agreement on Tariffs and Trade
IADB	Inter-American Defense Board
IA-ECOSOC	Inter-American Economic and Social Council
IDB	Inter-American Development Bank
IIAA	Institute for Inter-American Affairs
IMF	International Monetary Fund
ITT	International Telephone and Telegraph Corporation
MCC/CACM	Central American Common Market
NAM	National Association of Manufacturers
NJM	New Jewel Movement
OAS/OEA	Organization of American States
OECS	Organization of Eastern Caribbean States

OIAA	Office of the Coordination of Inter-American Affairs
OPEC	Organization of Petroleum Exporting Countries
PNP	People's National Party
SELA	Latin American Economic System
SNOIA	National Sugar Workers' Union
STPRM	Union of the Oil Workers of the Mexican Republic
UP	Popular Unity
URNG	Guatemalan National Revolutionary Unity

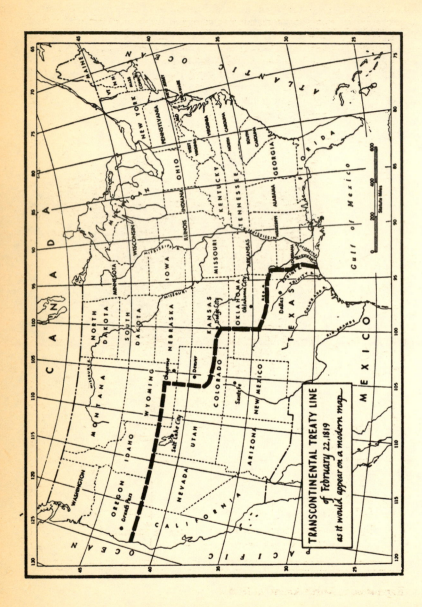

TRANSCONTINENTAL TREATY LINE
of February 22, 1819
as it would appear on a modern map

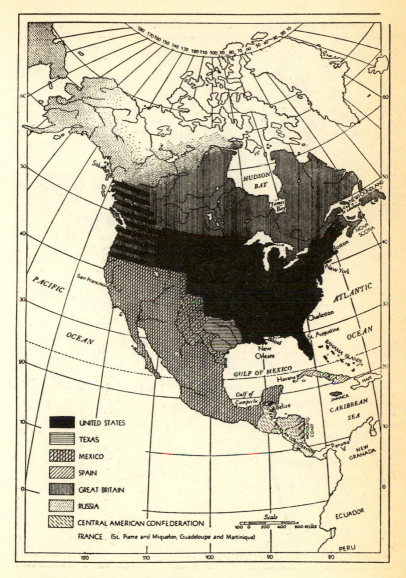

Expansion in North America, 1836

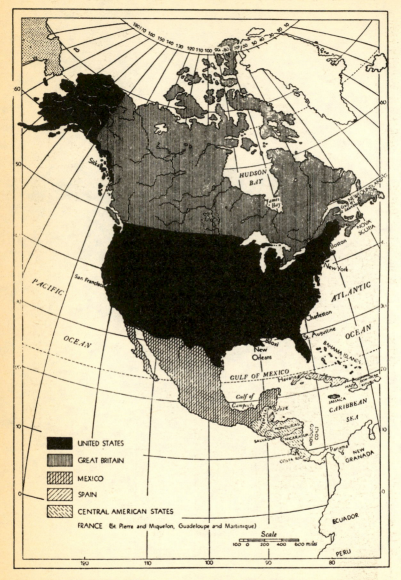

UNITED STATES

GREAT BRITAIN

MEXICO

SPAIN

CENTRAL AMERICAN STATES

FRANCE (St Pierre and Miquelon, Guadeloupe and Martinique)

Scale

100 0   200   400   600 miles

The United States in 1868

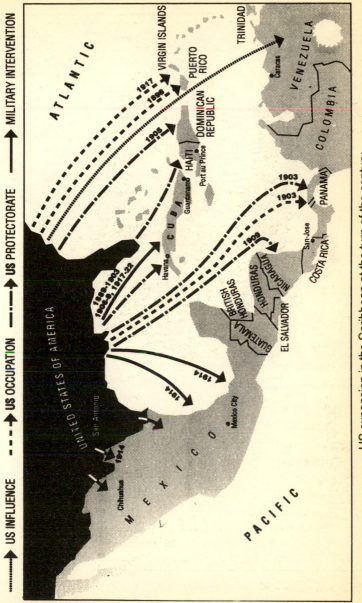

US expansion in the Caribbean at the turn of the century

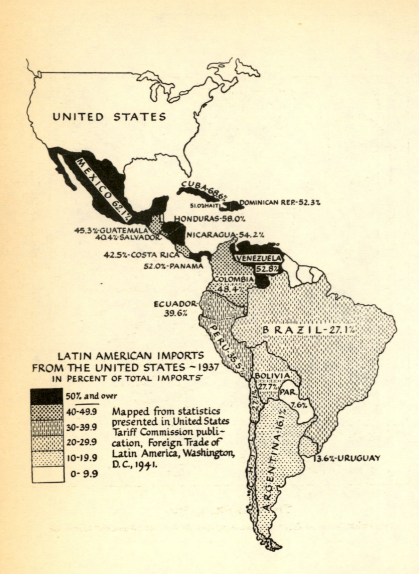

UNITED STATES

MEXICO 62.1%

CUBA-68.6%
51.0%HAITI
DOMINICAN REP.-52.3%
HONDURAS-58.0%
45.3%-GUATEMALA
40.4%-SALVADOR
NICARAGUA-54.2%
42.5%-COSTA RICA
52.0%-PANAMA
VENEZUELA 52.8%
COLOMBIA 48.4%
ECUADOR- 39.6%
B R A Z I L - 27.1%
PERU-35.5%
BOLIVIA 27.7%
PAR. 7.6%
13.6%-URUGUAY
ARGENTINA-16.1%
CHILE-27.1%

LATIN AMERICAN IMPORTS
FROM THE UNITED STATES ~1937
IN PERCENT OF TOTAL IMPORTS

50% and over
40-49.9
30-39.9   Mapped from statistics
20-29.9   presented in United States
10-19.9   Tariff Commission publi-
0- 9.9   cation, Foreign Trade of
               Latin America, Washington,
               D.C., 1941.

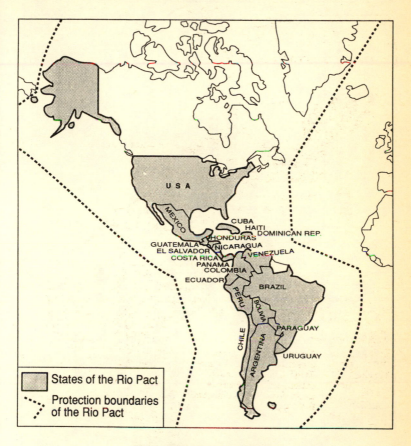

The Rio Pact, 1947.

(Heinrich von Siegler, Die Zusammenschlüsse und Pakte der Welt, Bonn/Wien/Zürich 1958, S. 20)

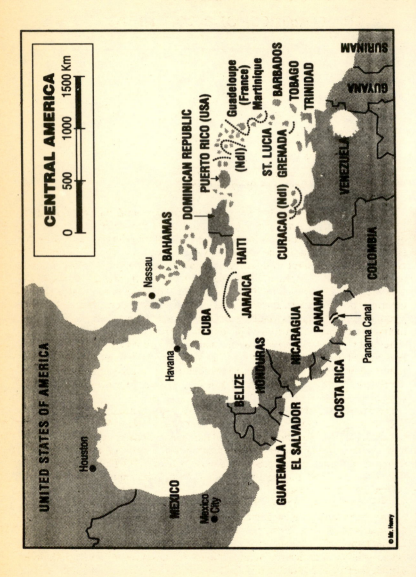

1. Westward movement: the conquest of a continent

The expansionist ideas of the founding fathers

The expansion of the United States southwards, beyond the Rio Grande to Mexico, the Central American isthmus and South America, was foreshadowed during the transformation of the former British colonies into a constitutionally strong federal republic by the leaders of the American Revolution. Rhetorically, at least, the politicians of the day occasionally felt the *Drang nach Süden*, the push toward the south. Disproving the myth of the founding fathers, weary of the diplomatic machinations, political immorality and wars of the old world, as determined isolationists, the first policy-makers of the new United States — Thomas Jefferson, James Madison and most others — cast an interested eye on their surroundings. They looked beyond the narrow confines of the original 13 states in a way that suggested that they had no intention of committing their new republic to territorial and political self-restraint for all time. The earliest expansionist desires of America's politicians focused on the island virtually on its doorstep — Cuba, the 'pearl of the Antilles', and a possession of a Spanish empire in decline.

The push to the south seemed natural enough, for historically the Americans had strong trade links with the Caribbean. From the seventeenth century onwards, New England merchants plied the region (in defiance of strict prohibitions by the mother country, which wanted to maintain its trade monopoly) selling semi-manufactured products, fish and slaves to the French, Spanish and British islands, and buying sugar and molasses to supply the innumerable flourishing distilleries scattered along the 1,000-mile coast from Maine to Georgia. The sale of rum in turn allowed them to buy 'black ivory', African slaves. Nearly every port in New England and nearly every merchant family — the Livingstones of New York, the Browns of Providence, the Dickensons of Philadelphia, and the agencies of Peter Faneuil of Boston and Richard Derby of Salem — in the American colonies profited from this three-cornered trade. With neither the British nor the Spanish colonial authorities able to put a stop to it, the enterprising merchants from New York and Boston had established a monopoly of trade with the Antilles by the middle of the eighteenth century. This initially illicit colonial trade marked the beginning of the history of inter-American relations. Once independent, the United States proceeded to send consular agents to southern commercial centres to facilitate the merchants' business transactions. One of the first of these agents was sent to Havana, the capital of Cuba.

So American fantasies of expansion southwards had a very real material basis, a thick web of economic interests. Moreover, since at this time the transport routes from north to south were much better developed than the east–west links across the continent, the Antilles were also nearer geographically than the expanse beyond the Appalachians. Accordingly, Benjamin Franklin in 1761 suggested Cuba and Mexico as goals of American expansion, and expressed the hope that one day the 'Spanish lake', the Caribbean, would become American.[1] Alexander Hamilton, writing in *The Federalist* in 1787, set forth how this might be done: in his view a small navy would enable the United States to hold the balance of power between the rival European colonial powers; once established as a naval power, if only a modest one, the United States would in due course be in a position to control economic and political events in the 'American Mediterranean'.[2] And John Quincy Adams called Cuba, which to him seemed simply an appendage to the Florida coast, 'the ripening apple which cannot choose but fall to the ground', destined one day to be absorbed into the union.[3]

Even at this time, only a few years after the foundation of the United States, some Americans looked far beyond the frontiers of the American Mediterranean. Thomas Jefferson and Henry Clay, for instance, the earliest influential advocates of the 'western hemisphere idea' and without doubt among the first American expansionists, envisaged an inter-American system with the United States at its hub. In 1786, three years after the Treaty of Paris and three years before the adoption of the federal constitution, Jefferson declared that 'Our confederation must be viewed as the nest, from which all America, north and south, is to be populated'; and in 1813 he wrote to his friend Alexander von Humboldt that 'America has a hemisphere to itself', a pithy statement anticipating Monroe's formal warning to the Europeans to keep out of America's back yard.[4] Clay, one of the most articulate advocates of the burgeoning 'American system', who would later serve as John Quincy Adams' secretary of state, predicted in 1818 that the governments of the new Latin American countries 'will be animated by an American feeling and guided by an American policy. They will obey the laws of the system of the new world', that is, the laws and regulations laid down by the United States in its constitution and policies.[5]

Even before the Latin Americans rebelled against the Spanish and Portuguese crowns, many Americans employed a rhetoric predicated on the incorporation of the southern continent into a US commonwealth of nations. In proposing the expansion southwards, whether in the form of annexations or peaceful economic co-operation, US politicians were motivated not simply by greed and a lust for power. Jefferson and Madison, for instance, advocated the push to the south because they were convinced that the new union could never thrive in commercial and continental isolation, but only by reaching far beyond its own frontiers.

The older political theory, according to which a republic had to be small and its workings transparent and accessible to assure peace and prosperity, was turned into its opposite. Recast in economic terms, this consensus held that the republic needed external markets as a valve for its own internal conflicts. This was revived 80 years later, when it was argued that a social revolution would consume the country unless it found markets for its surplus products. In any case, it is clear that the epigones of the expansionists Jefferson and Clay were not the first to proclaim the concept of an American empire. That concept, and the main outlines of the empire's future growth, was fully developed by the end of the eighteenth century. And one way or another, Latin America would be part of that empire.

The Louisiana Purchase

For the time being, however, America's politicians had to shelve their designs on Spain's colonial empire. They had more urgent matters to attend to closer to home, such as satisfying the settlers' hunger for land, not just in the fertile region between the Appalachians and the Mississippi, but also in the immense French and Spanish territories beyond the Mississippi. Furthermore, before they could consider extending their influence southwards they had to secure and improve the new union's access to the world markets. In particular, they had to find an outlet for the western territories, which from 1790 onwards began to produce large quantities of tobacco, wheat and cotton.

For most western farmers the Mississippi river provided the quickest transport route to the port of New Orleans. But this gateway to the world was controlled by a foreign power, Spain. Although the Spanish government gave the Americans free navigation of the Mississippi and confirmed the right of deposit for their goods awaiting trans-shipment to ocean-going vessels in the Treaty of San Lorenzo of 27 October 1795 (also known as Pinckney's Treaty), this was not enough for the Americans, who disliked, with good reason, still being at the mercy of arbitrary decisions by individual officials. The unilateral repeal of the right of deposit by the governor of New Orleans in October 1802 caused great consternation, not assuaged by its restoration in April of the following year, and brought home to the federal government the extent to which the fate of the western territories depended on the good will of the colonial powers — which were also America's chief competitors for raw materials and market shares.

The Americans sought a general and lasting solution to the problem. This must have seemed even more intractable after Spain, which had acquired New Orleans and Louisiana from France in the 1762 Treaty of Fontainebleau, returned this area to France by the secret Treaty of San Ildefonso, signed on 1 October 1800. The retrocession, confirmed in the Treaty of Madrid, signed on 21 March 1801, greatly alarmed the Jefferson administration, not least because little good could be expected of Napoleon Bonaparte's imperialist desire to revive the French colonial empire in North America. In this critical situation the administration reiterated the right of the United States to free trade and navigation, and informed its Spanish and French counterparts that the country's vital interests required possession of the port of New Orleans and both East and West Florida. (Regarding the latter, the aim was not territorial expansion as such, but control over the other main rivers apart from the Mississippi which flowed into the Gulf of Mexico, the Mobile and the Apalachicola.) As a precautionary measure, just in case the two governments would prove unwilling to come to an amicable settlement, the administration also publicly announced the annexation of the territories in question.

On 18 April 1802, President Jefferson instructed the US ambassador in Paris, Robert R. Livingston, to negotiate with France for a tract of land on the lower Mississippi for use as a port or, failing that, to obtain an irrevocable guarantee of free navigation and the right of deposit. To give weight to the American claims, James Monroe was sent to Paris as a special envoy in January 1803 with a congressional appropriation of $2 million (an amount which he was authorized to raise to $10 million if need be). But even before Monroe arrived in France, Napoleon had abandoned his ambitious scheme for a colonial empire. The attempt to found a Caribbean empire, centred on Haiti, had already cost 25,000 lives, and rather than continue to pay for the suppression of the slave revolt in the Antilles and the defence of Louisiana, the emperor decided to grant independence to Haiti and to sell French North America.

When Monroe and Livingston sealed the bargain with the French finance minister, François de Barbé-Marbois, on 30 April 1803, the United States had made an excellent deal. With the Louisiana Purchase, approved by the Senate on 20 October, the United States obtained a huge territory of around 828,000 square miles between the Mississippi and the Rocky Mountains for a knockdown price of $15 million or 60 million francs. With one blow it doubled its area, with the future states of Arkansas, Iowa, Louisiana (most importantly, with the port of New Orleans), Missouri, Nebraska and South Dakota, major parts of Kansas, Montana, North Dakota, Oklahoma, Wyoming and parts of Colorado and Minnesota all becoming part of the union.

The only disadvantage of this otherwise very generous treaty was the omission of the negotiators to define clearly whether West Florida, the area between the Mississippi and Perdido rivers, was included in the area sold by France. But the Americans, having completed the first stage of their westward expansion, were not unduly perturbed and soon found a way to annex this territory as well. In 1810, southern expansionists led a revolt against Spanish rule and proclaimed the independent republic of West Florida. Two years later, on 14 May 1812, Congress gave its blessing to this aggression by incorporating West Florida into the Mississippi Territory.

The acquisition of Florida

As part of its effort also to gain possession of East Florida, a subdivision of the vice-royalty of New Spain, the Americans continually accused the Spanish of not being in control of their colonial back yard, claiming that their authority extended no further than the ports of Pensacola and Saint Augustine and that they were aiding and abetting criminals, adventurers and runaway slaves in attacks on law-abiding US citizens in the territory. A further major irritant for Americans was the Seminole Indians, who had occupied Fort Apalachicola after the Anglo-American War of 1812 and from there posed a serious threat to the Georgian border. The fort was destroyed by a US expeditionary force in July 1816, but this did not yet secure, in the eyes of the government, the country's south-eastern flank. In the spring of 1818, President Monroe instructed General Andrew Jackson, the regional commander, to pursue 'hostile elements' across the border if necessary. Jackson, who had previously claimed he could conquer Florida within 60 days, saw his chance. He marched into Florida in the spring of 1818 and seized Pensacola at the very moment that the secretary of state, John Quincy Adams, was conducting discussions on a peaceful settlement of the Florida question with the Spanish ambassador, Luis de Onís y González.

Jackson's military success suited Adams. Declaring that the United States had acted in self-defence against the Seminole, he put a simple ultimatum to the Spanish: either maintain order in Florida, or cede it to the United States. Largely because they had their hands full in trying to suppress independence movements in the southern vice-royalties of New Granada and Peru, the Spanish acceded to the US demands. Under the so-called Adams–Onís Treaty, signed in Washington on 22 February 1819, Spain ceded East Florida to the United States for a mere $5 million.

Although the union's coastal frontier had thus been successfully rounded out in the south, the Americans were still far from satisfied. They had already set their sights on the third stage of expansion westward, on Texas and beyond. The fact that the United States had renounced all claims to Texas in the Adams–Onís Treaty did not stop it from resolutely pursuing the annexation of this formerly Spanish and now, since the declaration of independence from Spain in February 1821, Mexican territory.

The annexation of Texas

The Adams–Onís Treaty had also clearly defined the western frontier of the United States with New Spain. It would run along the course of the Sabine River from its mouth on the Gulf of Mexico north, then due north to the Red River, along its course north-west, then due north along the 100th meridian to the Arkansas River, along its course north-west, then due north (along the Rocky Mountains) to the 42nd parallel, and then due west to the Pacific coast. But the ink was barely dry on the treaty when the first voices could be heard bemoaning America's misfortune that it had been denied the territories west of this line. The expansionists especially envied the newly independent Mexicans their posses-sion of Texas, where American cattle farmers and cotton planters had settled. But the territory was of great economic interest not just to them. The New England entrepreneurs and traders wanted to buy cotton for their textile mills and hoped one day to capture new markets for their products there. Entrepreneurs and settlers from the southern states also had their eyes on the fertile Texan expanse. These interests found an articulate advocate in Adams, who did not take seriously the 1819 treaty he had negotiated. In 1823 he wrote that 'The world shall be familiarized with the idea of considering our proper dominion to be the continent of North America'.[6] Here 'the world' meant not just the rival European powers, but also the United States' southern neighbour.

Soon after his election as president, in 1824, Adams began to put pressure on Mexico to persuade it to agree to a 'rectification' of the frontier. Any of the Texan rivers west of the Sabine (the Brazos, Colorado or Nueces) was considered acceptable as a new frontier, but the Rio Grande was already the preferred option. The secretary of state, Henry Clay, was still relatively restrained in his letter of instructions to the US ambassador in Mexico, Joel R. Poinsett, declaring that the administration could accept an offer of possession of the navigable sections of the Red and Arkansas rivers. (As some years earlier, the issue of north–south transport routes was uppermost in Washington's mind.) Poinsett was authorized to offer the Mexicans $1 million.[7] But all proposals were rejected out of hand by the Mexican government.

In August 1829, Poinsett received a similar communication, this time from Clay's successor, Martin Van Buren. He instructed him to try to purchase as much of Texas as possible, and authorized him to pay up to $4 million for the territory. In the same way that Adams had used all his power of persuasion to convince the Spanish colonial government of the disadvantages of holding on to Florida, Van Buren wanted to convince the Mexican government that it would relieve itself of a huge burden by handing Texas over to the United States. In particular he pointed out that the very costly task of keeping the belligerent Comanche, Shawnee, Cherokee and Kickapoo under control, and protecting the white settlers, would then fall to the United States.[8] Although the cash-starved Mexicans may have been tempted by the advances, they again turned down all offers, no doubt because like the Spanish before them they feared American ambitions.

The Mexicans had pursued a liberal immigration policy since 1820, when they had granted a concession to Moses Austin to distribute Texan land to American settlers for colonization. His son Stephen was allowed to continue to act as a 'contractor' (*empresario*). The new arrivals from the north soon raised demands for regional autonomy, to which the Mexican Congress responded by enacting a law on 8 April 1830 prohibiting the introduction of more slaves to Texas and further settlement by immigrants from the United States. The settlers reacted angrily to the closing of the border and the denial of autonomy, and their aggressive tones reverberated in Washington like an ideological echo — one senator, Thomas Brenton, even went so far as to assert that 'the laws of God and nature' had intended the Rio Grande for the United States.[9]

What the US government, Austin and the settlers could not obtain from Mexico willingly, they took by force. A group of settlers led by William B. Travis stormed and seized the garrison of Anahuac on 30 June 1835. Mexico's dictator, President Antonio López de Santa Ana, replied by raising an army of 6,000 men against the Texan rebels. Although he achieved some military successes, his forces were unable to break the Texans, whose resolve was only strengthened by the massacres which he ordered against them — at Goliad, for instance, 300 rebels were executed. In reference to another such massacre, the Texans rallied under the famous slogan 'Remember the Alamo!' In the battle of San Jacinto on 21 April 1836, the Mexican army was decisively defeated and Santa Ana was taken prisoner. Six months later, on 22 October, the Texan settlers proclaimed an independent republic and installed as president their military commander, General Sam Houston.

This idyllic situation did not last long, however. A first attempt to incorporate Texas into the United States — a treaty signed by presidents Tyler and Houston in April 1844 — foundered in the Senate on the resistance of the anti-slavery lobby, which baulked at the idea of allowing another slave state into the union. But in the end economic interests, in particular those of the land speculators, prevailed over the territorial moderation of the abolitionists. The deadlock was broken by the victory of the expansionist James K. Polk over the more cautious Henry Clay in the presidential elections of 1844. By a joint resolution of both houses of Congress, Texas was formally admitted to the union on 1 March 1845.

The war with Mexico

The Mexicans were understandably extremely indignant at this development and refused to accept the loss of such a large part of their territory. Already, in August 1843, President Santa Ana had informed the United States that the Mexican government would consider the incorporation of Texas equivalent to a declaration of war. On 28 March 1845, four weeks after the US Congress had given its blessing to the annexation, the Mexican government broke off diplomatic relations with Washington. At the same time, preparations were set in motion to try to prevent the planned annexation by military means. Thus Mexico's refusal to accept the facts as created by the United States as immutable or even divinely ordained, together with financial disagreements and recurring border disputes, led to war between the two countries in 1846. The Polk administration, which had been intent on war from the beginning, managed elegantly enough to shift the blame for the outbreak of war onto the Mexicans.

On 26 July 1845, US forces led by General Zachary Taylor, the commander in the south-west, marched into Texas and took up position on the southern bank of the Nueces River near Corpus Christi, only 150 miles from the Rio Grande, the 'dream frontier'. With both American and Mexican forces ready for action but still at a distance from each other, President Polk tried once again to obtain land and people by diplomatic means. When the Mexicans showed an interest in resuming diplomatic relations, Polk dispatched John Slidell on a secret mission to Mexico with a blank cheque, as had become customary since the earliest days of the United States' westward expansion. Slidell had instructions to offer the Mexicans sums ranging from $5–30 million, depending on how much land they were prepared to sell. The smaller amount was to be offered for the purchase of New Mexico, the territory outside Texas north of the Rio Grande; the higher amount for California, including San Francisco Bay.

Possession of San Francisco Bay was all-important as far as the Polk administration was concerned. A number of American traders and fishermen had already trickled into this economically increasingly important region — a few hundred whaling ships were based in the bay — in which the British and French were also active. As would emerge subsequently, the Texan border dispute over which the United States went to war with Mexico was actually little more than a diversion. The Americans' real goal lay further west, on the Pacific. This had become clear in President Polk's annual message to Congress on 2 December 1845, when he invoked the Monroe Doctrine and warned Britain and France that the United States could not allow any interference by them on the North American continent.[10] (He used the same occasion to address highly critical remarks to Mexico, apparently not deterred by the effect this might have on Slidell's mission and the prospects of a land purchase.)

Fearful of domestic reaction against even the slightest hint that he would give in to diplomatic pressure from the north, President José Joaquín de Herrera refused even to receive Slidell. Of course, regarding this as a slap in the face, the US administration showed no hesitation in abandoning the diplomatic approach. The day after the report of the complete failure of Slidell's mission reached Washington (13 January 1846), President Polk dispatched orders to General Taylor to march into disputed territory and proceed to the Rio Grande. At the same time he instructed a navy squadron to seize San Francisco Bay and Monterey. Taylor's advance on the Rio Grande had the expected result. After a futile Mexican demand that the Americans evacuate the territory, an armed clash ensued. Although the main battle was fought on the river's south bank on 24 April, the first shot was fired on the north bank. Polk had the trump card he needed to sway Congress. When news of the battle reached Washington he could claim that the Mexicans 'had invaded our territory and shed American blood upon American soil', thus pretending that the US already held a legal title to the areas beyond the Nueces.[11] Congress duly declared war on Mexico on 13 May.

The war lasted just under two years, and ended with the defeat of Mexico and the Treaty of Guadelupe Hidalgo signed on 2 February 1848. Under its terms, Mexico ceded an area of around 850,000 square miles to the United States, thereby losing half its territory, while the United States increased its territory by a fifth. The frontier between the two countries now followed the course of the Rio Grande from its mouth on the Gulf of Mexico north-west to the border of New Mexico, then 200 miles due west and due north to the Gila River, west along its course to the Gila's confluence with the Colorado River, and then due west (along the border of Upper and Lower California) to the Pacific coast. This huge area included the present states of Arizona, California, Nevada, New Mexico and Utah, and part of Colorado and Wyoming. While the Polk administration had been prepared to pay up to $30 million for these territories at the time of the Slidell mission, it now needed to pay only half, $15 million, in compensation to the Mexicans.

Two further acquisitions rounded off the great transcontinental expansion of the United States. As arms were deciding matters further south, a stroke of good fortune enabled the Americans to settle by peaceful means the long-standing dispute with Britain over Oregon in the north-west, with the partition treaty of 15 June 1846 settling the final frontier between the United States and Canada at the 49th parallel. And the Mesilla Valley south of the Gila river in the south-west, the preferred route for a southern railway link to the Pacific, was obtained from Mexico in the so-called Gadsden Purchase of 30 December 1853 at a cost of $15 million, later reduced to $10 million, and a further deterioration in bilateral relations.

Between the Louisiana Purchase in 1803 — which had already turned out to be a more profitable investment than the Americans could have imagined in their wildest expansionist dreams — and the Gadsden Purchase in 1853, the United States had made the best property deals in world history. It had obtained the bulk of its territory for $45 million ($15 million for Louisiana, $5 million for East Florida, $15 million for California and New Mexico, and $10 million for the Mesilla Valley). It had achieved this by following purposeful and aggressive expansionist policies, and not without holding a pistol to the heads of its various negotiating partners — and in the knowledge that everything had its price, even foreign land.

The purchase of the Mesilla Valley did not sate the Americans' hunger for land; on the contrary, it only inspired them to indulge geopolitical fantasies. The acquisition of the new territories focused attention on Central America and the Caribbean. Already under Polk the construction of a canal somewhere in the Central American isthmus to link the Atlantic and the Pacific, had become one of main objectives of US foreign policy. At the time, the sea voyage from New Orleans to San Francisco seemed far less strenuous and dangerous than overland journeys across the Rocky Mountains, and a canal would shorten trade routes and facilitate military movements between the east and west coasts of the United States.

Under the circumstances it was inevitable that the United States would come into conflict with European interests in Central America. This was the case in Nicaragua, for example, one of the projected locations for an interoceanic canal, Nicaragua. In 1848, the British established a protectorate over both the Miskito Indians on the Atlantic coast and the town of San Juan del Norte (which they called Greytown), a strategic location at the mouth of the San Juan River, itself the planned eastern link of the interoceanic canal. The United States did not have the power, specifically the sea power, to pose a serious challenge to the British. Nevertheless, John M. Clayton, the new secretary of state under President Taylor (who had succeeded Polk in 1849), informed the British in 1850 that the the United States would not recognize its protectorate over the Mosquito coast, let alone its hold over the San Juan river. Discussions on this sensitive issue between Clayton and the British ambassador in Washington, Henry Lytton Bulwer, resulted in the so-called Clayton–Bulwer Treaty of 19 April 1850, in which both sides undertook never to attempt to gain sole control over a future interoceanic canal. More generally, they also undertook to refrain from any colonization, occupation or even domination of Central America.

In the light of the then prevailing balance of power between the two countries, the British made more concessions than the Americans in the Clayton–Bulwer

Treaty, which remained in effect until 1901. Even so, it was highly unpopular in the United States, particularly among the anglophobes and the expansionists. For them the US foreign-policy agenda was concerned with *gaining* control, not renouncing it. In their view the treaty also interfered with the objective of acquiring Cuba, the quietly nurtured dream they began to articulate anew from the 1850s onwards. Their argument ran as follows: now that the United States owned the south-west of the North American continent, which was to be linked to the east with a canal through Central America, strategic control over the canal entrance in the Caribbean would have to be secured; and possession of Cuba (which providence had allocated to the United States in any case) would provide the best possible position from which to defend the new strategic interests. In the 1850s, and for some decades afterwards, these grandiose plans had to remain in the realm of fantasy. The expansionists, for whom taking Cuba from the Spanish could not happen soon enough, had to restrain themselves, not least because there was still much to do on the North American continent.

The genocide of the Indians

The acquisition by the United States of all the land between the Atlantic and the Pacific by diplomatic, financial and military means did not of course lead immediately to the integration of these huge expanses into the economic and political framework of the union. It was not until 1890 that the census authorities could declare — to the chagrin of the land- and money-hungry — that 'there can hardly be said to be a frontier line' and that between the mid-west and the west coast there was no more 'unoccupied' land available for white settlement.[12] In the meantime the original inhabitants, the Indians, who had already been expelled from the areas east of the Mississippi, had been decimated because they were in the way of the prospectors, trappers, traders, ranchers, farmers and railway workers.

The white settlers, imbued with a secularized puritanical sense of mission to bring civilization to the New World, regarded it as their solemn duty to eliminate the 'savages'. But it was the settlers, not the Indians, who were shown up as the savages, perhaps most dramatically in their destruction of one of the Great Plains' most valuable resources, the buffalo. The Indians killed only as many buffalo as they needed for survival and used all parts of the animal, even cutting the horns into spoons and cups and weaving the hair into ropes and belts. But the white hunters killed at random (some 3.7 million buffalo were slaughtered between 1872 and 1874 alone), skinned the animal and ate or sold the meat, but left the rest of the carcass to rot. Within the space of a few years the huge buffalo herds, whose numbers had remained stable for centuries, were all but destroyed — as was the livelihood of the plains Indians. The gold- and land-obsessed whites behaved like savages also towards the native inhabitants. The Indians — who at first had innocently offered to share the land with the newcomers, since the Great Spirit had not granted it to anyone as private property — were often shot like rabid dogs.

If the whites ever bothered to justify their actions by arguing that the Indians deserved no better fate because they roamed the countryside like wild animals without developing the land and exploiting its resources, they were lying. For the civilization of the Indians of North America was in large part based on agriculture. Of the 600 tribes which inhabited the continent before the arrival of the Europeans, only a dozen, those of the plains, subsisted on hunting and fishing. The Iroquois of the north-east lived in log cabins (which they had invented, not the trappers) and founded a sophisticated political alliance, the League of Six Nations. The Cherokee, Creek, Seminole and Chickasaw of the south-east lived in settlements protected by stockades, grew crops and built large temples. The Indians of the Great Lakes cultivated 30 different types of vegetable. And the Pueblo and Zuñi farmers of the south-west built complex irrigation systems (destroyed by the incoming whites, who wanted pasturage).

The advance of white settlers into Indian territory was in effect sanctioned by the Northwest Ordinance, adopted by the congress of the newly independent confederation on 13 July 1787. Specifically intended to regulate the administration and political representation of the Northwest Territory, the act also provided the framework for the continental expansion of the United States. Like so many subsequent agreements with the Indians, the ordinance solemnly promised that their land and property would never be taken from them without their permission. At first a semblance of legality was indeed maintained, as the federal government entered into a number of state treaties with the Indian tribes between the Appalachians and the Mississippi in the 1790s and 1800s. But they would not be kept. The government negotiated no less than 387 Indian treaties between 1789 (with the Wyandot, Delaware and others) and 1868 (with the Nez Percé). But the Indian chiefs, often enough drunk with firewater, made their crosses on treaty after treaty only to discover that the whites would break their undertakings shamelessly at the first opportunity. During the Jackson administration, for instance, legal titles to land were renegotiated under coercion on 94 occasions when Indian chiefs refused to yield willingly.

The Indians of the old north-west and the south-east did attempt to resist the whites' encroachment. Having called on all Indians to defend their ancestral land rights, the Shawnee chief Tecumseh in the autumn of 1811 was able to form a tribal alliance opposed to further white settlement. The white settlers were highly suspicious of even this essentially defensive move and persuaded the territorial governor, William Henry Harrison, to act. With 1,000 men he marched on Tecumseh's headquarters on the Tippecanoe river. In the ensuing battle, the white forces suffered heavy losses, but nevertheless claimed a great victory. Although not decisive, the defeat at the Tippecanoe was a serious setback for the Shawnee because they lost their headquarters (which Harrison ordered to be razed to the ground) and food supplies. It also put great strain on the already fairly loose tribal alliance. Its power, and with it that of the Indians of the old north-west, was finally broken two years later, with the defeat of the Shawnee and the death of Tecumseh in the battle of the Thames on 5 October 1813. The success in the old north-west was then repeated in the south-east by General Jackson, whose forces defeated the Creek in Alabama in 1814 and the Seminole in Florida in 1818. This broke Indian resistance and opened up white settlement of Georgia, Alabama and Tennessee.

Once the Indians had been defeated, decimated and demoralized, the whites could put long-cherished plans into effect. Much earlier, influential politicians had agreed among themselves on the eventual expulsion of the 'redskins' from the territories reserved for them between the Appalachians and the Mississippi. A plan referred to with some understatement as the 'removal policy' was drawn up by John C. Calhoun, the secretary of war, in 1823 and announced by President Monroe in 1825. President Jackson — whom the Indians knew from his army days as the butcher of the Seminole and called 'Sharp Knife' — prepared to put the policy into operation immediately upon taking office in 1829. In his inaugural address he still promised the Indians 'a just and liberal' policy; but later that year, in his first message on the state of the union, he recommended their wholesale transfer to lands far across the Mississippi, to Kansas and Oklahoma, also unashamedly declaring that 'this emigration should be voluntary'.[13] But the forced exodus of those who had survived the battles and massacres began even before the passage of the Indian Removal Act on 10 March 1830.

The Indians would not be driven westwards like cattle. The Sauk and Fox on the upper Mississippi, for instance, fought against the deportations in the Black Hawk War of 1832, and the Seminole tried to defend themselves in the Second Seminole War of 1835–42. But all resistance was crushed, and a wretched fate awaited the eastern tribes. The Cherokee nation, which had survived more than 100 years of the whites' wars, diseases and whisky, was nearly blotted out during the great removal. On the long winter trek, one of every four Cherokees died from cold, hunger or disease; they called the march their 'trail of tears'. Many other once mighty tribes — including the Choctaw, Chickasaw, Cree and the Seminole in the south, and the surviving remnants of the Shawnee, Miami, Ottawa, Huron and Delaware in the north — had to give up their homelands and walked or travelled by horseback and wagon beyond the Mississippi, 'carrying their shabby goods, their rusty farming tools, and bags of seed corn. All of them arrived as refugees, poor relations, in the country of the proud and free Plains Indians.'[14]

The expelled eastern Indians were not exactly welcomed with open arms by the Plains Indians. Nor were they well served by a Congress decision to set up the Bureau of Indian Affairs to help them to survive in the west. Rather than developing into an office *for* Indian affairs, the bureau increasingly became an office *against* Indian interests, headed by whites who showed little inclination to interpret official policy to the benefit of the Indians (the one exception to this rule being Ely Parker, a Seneca chief, who was however forced to resign in 1871 after only three years in office).

When all land west of the Mississippi, with the exception of Louisiana, Missouri and Arkansas, was declared Indian territory, it should in theory have been closed to white settlement, or at least to the much-maligned traders. But the eternity for which the Mississippi was guaranteed as the 'permanent Indian frontier' proved very short indeed. It lasted until the late 1840s. When rumours spread in the east that huge amounts of gold were to be found in California, thousands of hopeful prospectors and adventurers set off for the south-west. The fertile Oregon territory attracted settlers who wanted to make their fortune as farmers and ranchers. What had been a relative trickle in the 1850s turned into a flood of settlers surging westward after the end of the civil war in 1865. Soon stage coaches, railways and roads traversed the lands allocated to the Indians. Those buffalo and other game which escaped the white hunters' guns migrated elsewhere, thus putting ever greater strain on the Indians' livelihoods.

Initially the Indians accepted, albeit grudgingly and with growing resentment, how the whites systematically broke all the treaties they signed (the 1851 treaty with the Cheyenne, Arapaho, Sioux and Crow providing a notorious example). But when it became clear that their very survival was at stake, they turned to armed resistance. Using hit-and-run guerilla tactics they attacked wagon trains, transport installations, pioneer settlements and, not least, the army's advance posts, like Fort Laramie on the Platte River. Open war broke out in 1861 in Colorado, when the Cheyenne and Arapaho took up arms against large numbers of miners encroaching on their territory. Since they had nothing to set against the army's repeating rifles (introduced in 1860) and the cavalry charges but their cunning, mobility and courage, their desperate struggle was doomed from the beginning. As was that of the Apache and Navaho, who rose against the advancing whites a few years later. The wars ended in 1865 with the Indians' subjugation and their forced removal to reservations, where they were crowded together, refugees in their own country, on infertile land whose meagre harvests could not feed their children. They had to beg for food at the reservation posts, usually receiving only starvation rations. And the whites did everything to humiliate them: one army major made the Apache wear metal tags like dogs.[15]

An attempt by the US army to construct a road from Fort Laramie to Bozeman in Montana sparked off the first war with the Sioux in 1866. It ended two years later with their defeat. So too did the war with the Apache in New Mexico, which began with the massacre of a hundred Indians in Camp Grant in April 1871 and ended with the capture of the Apache leader Geronimo in the autumn of 1886. The Sioux, led by chiefs Sitting Bull and Crazy Horse, launched a second war in 1875–76 to defend the sacred Black Hills against an invasion of whites in violation of the treaty signed with the federal government in 1868. Although they achieved a famous victory over General Custer and his men at the battle of Little Big Horn on 24 June 1876, they also had to accept defeat in the end. In 1877, the Nez Percé, under Chief Joseph, were forced to declare war after whites greedy for land and gold began to invade their territory in violation of an 1873 executive order prohibiting white settlement. They were defeated in October 1877. The massacre of some 300 Sioux women, children and men by the US army at Wounded Knee on 29 December 1890 marked the last act in the tragedy of the Indians.

It was earlier that year that the director of the US census office had declared that the 'frontier' — which had been pushed westward for over two and a half centuries and where enterprising and adventurous whites had sought their fortune — had been extinguished. The great westward expansion across the North American continent was complete. Now the southward expansion could be put on the agenda.

The Monroe Doctrine

The Americans had prepared the ideological ground long before they could set about incorporating the southern continent into their empire, at least as a sphere of influence if not as a formal component. Their firm belief that the United States had been chosen by providence to demonstrate to the world how a true republic, a mature democracy and a thriving economy should function played a major part in these ideological preliminaries — the outstanding symbol of which is of course the Monroe Doctrine of 1823 — to the southward expansion. The Americans' hopes of eventually dominating the western hemisphere were already raised soon after the Latin Americans, led by Simón Bolívar, José de San Martín and others, threw off the Spanish colonial yoke. At this time they still lacked the power to enforce their domination of the emerging southern countries. Nor did there exist, a few years after the acquisition of Florida and 70 years before the disappearance of the western frontier, any significant economic pressure to reach out to the south. But the US politicians decided nevertheless, as a precautionary measure, to extend their claims of continental hegemony over Central and South America as well.

The Monroe Doctrine, the geopolitical principle of 'hands off the Americas', warned the European powers against any interventions in Latin America and at the same sought to elevate a protective US umbrella over that continent to the level of international law. It is as illustrative of American foreign-policy ideology as no other instrument, in that it upheld concrete power-political interests under a pretext of anti-imperialist altruism. What Dexter Perkins, the author of the standard work on the doctrine, has called 'the most significant of all American state papers', has retained its power as a fundamental maxim of US ideology. On the hundredth anniversary of Monroe's message, Mary Baker Eddy, the founder of the Christian Science Association, announced in a full-page advertisement in the *New York Times* that she believed 'strictly in the Monroe Doctrine, in our constitution and in the laws of god'.[16] The doctrine is considered as relevant today as it was in 1823, although its thrust has changed. It is no longer aimed at the former European colonial powers as potential rivals in the western hemisphere but at the Soviet Union — and, by extension, communism — as the 'foreign' power.

The Monroe Doctrine's ideological antecedents go back a few decades to the early days of independence. The founding fathers of the United States held the historical-philosophical view that they were involved not just in the creation of a new country but in the evolution of a new social order of progress, democracy and equality. Contrasting their new world with the old world of corrupt, warmongering autocratic regimes and the fetid air of feudal society, they developed what twentieth-century publicists have called the 'doctrine of the two spheres'. Thomas Jefferson expressed this with crystal clearness when he divided the world into two systems, the 'American ... with its own hemisphere' on the one hand and the 'European ... which occupies a separate division of the globe' on the other.[17] The conception of the separation between the 'old' and the 'new' worlds, which had its roots in the Americans' particular economic interests and their very conscious desire to emancipate themselves from the old society, gradually hardened into a political article of faith.

This conception was articulated by the most influential political leaders of the day, and moulded US foreign policy especially in the early years. Already in 1775 the great pamphleteer of the revolution, Thomas Paine, had argued in *Common Sense* that 'It is the true interest of America to steer clear of European contentions, which she never can do ... by her dependence on Britain'.[18] The first three presidents of the new republic were essentially of the same view: in his farewell address, George Washington urged America 'to steer clear of permanent alliances'; John Adams advised that 'we should make no treaties of alliance with any European power, that we should consent to none but treaties of commerce, that we should separate ourselves ... from all European politics and wars'; and in his famous inaugural address Thomas Jefferson declared that his administration would seek 'entangling alliances with none'.[19]

Mindful of these weighty admonitions, the next generation of US politicians certainly tried to stay out of the dynastic and power-political struggles in Europe. In return, they of course expected the European powers to stay out of the western hemisphere, at least not to intervene in the countries which were in the process of shaking off the Spanish yoke or whose emancipation from colonial rule seemed only a question of time.

Latin America was truly in ferment at this time. Rebellion had broken out in Mexico in 1810, and the country proclaimed its independence in 1821. Gran Colombia was formed by the union of New Granada (Colombia) and Venezuela in 1819 under the presidency of Bolívar. Peru's independence was assured after the battle of Ayacucho in 1824. Paraguay gained its independence in 1811 in the wake of the revolution in Buenos Aires. The declaration of independence of Tucumán in 1816 transformed the former vice-royalty of La Plata into the United Provinces of Rio de la Plata (Argentina). Chile was liberated by the forces of San Martín and Bernardo O'Higgins, victorious at the battle of Maipú in 1818. Brazil separated from Portugal peacefully with the proclamation of an independent empire in 1822. Under Antonio José de Sucre, Bolivia separated from Peru in 1825. Uruguay gained its independence in 1828 in the wake of a war between the United Provinces and Brazil. In the Caribbean, Haiti liberated itself from France in 1804 and established a republic two years later; and the Dominican Republic declared its independence in 1821.

At first, enthusiasm in the north for the liberation movements of the south was somewhat muted, not least because most Americans knew very little about their southern neighbours, and many were arrogant enough to doubt the Latins' ability to develop a republican form of government. In addition, the United States' hands remained tied while the conflict with Spain over the Floridas smouldered. Henry Clay, the expansionist from Kentucky, was one of the few political leaders in Washington who championed the cause of 'our southern brethren', and he and his supporters launched a campaign for the diplomatic recognition of the independence of the new Latin republics in 1817.[20] But a year of efforts merely showed that Congress was not yet prepared to do so.

At least President Monroe felt impelled by the rising tide of public sympathy for the new states to send a fact-finding mission to South America to report on the progress of revolutionary and anti-colonial developments. On their return from Buenos Aires in July 1818, its three members were unable to submit a joint report. They agreed that it would be impossible for the Spanish crown to re-establish its authority over the United Provinces; but on everything else they were hopelessly divided. The fact that the members of the mission disagreed so fundamentally on how to interpret the facts they had found on the ground dampened the public's growing enthusiasm for the independence of the new republics. But despite this somewhat confusing situation President Monroe was nevertheless swayed by the arguments for recognition. In this he over-ruled his secretary of state, John Quincy Adams, who made no secret of his scepticism of the Latins Americans' ability to govern themselves.

The signing of the Adams–Onís Treaty on Florida in 1819 and especially its taking effect two years later changed the mood in Washington dramatically. It was no longer necessary for the US government to remain politically neutral and exercise diplomatic caution towards the former Spanish colonies. Once it had become clear that Spain had abandoned any serious attempt to recover the rebellious provinces (around 1821), President Monroe sent a message to the House of Representatives on 8 March 1822 in which he declared that 'the contest [between Spain and its colonies] was manifestly settled' and therefore 'we are compelled to conclude ... that the provinces which have declared their independence, and are in enjoyment of it, ought to be recognized'.[21]

Monroe's view that the United States could no longer withhold diplomatic recognition of the new republics was accepted readily enough by Congress. By 4 May, both houses had appropriated $100,000 requested by the executive to set up and meet the expenses of the first diplomatic missions in Latin America. The near-unanimous votes — the House approved the measure by 167 votes to 1, the Senate by 39 votes to 3 — showed the degree to which the mood on recognition had changed in the four years since 1818 which had seen success for the liberation movements and the annexation of Florida. The United States became the first country to recognize one of the Latin American republics on 19 June 1822, when, 'in a moment of great and sincere emotion', President Monroe formally received Manuel Torres as the chargé d'affaires of Colombia.[22]

Meanwhile other countries, Britain in particular, chose to defer recognition for the time being, since there still seemed a possibility that it might prove precipitate and inopportune. That this possibility might become a probability became clear at the Congress of Verona in November 1822, when the reactionary Holy Alliance (Austria, Naples Prussia, Russia and Sardinia) approved plans to mandate France to suppress the liberal movement in Spain and, by extension, reconquer the Latin American states on behalf of Spain. US leaders were greatly alarmed when French troops crossed the Pyrenees in April 1823, occupied all of Spain within a few months, crushed the liberals and restored the conservative king, Ferdinand VII. There could be little doubt that this heightened the danger of an attempted reconquest of the former Latin American colonies, and as far as the Americans were concerned such an attack would merely be a prelude to an attack on the United States itself.

The British government was not exactly enamoured either of the Holy Alliance's intention to assist Ferdinand VII in launching a counter-revolution in Latin America once the liberal and revolutionary movements in Europe had been suppressed. Steeped in a tradition of political liberalism, the British viewed the prospect of such a reactionary enterprise with apprehension. But what prompted them to act was concern for the vast commercial interests they had built up in Latin America during the previous quarter century. So in both Britain and the United States ideological and economic motives — albeit in different measure — coalesced into a determination to prevent the recolonization of Latin America.

Adams had begun to formulate, long before 1823, the so-called 'non-colonization dogma', which was supposed to exclude European influence from the American continents. Adams disliked colonialism not only because it ran counter to his political principles, but also because it was connected in his mind with commercial monopoly and the exclusion of the United States from the markets of the new world. For that reason, and in contradistinction to British interests and ambitions, he saw another danger to the United States in addition to French intervention in Latin America and the restoration of the Spanish empire by the Holy Alliance, namely the Russian presence in the north-west. In September 1821, Tsar Alexander I had issued an edict setting out Russian claims on the North American continent from Alaska down the Pacific coast to the 51st parallel. Particularly grave as far as Adams was concerned — and his reason for developing the non-colonization dogma further — was the fact that the edict claimed exclusive rights for Russian economic interests. It granted only to Russian subjects the pursuits of commerce, whaling, fishery and all other industry in the designated coasts and islands, and prohibited, on pain of capture and confiscation, foreign ships from approaching within a hundred miles of the coast. Adams instructed the US ambassador in Petersburg, Henry Middleton, to reject the Russian claims energetically and claim instead (in so many words) America for the Americans.[23]

Adams accepted that there existed a 'coincidence of principles' between London and Washington, albeit only one of *political* principles, since economically the United States and Britain were competitors especially in Latin America. During the summer of 1823, he held several meetings with the British ambassador to the United States, Stratford Canning, on how both countries could join forces to prevent a reconquest of Latin America for Spain. In the course of these discussions he became increasingly distrustful of the British, whom he suspected of pursuing objectives inimical to American interests.

On 16 August 1823, the British foreign secretary, George Canning, a supporter of trading interests who had been appointed the previous September and had already broken with the Holy Alliance, made a first diplomatic approach to the US ambassador in London, Richard Rush, with the aim of gaining American support for concerted action against the Latin American policy of the reactionary European powers. Considering the matter both urgent and sensitive, Rush informed Adams almost immediately of the content of his meeting with Canning. He reported that Britain 'disclaimed all intention of appropriating even the smallest portion of the late Spanish possessions in America' and that Canning 'was also satisfied that no attempt would be made by France to bring any of them under her dominion' (a surprising statement in view of current events). Canning had suggested that both countries should go 'hand in hand' in case France did contemplate direct interference in Spanish America. World opinion would be impressed by 'the large share of the maritime power of the world which Great Britain and the United States shared between them' and by their 'common opinion'. Britain recognized Spanish prerogatives in Latin America, but wanted 'as favoured a footing as any other nation' — read: access to markets — in the region.[24]

On 20 August, Canning sent a five-point confidential note to Rush putting the British position in more formal terms. The note stated that:

(i) We conceive the recovery of the colonies by Spain to be hopeless;
(ii) We consider the question of recognition of them, as independent states, to be one of time and circumstance;
(iii) We are, however, by no means disposed to throw any impediment in the way of an arrangement between them and the mother country by amicable negotiation;
(iv) We aim not at the possession of any portion of them ourselves; and
(v) We could not see any portion of them transferred to any other power with indifference.

Why, Canning concluded, should America and Britain not declare their common opinions in the face of the world?[25]

Although Rush did not have a mandate to reach an agreement with the British government, he intimated in his reply that the Monroe administration would view the proposal favourably.[26] And it was true that President Monroe, deeply concerned that an attack on the former Spanish colonies would inevitably lead to an attack on the United States, inclined towards acceptance. But he had his doubts on this momentous issue and consulted his predecessors Jefferson and Madison. Both supported concerted Anglo-American action, with Madison expressing the view that backed by British power and the British navy the Americans had nothing to fear from the rest of the world.[27]

Adams, however, was frankly opposed to such co-operation for the 'protection' of Latin America. He particularly disliked the assumption underlying Canning's proposal that in opposing any attempts by or on behalf of Spain to recover its colonies the United States and Britain should also disclaim any territorial ambitions themselves. The US foreign-policy establishment had already set its heart on the eventual annexation of Cuba and Texas, and Adams saw no advantage for the United States in publicly declaring its intention to refrain from a policy of territorial expansion in the south and south-west. Moreover, unlike President Monroe and John C. Calhoun, the secretary of war, he thought the likelihood of France appearing in Latin America as the new colonial power in the service of Spain much exaggerated.

And indeed, by the autumn of 1823, the danger of French intervention had all but disappeared, although the politicians in Washington could not yet have

realized this. During a diplomatic silence between the US and British governments, the latter made unilateral efforts to counter any interventionist policies
being contemplated by the French. Canning warned the French government, via
the ambassador in London, Jules de Polignac, most emphatically against any
colonial adventures in Latin America. As a result, the French foreign minister,
René de Châteaubriand, dictated a memorandum to Canning on 9 October
(named after Polignac) in which France formally disclaimed 'any intention or
desire ... to appropriate to herself any part of the Spanish possessions in
America'.[28]

Ignorant of this development, the Americans continued to work on their anti-
colonial declaration. Adams was able to win over the president and his cabinet
colleagues to his view that unilateral action by the United States, and not a joint
Anglo-American initiative, would be in the country's best interest. Most important, he was able to convince the president that the intended declaration would
have much greater political impact if it focused exclusively on American issues
and not deal with European concerns (such as the liberation struggle of the
Greeks) — 'to make our American cause, and to adhere inflexibly to that', as he
put it.[29] What became known as the Monroe Doctrine showed the hand of the
secretary of state so clearly that it might just as well have entered the history
books as the 'Adams Doctrine'.

After the Russian ambassador in Washington submitted a note which in
essence reiterated the policy of the Holy Alliance, the US government reacted
promptly and decisively. Monroe immediately drafted a reply vigorously censur-
ing Europe's interventionist policy. Adams suggested that the declaration, which
set out the fundamental the principles of US foreign policy, should be transmitted
to European governments in confidential diplomatic correspondence, almost in
the manner of the secret diplomacy so despised in the new world. But President
Monroe was of a different opinion. He used the very public vehicle of his annual
message to Congress on the state of the union, delivered a few days later on 2
December 1823, to put the European powers in their place.

In his message Monroe outlined a number of theses. First, 'The American
continents are henceforth not to be considered as subjects for future colonization
by any European powers'. Second, in the new world a political system had
emerged which was wholly different from that of Europe and separated from it.
That is why, third, the United States would view attempts on the part of any
European powers to extend their system to any portion of the hemisphere, to
recover former colonies or cede colonies to another power as 'dangerous to our
peace and safety' and a 'manifestation of an unfriendly disposition toward the
United States'. To assuage the Europeans, who would have been unaccustomed
to such provocative language, Monroe declared that, fourth, the United States
would not interfere in any way in the affairs of Europe or its remaining colonies
in the western hemisphere. In conclusion, he even called for friendly relations
between the United States and Europe.[30]

Quite the opposite of what many historians have tried to pretend, the Monroe
Doctrine and its strong message directed at Europe was anything but a bold and
unselfish declaration of human freedom challenging all the world in a crusading

spirit to keep 'hands off' the western hemisphere, specifically, Latin America. Rather, its hidden purpose was to lay the foundations of US hegemony in the Americas. The real motive behind the ostensibly altruistic gesture was clearly the US government's desire to stake at least a verbal claim as the hemisphere's leading power, with words to be followed by deeds as soon as the country's political and economic strength permitted. Under the semblance of an anti-imperialism directed against the corrupt colonial powers, the Monroe Doctrine merely prejudiced the United States' own imperialism. Significantly, the doctrine subsequently never managed to be applied *against European* intervention, but always served as a justification *for US* intervention.

The Monroe Doctrine in practice

But the United States could not yet do as it pleased in Latin America. Many Latin Americans, all too conscious of their still precarious independence, welcomed the US government's self-confident declaration that it intended to prevent any European effort to recover lost colonies. But the Europeans were extremely irritated by the effrontery shown by the Johnny-come-lately among the nation states. But more important, they did not take very seriously the postulates contained within the Monroe Doctrine, whether it be the non-colonization dogma, the non-intervention principle or the no-transfer doctrine. The Europeans could cast derision on Monroe's early excursion into world politics because they knew that his threats were empty as long as the United States could not count on the support of Britain and its powerful fleet — a handicap of which the American politicians of the 1820s and 30s were very well aware.

At the time it was enunciated, the practical value of the Monroe Doctrine appeared to be nil. And the US government showed great reluctance to address the discrepancy between ideological pathos and political passivity or to translate the doctrine's principles into any kind of effective action. For example, in July 1824, Washington ignored a request from Colombia for a treaty of alliance as protection against rumoured French steps to establish a monarchy there. And the following year, Washington refused to give Brazil guarantees of defensive aid should Portugal, alone or in conjunction with another power, attempt to regain its former colony.

Even Britain, which had originally proposed concerted action to thwart colonial conquests or reconquests by the other European powers, did not hold Monroe's principles in very high regard when the extension of its own South American economic empire was at stake. The occupation of the Falklands/Malvinas in January 1833 constituted a flagrant violation of the Monroe Doctrine, but it went unchallenged by the Americans, who argued that they were not a party to the controversy between Argentina and Britain over these South Atlantic islands (which from a contemporary US perspective must in any case have seemed god-forsaken and irrelevant to the national interest). Apart from delivering a weak protest to London, the administration took no diplomatic steps or political action when the British seized Roatán, one of the Bay Islands off the coast of Honduras. The same happened three years later when the British occupied the port of San Juan del Norte, at the mouth of the river of that name, in Nicaragua. The French occupation of the Mexican port of Vera Cruz and the island of Martín García in the Río de la Plata in 1838 also went unpunished.

The Americans did not react against these European interventions in the western hemisphere because they had no immediate implications for US interests and security. Political and economic relations between the United States and the Latin American states were still far too loose during the 1830s and 40s for the southerners to be able to call on northern assistance in the event of an external threat or for the northerners to have a vested interest in developments in the south.

The year 1842 witnessed the first attempt by a US administration to put teeth into the Monroe Doctrine. Self-interest precipitated this change of policy. The United States was now being challenged in its own back yard on the North American continent by Britain and France, which were giving active support to Texan groups opposed to the impending annexation of their country by the United States. This prompted President Tyler, in his annual message to Congress, to reiterate the principles set down by Monroe and to warn the European powers to keep out of the affairs of the new world just as the United States kept out of European affairs.[31]

As the appetite of the burgeoning 'colossus of the north' for Texas, Oregon and California grew, so the languishing Monroe Doctrine was revived. It remained for Tyler's expansionist successor, James Polk, to bring it out of the stockroom of US foreign policy and dust it off. In his first annual message to Congress, on 2 December 1845, he stated categorically that, first, 'the people of this continent alone have the right to decide their own destiny'; second, the United States could not permit European interventions in North America which aimed to prevent the incorporation of a state into the union merely because it might disturb Europe's view of the balance of power; and, third, the United States would not tolerate the establishment of European colonies or dominions in North America in the future.[32] However aggressive this declaration, which became known as the Polk Doctrine, must have sounded to European diplomats, it did amount to a temporary moderation of the claims for hemispheric hegemony enshrined in the Monroe Doctrine. Because his administration still lacked the means to extend the legal-diplomatic protective umbrella of the Monroe Doctrine over the whole of the western hemisphere, Polk restricted its purview to North America. This may have contributed to the fairly muted reception of his message by critics and supporters both at home and abroad, and to the doctrine's negligible impact on foreign policy.

The Americans, thus far singularly ineffective in asserting the non-colonization dogma and the non-intervention principle, had more success with the no-transfer doctrine. This was no doubt partly because a transfer or exchange of a colony involved by definition two European powers, which frequently could not agree terms between themselves, irrespective of any American threats. Throughout the nineteenth century, US administrations applied the policy based on this doctrine: to Cuba in 1823 (which for practical reasons Washington preferred to remain in Spanish hands rather than those of any other European power); to California in 1845 (when a fear spread in Washington that the British had designs on this territory and might try to shut the United States off from the Pacific); to the Danish possessions in the Caribbean in 1869; and to the Dominican Republic in 1870.

That the Dominican Republic did not precede Cuba into the American system was no fault of a group of New York adventurers who, awestruck by the brilliant prospects of developing the rich natural resources of this part of Hispaniola, easily secured the backing of respectable capitalists like Cyrus M. McCormick, Ben Holliday and the Spofford and Tileston banking house. President Grant, an experienced warrior and therefore the 'right' man for such an undertaking, was all in favour of this plan, not least because against all the available evidence he persuaded himself the North German Confederation (dominated by Prussia) might pre-empt the United States and occupy the strategically important Samaná Bay. Hamilton Fish, the more cautious secretary of state, would have accepted a US protectorate over the Dominican Republic, but his fear that 'the incorporation of these people ... would be but the beginning of conflict and anarchy' set him against the president's scheme.[33]

Grant's cabinet rejected his draft annexation treaty to a man. Undeterred, he submitted a more formal draft to the Senate on 18 January 1870, where it met a similar fate. Some senators, including the influential Charles Sumner from Massachusetts, shared Fish's reservations and furthermore feared that the annexation of the Dominican Republic would ultimately lead to the seizure of Haiti. With Sumner subjecting the project to a scathing denunciation, it was rejected by the foreign affairs committee and finally thrown out of the Senate on 30 June.

The annexation scheme was abandoned, but the affair turned out to be far more than a mere footnote in the history of American expansionism. To give his plan a principled gloss, Grant had invoked the spirit of his predecessor Monroe. In a last-ditch attempt to save the treaty he had even described the annexation of the Dominican Republic as an 'adherence of the Monroe Doctrine' and had reiterated the equally important principle that no American territory could be transferred from one European power to another.[34]

Yet another doctrine was born. The no-transfer doctrine had been a cardinal principle of US Latin American policy from 1811 onwards, when Congress had tried to prevent the transfer of Florida from Spain to Britain. In the guise of the Grant Doctrine it remained a significant element of US policy until well into the twentieth century, when the remaining British, French and Dutch possessions in the Caribbean threatened to fall into the hands of a victorious Nazi Germany in 1940. Fish affirmed this principle of US foreign policy in a detailed memorandum of 14 July 1870, and linked it explicitly to the Monroe Doctrine. He added that the United States 'looks hopefully to the time when, by the voluntary departure of Europe's governments from this continent ... America shall be wholly American'.[35] It should be remembered, however, that not even in Grant's time was the United States capable of enforcing the Monroe Doctrine and its no-transfer principle in the face of opposition from a foreign power.

The Americans actually applied the Monroe Doctrine for the first time in 1895, when they flexed their muscles in a dispute between Britain and Venezuela over the latter country's eastern border with British Guiana. Washington turned words into deeds and on the ideological basis of the doctrine set itself up as the regional policeman who had to bring the two rivals to their senses. Britain, plagued with numerous foreign-policy problems and hence reluctant to risk a clash with the United States, backed down and met the US' demands, also in effect agreeing not to violate the Monroe Doctrine in future. The doctrine — hitherto only a piece of paper — had proved its practical value for the first time.

It still remained very much a unilateral affair, however. While the politicians around President Monroe had discussed among themselves the best diplomatic and ideological means of establishing their country's claim to hemispheric hegemony, they had not solicited any Latin American views on the matter. Self-righteous and self-confident as ever, they had declared the Latin Americans in need of protection without even bothering to inquire whether they would welcome such protection. And in proclaiming the Monroe Doctrine unilaterally, the Americans ensured that its application could never be mandatory. Whether or not Washington helped southern neighbours to defend themselves against European encroachment depended invariably on US political and military dispositions. On every occasion the Latin Americans had to accept whatever decision Washington came to, whether regarding the doctrine's practical application or otherwise.

This state of affairs obtained until well into the twentieth century. As late as 1923 the Americans made it clear that they did not have the slightest interest in modifying the unilateral character of the Monroe Doctrine. Only at a special Pan-American Conference convened under the looming fascist threat in Buenos Aires in 1936 did the US government accept the principle of multilateral consultation in case of an outside threat. It condescended to this step presumably in the recognition that it would have considerable difficulty in singlehandedly asserting the doctrine against the fascist powers.

'Manifest destiny': the ideology of expansionism

US politicians had at their disposal, in the Monroe Doctrine, a proven means of concealing their designs on Latin America under a cloak of legitimacy. But they were not short of additional ideological legitimations for their actions and policies. The establishment of the United States and its continental expansion stimulated a range of ideological reflexes which coalesced into a specifically American sense of destiny. Derived from puritan notions of predestination, salvation and covenant, it acquired its unmistakable form through secularization and the legal-rationalist interpretation of the social contract. This consciousness was also moulded by the conception, as pretentious as it is self-righteous, of the unique historical destiny of the United States and its chosen people. Spell-bound by what they considered the transcendent success of their experiment, the Americans insisted on the universality and permanence of the principles underlying it and even enthused with millenarian conviction about having realized the moral purpose of the world. Following the political imperative inherent in the puritan ethos of success and the tradition of the enlightenment, they preached their civilizing and democratic message from the summit of the mountain of progress.

It was only a small step from this rather passive sense of destiny and mission — content to show the way by conduct and example — to the zealous presumption that the rest of the world, starting with Latin America, had to be assimilated to the American way of life. That step was taken by the ideologues of 'manifest destiny', who held that it was incumbent on the United States to subjugate the world around it, or at least to adapt it to its political model and lifestyle. The originator of the phrase was the journalist John L. O'Sullivan, who declared in an article in the July–August 1839 issue of *United States Magazine and Democratic Review* that it was 'the fulfilment of our manifest destiny to overspread the continent allotted by providence for the free development of our millions'.[36] O'Sullivan did not invent anything new here, but merely gave elegant expression to a widespread ideological sentiment of his age. The New York *Morning News* took up the term 'manifest destiny' and transformed it into a slogan in late 1845, significantly at the very time that the expansion-minded President Polk revived the neglected Monroe Doctrine in his annual message to Congress.

Many elements of the Americans' traditional sense of destiny flowed into this blanket legitimation of the crudest and most aggressive foreign policy. Among them were: the belief that as the secular 'new Jerusalem' or the 'city on the mountain' the United States should guide the world on the path of progress; the heritage of puritanism, which held that success on earth, also in business, ensured happiness in the hereafter; the notion of the United States as the final link in a historical westward progression of empires (from China to Persia, Greece, Rome, Germany, France and Britain); and the view that with the rise of the United States humanity had reached the summit of civilization. Once manifest destiny had been distilled from this ideological brew, the democratic mission of the United States stopped being an object of contemplation and an injunction to educate the world by example. In the new ideology, the hitherto rather abstract and vague sense of purpose was transformed into an active, dynamic principle of practical politics.

The North American continent provided an ideal geographical framework for this new aggressive zeal. Taking manifest destiny seriously meant, for most of the nineteenth century, extending the political borders of the great republic to its natural frontiers. Once that task had been completed, around 1890, manifest destiny's universalism, the corollary of this philosophy of history, came into play. This meant, simply, that as part of the great historical plan the rest of the world would in due course partake of the benefits of American civilization, even if these had to be imposed.

Small wonder, then, that during the 1890s, when the United States became the world's leading industrialized country and all foreign-policy considerations centred on where and how to sell surplus goods and invest surplus capital, the American imperialists eagerly revived the concept of America's manifest destiny, which had been almost forgotten in the previous 20–30 years. For like no other world view it provided the ideological justification for the thrust of the expansionism of that period. The historian Max Lerner has succinctly described manifest destiny as 'the rationalization the Americans gave to their expansive thrust and hunger for land and power, for profits and bigness'.[37] Manifest destiny transfigured the United States' southward expansion into an inevitability, not in the fatalistic sense of an impending natural disaster but rather as a stroke of extraordinarily good fortune for the fated countries. Accordingly, Latin Americans could look forward to receiving the achievements of American civilization, quite regardless of much or how little they themselves had contributed to progress and prosperity in their countries. The ideological label of 'manifest destiny' miraculously transformed imperialism into an altruistic mission which it was incumbent on the Americans to fulfil, more in the interest of others than their own.

With the general ideological backdrop to the rise of American imperialism in place, William Henry Seward, secretary of state from 1861 until 1869 under Lincoln and Johnson, provided the practical directions. Counselling against imposing a formal colonial administration on the neighbours south of the Rio Grande, which would only swallow up money and require the deployment of large numbers of soldiers and civil servants, Seward instead recommended the creation of an 'informal' or commercial empire. To achieve this goal, this prophet of economic imperialism advised, the United States would need no more than treaties, consulates and gunboats.[38] For the time being, however, Seward's prescriptions and all the talk of an obligation to spread American values were no more than illusion and conceited rhetoric, largely because the gunboats only existed in theory.

The United States' pan-American policy, and its imperialism, began to take shape in the 1880s, when the naval strategist Alfred Thayer Mahan developed his theory of the pivotal importance of sea power in world politics.[39] In 1881, three years before Mahan started his influential lectures at the newly created Naval War College, Congress approved the construction of a new navy. And in 1890 the secretary of the navy, Benjamin F. Tracy, recommended the construction of 20 battleships, sufficient to command the western Atlantic, the eastern Pacific and above all the Caribbean, the *mare nostrum*. No sooner said than done. Previously, Congress had only authorized the building of small, unarmoured cruisers in the 7,000-ton class, vessels which at most could be used for hit-and-run destruction of commerce; it now approved Tracy's proposals, and the first battleship left the slips later that year. The new ships could challenge those of the other powers competing for economic and territorial control in the hemisphere because they could store more coal and therefore had a much greater operating range.

Between 1880 and 1897, the federal budget for the navy was raised from $3.5m to $34.5m, equivalent to a doubling of its share of the total budget from 5% to 10%. These outlays gave birth to the modern American navy. When Benjamin Harrison was sworn in as president and Tracy was appointed secretary of the navy in 1889, the US navy ranked probably not even among the 15 largest in the world. When four years later both politicians cleared their desks in Washington, the US navy occupied seventh place. With both Congress and the executive heeding the advice of Mahan and Tracy to create a fleet of modern battleships as the backbone of national foreign policy, especially of an aggressive commercial strategy, the expansion continued in the following years, so that even before the turn of the century the United States could claim third place among the world's sea powers. This resource was put to use at the first opportunity.

Notes

1. Quoted in Van Alstyne 1960 p. 148.
2. Ibid.
3. Letter to Hugh Nelson, 28 April 1823, quoted in Gantenbein (ed.) 1950 p. 426.
4. Letter to Archibald Stewart, 25 January 1786, quoted in Van Alstyne, op. cit., p. 81; letter to Alexander von Humboldt, 6 December 1813, quoted in Whitaker 1954 p. 29.
5. Address to the House of Representatives, 24 March 1818, quoted in Perkins 1941 p. 4.
6. Letter to Richard Rush, 22 July 1823, quoted in Van Alstyne, op. cit., p. 96.
7. Letter to Poinsett, 15 March 1827, quoted in Bemis 1949 p. 563.
8. Letter to Poinsett, 25 August 1829, quoted in US Congress 1837 p. 13ff.
9. Quoted in Van Alstyne, op. cit., p. 102.
10. Annual message to Congress, 2 December 1845, quoted in Gantenbein (ed.), op. cit., p. 552.
11. Message to Congress, 11 May 1846, quoted in Gantenbein (ed.), op. cit., p. 552.
12. Quoted in Morris (ed.) 1976 p. 615.
13. Inaugural address, 4 March 1829, quoted in US Congress 1969 p. 57; annual message to Congress, 8 December 1829, quoted in Brown 1970 p. 5.
14. Brown, op. cit., p.7ff.
15. See ibid., p. 208.
16. Advertisement in the *New York Times*, 2 December 1923, quoted in Perkins, op. cit., p. ix.
17. Letter to Alexander von Humboldt, 6 December 1813, quoted in Perkins, op. cit., p. 22.
18. Quoted in Perkins, op. cit., p. 5ff.
19. Washington, farewell address, 17 September 1796, quoted in Gantenbein (ed.), op. cit., p. 5; Adams, message to Congress, 16 May 1797, quoted in Perkins, op. cit., p. 6; Jefferson, inaugural address, 4 March 1801, quoted in Gantenbein (ed.), op. cit., p. 6.
20. Quoted in Bemis, op. cit., p. 344f.
21. Message to the House of Representatives, 8 March 1822, quoted in Gantenbein (ed.), op. cit., p. 15.
22. Quoted in Bemis, op. cit., p. 359.
23. Letter to Henry Middleton, 22 July 1823, quoted in Gantenbein (ed.), op. cit., p. 306f.
24. Letter to Adams, 19 August 1823, quoted in Gantenbein (ed.), op. cit., pp. 307–9.
25. Letter to Rush, 20 August 1823, quoted in Gantenbein (ed.), op. cit., p. 310f.
26. Letter to Canning, 23 August 1823, quoted in Gantenbein (ed.), op. cit., p. 311.
27. Letter to Monroe, 30 October 1823, quoted in Gantenbein (ed.), op. cit., p. 319.
28. Memorandum to Canning, 9 October 1823, quoted in Perkins, op. cit., p. 52.
29. Quoted in Perkins, op. cit., p. 44.
30. Annual message to Congress, 2 December 1823, quoted in Gantenbein (ed.), op. cit., pp. 323–5.
31. Annual message to Congress, 30 December 1842, quoted in Lieuwen 1965 p. 15ff.
32. Annual message to Congress, 2 December 1845, quoted in Gantenbein (ed.), op. cit., p. 328ff.
33. Diary, 5–6 April 1869, quoted in LaFeber 1963 p. 39.

34. Message to Congress, 31 May 1870, quoted in Perkins, op. cit., p. 158ff.
35. Memorandum to Grant, 14 July 1870, quoted in Gantenbein (ed.), op. cit., p. 338.
36. Quoted in Morris (ed.), op. cit., p. 230.
37. Lerner 1958 p. 887.
38. See LaFeber, op. cit., pp. 25–8.
39. See ibid., p. 88.

2. The rise of American imperialism

Economic crisis and expansion

The expansion of the United States southwards did not follow on the heels of the rhetorical excesses and the construction of a modern navy. Certain conditions had to be fulfilled before the verbal push to the south could be turned into deeds. The principal condition was provided by the economic crisis in the final years of the nineteenth century. The phase of rapid industrialization in the United States from 1865 until 1897 was interrupted by three major depressions, in 1873–79, 1882–85 and 1893–97. More than half of the 25 years after 1873 were years of economic decline, and as each recession struck Americans became convinced it was worse than the previous one. The 'great depression' of the 1870s and 1880s culminated in the economic crisis of 1893–97. Its direct cause was loss of financial confidence, but it also marked both the end and the low point of a longer-term recessionary period for the agricultural sector, coupled in a remarkable way with a period of rapid growth in the manufacturing sector.

Commercialization and mechanization in agriculture had led to a situation in which the country's farms produced far more than the people could consume. As production soared beyond all previous figures, prices plummeted. Cotton production, for example, increased from 4.3 to 6.9 million bales between 1870–82 and 9.0 million bales in 1891; prices meanwhile dropped from 18 to 10 cents per pound weight between 1871–80 and to a little over 7 cents in 1891. The figures for wheat tell a similar story. Wheat production rose from 368 to 555 million bushels between 1873–82; but prices dropped from $1.50 per bushel in 1866 to 77 cents in 1878, to 68 cents in 1887 (following a short recovery) and to 54 cents in 1893.

The year 1892 showed an upturn for heavy industry in particular, but the failure of the Philadelphia & Reading Railroad and the National Cordage Company in the spring of 1893 already gave warning of the end of a short-lived boom. By the end of the first year of recession, some 500 banks and 15,000 businesses had been bankrupted, and thousands of farmers had lost their livelihoods. The sharp drop of investment in railway construction in particular contributed to the severity of the recession. Some 4,584 miles of new railway track were laid in 1892, but only 1,938 miles in 1895, a drop of 58%; orders for rails fell by 75%. Two hundred and thirty carriages and 205 locomotives were ordered every quarter in 1892, but only

11 carriages and 29 locomotives in the first half of 1894. Compared to its rapid development in previous years, railway construction had virtually halted by 1886. This hit the American economy particularly hard because of its role hitherto as a key growth sector. Iron producers, for instance, had difficulties in disposing of their ever-increasing stocks. Moreover, many of the 200,000 construction workers employed by the railway companies in the early 1880s lost their jobs. They were not the only ones, however: during the recession the number of unemployed increased to around 2.5–3 millions, or 12 to 14% of the labour force.

A palpable mood of crisis took hold, but not only as a result of the immediate calamitous effects of the depression, including a fall in the standard of living. Doubts began to be expressed about the continuance of economic growth and prosperity and the durability of the country's social and economic structures. Such doubts fed off an increasing awareness of other concurrent developments, notably a loss of confidence in economic liberalism and the disappearance of the continental frontier.

Rapid concentration of the ownership of industrial enterprises, which had accompanied the industrial revolution in the United States and received a hefty stimulus in the aftermath of the civil war, destroyed for many their faith in economic liberalism or *laissez-faire*. Small businesses had been characteristic of the American economy both before 1861 and immediately after 1865. Out of this heterogeneous structure there developed — with scant regard for companies that went under — in the course of the next 30 years what has since been called 'big business'. Apart from a few large railway companies, US manufacturing industry in 1850 was dominated by small businessmen whose firms relied on locally available raw materials to manufacture goods for local consumers; by 1914 it was dominated by a small number of huge conglomerates which controlled the domestic market as oligopolies (and in some cases even as monopolies) and branched out increasingly overseas. The 1900 census showed that 185 concerns (almost all the product of the mergers of the 1880s and 90s) controlled a third of US manufacturing industry, holding capital assets of $3 billion. The more *laissez-faire* capitalism had to make way for organized capitalism and its trusts, cartels and monopolies, the more the notion of 'free enterprise' lost meaning. Under these conditions, the rags-to-riches legend of the shoeshine boy who made a million would prove increasingly fanciful.

The conclusion of the 1890 census that there was no more land available for settlement, that the frontier had been extinguished, also filled many Americans with dread. In national mythology the western frontier was seemingly equivalent to a gate to freedom, and its disappearance deprived farmers, artisans and shopkeepers of opportunities to escape social and economic deprivation in the cities of the east. This 'safety valve' in the west was now blocked. This realization sent an intellectual and political leadership already racked by doubts over the fate of the American dream into something little short of panic, since, it was thought, the social boiler would one day explode under the pressure of the social contradictions.

The apparent difficulties encountered by the United States in breaking into the increasingly important world markets provided a further contributory factor to the panic. The Americans could only look on enviously and impotently as the British extended their commercial interests in Latin America, while US trade with the region remained persistently in deficit.

In the hothouse of public opinion all these elements fused into a nightmare vision of a society cheated of its 'manifest destiny' and shaken to its foundations by social tension, civil strife and perhaps even revolution.

The industrial conflicts of the 1880s and 1890s showed that the fear of social discord was not mere fantasy. Despite the widespread parochial, pliant and reformist attitudes — perhaps best personified by the labour leader Samuel Gompers — which hampered the emergence of working-class solidarity, the organized labour movement was able to mount a series of protests and strikes: in May 1886, thousands demanded the right to the eight-hour working day at the Haymarket Square protest in Chicago; in June 1892, some workers were killed during a strike at the Homestead plant of Carnegie Steel in Pennsylvania, called by the Amalgamated Association of Iron, Steel and Tin Workers over wage differentials; and the American Railway Union, led by Eugene V. Debs, organized a strike at the Pullman Company in May 1894, a dispute which ended with the Chicago massacre. What alarmed capital and its supporters most was the fact that the unemployed were no longer resigned to their fate but, led by populists like Jacob S. Coxey from Ohio, began to organize themselves. Coxey's proposal to lead an 'army of unemployed' to Washington to create work for them there (by building roads, for example) was put into practice after the panic of 1893. Hundreds of thousands of unemployed converged on Washington to demonstrate in the first days of May 1894, albeit to no avail.

In the short term, the bourgeoisie succeeded in suppressing the labour movement, not least by calling on the courts and the army. But in the long term it still had to address the causes of the economic and social convulsions and find solutions: how to escape the cycle of boom and bust; how to maintain economic stability under conditions of high employment and high consumption; how to counter the concentration of industry in the hands of a few trusts; and most important of all, how to solve all these problems without changing the fundamental elements of the country's economic and social system.

It is a moot point whether the solution which emerged from these considerations, namely easing social tensions through the export of surplus production, served the interests of its originators or whether an alternative was available. It was undeniable that in the second half of the century economic gains and growth of trade bore no relation to high expectations, and that contrary to the expansionist rhetoric the domestic market was by no means saturated. What matters in the context of US Latin American policy, which acquired its expansionist thrust during the crisis of 1893–97, is that this magic formula — export of internal problems through expansion — remained the conventional wisdom within both the agricultural and the manufacturing establishments for decades to come.

In the proposed solution the future prosperity of the American economy was dependent on a rapid growth of foreign trade. According to the expansionists, the social fabric of the country would unravel if the United States failed to compete successfully with the colonial powers over markets for surplus goods and investment opportunities for surplus capital. Expressions of this sentiment by foreign-policy experts were legion. In 1897 Albert Beveridge, a senator from Indiana and an arch-nationalist and -imperialist, summarized the anxieties and desires of America's politicians by linking hard economic calculations to blind faith in manifest destiny: 'American factories are making more than the American people can use; American soil is producing more than they can consume. Fate has written our policy for us; the trade of the world must and shall be ours'.[1]

The priority of economic interests in the context of the expansionist strategy was rarely denied. More often than not it was explicitly referred to and stressed, at times with such determination that some diplomats, officials and politicians openly put their services at the disposal of the big corporations. The economic mentality eventually became second nature to the foreign-policy establishment to such an extent that its representatives often calculated and operated, or thought they were doing so, in more economic terms than the representatives of big business themselves. In 1915, the secretary of state, William Jennings Bryan, sanctioned this inter-relationship with stunning directness: paraphrasing the Latin American expression 'my house is your house' in a speech to a group of businessmen, he declared that 'my department is your department; the ambassadors, ministers and the consuls are all yours. It is their business to look after your interests and to guard your rights'.[2]

The untapped Latin American market

To establish the commercial empire in Central and South America to which the Americans considered themselves legitimately entitled, it was necessary first to take stock of existing trade relations between north and south. A proposal in 1882 to send a study commission to Latin America to provide Congress with reliable information was initially shelved, but soon under discussion again as the crisis of the following years cast a shadow over the overproducing American economy. After nearly two years of recession and the spread of panic that American society would collapse under its economic surplus, Congress on 7 July 1884 authorized the necessary funds to send a commission to the south with a remit 'to ascertain and report upon the best modes of securing more intimate international and commercial relations between the United States and the several countries of Central America and South America'.[3]

Before setting off on their arduous journey, the four commission members — three politicians: George H. Sharpe (chair), Thomas C. Reynolds and Solon O. Thacher; and a journalist with some knowledge of Latin American affairs, William E. Curtis — deemed it their first duty to ascertain the views of American merchants and manufacturers with experience in dealing with Latin America. They held conferences in Boston, New York, Baltimore and Philadelphia, but also extended their information gathering far beyond the major eastern cities. Major railway companies (including the Santa Fé, the Southern Pacific and the Mexican Central) contributed lavishly to their tickets for a 9,000-mile round trip to visit local businessmen in San Francisco, Mexico City and New Orleans.

The commissioners heard the same lament with monotonous regularity wherever they went. Latin America, the continent preordained to be the United States' 'natural trading partner' and whose peoples looked up to the United States 'as the mother and model of republics', was almost exclusively controlled by the British and the Germans.[4] Those questioned agreed unanimously that 'every commercial signboard points to the nations of Central and South America as offering the most extensive and profitable, the most natural and convenient field for our commerce'.[5] Yet America's entrepreneurs had paid little attention to external trade, sustaining themselves instead on the proceeds of the domestic market. 'Foreign commerce has been comparatively forgotten.'[6]

At the beginning of the 1880s, American manufacturing industry produced goods valued at $5.7 billion, of which only about 1.5% was exported; of the total gross domestic product, including agriculture, less than 10% was exported. Detailed figures showed that commercial relations with Latin America were particularly underdeveloped. The US share of total trade with the region was far smaller than those of its major European competitors, and stood at only $130 million out of a total of $850 million. It hurt the Americans particularly that the balance of trade was consistently negative. They bought more than twice as much as they sold to Latin America, with imports accounting for $90 million and exports for $40 million. In general, taking their economies as a whole rather than specific sectional interests, the United States and Latin America seemed hardly to exist for each other at this time. Only 7% of US exports went to Latin America, and only 10% of Latin America's imports came from the United States.

American merchants complained time and again that the southern neighbours bought from their traditional trading partners on the other side of the Atlantic the very merchandise which they had for sale (such as railway track and supplies, farming machinery, cotton and wool goods, cured meat, tinned fruit, flour, boots and shoes, pianos, sewing machines, petroleum). Once the British had established a near-monopoly in trade with Latin America after the collapse of Spanish colonial rule, the Americans could do little to alter their trade balance with the region, which was closed on the wrong side of the ledger year after year. Between 1865 and 1884, the cumulative deficit amounted to $766 million, and on average imports from the south exceeded exports there by $38 million annually.

Already pained by the realization that the United States figured merely among the also-rans in Latin American trade as a whole, the expansionists on Wall Street and the White House were doubly irritated by the lack of penetration in Central America, a region where US domination could have been expected. After all, these countries were 'almost opposite the mouth of the Mississippi river, which is the throat through which should pour the products of the greatest agricultural valley in the world'.[7] But the surplus remained stuck in the throat. Although Central America should have been one of the most inviting fields for US commercial enterprise, trade between the region and the United States remained very modest indeed, and in deficit, in the 20 years after the civil war (see Table 2.1).

It annoyed the Americans that they had to pay in cash for most of the raw materials they imported from Central America (such as coffee, rubber, hides, dyes, fruit, sugar and cocoa), rather than being able to exchange them for manufactured products. Here too the Europeans were ahead, with British industrial exports to Central America, for instance, valued at $3.6 million in 1883, against American exports of $1.8 million. The difference was particularly glaring in one item, cotton goods: the British competitors sold $2.5 million worth of shirts, jackets and so on, while the Americans sold only $124,000 worth. Even though their export position was strongest further south, in Argentina for instance, the British left the Americans behind by a considerable distance in Central America as well (see Table 2.2).

Table 2.1
United States trade with Central America, 1865–84
(in US dollars)

	exports	imports	total
1865	162,000	376,000	538,000
1870	232,000	735,000	967,000
1875	784,000	2,435,000	3,219,000
1880	1,785,000	3,313,000	5,098,000
1881	1,626,000	3,160,000	4,786,000
1882	1,644,000	4,735,000	6,379,000
1883	2,003,000	5,121,000	7,124,000
1884	3,302,000	6,249,000	9,551,000

Source: US Congress, *Report of the Commission [on trade with Latin America]*

Table 2.2
US and British exports to Central America, 1865–82
(in US dollars)

	United States	United Kingdom
1865	162,000	760,000
1870	232,000	1,849,000
1875	784,000	4,261,000
1880	1,785,000	3,316,000
1881	1,626,000	4,706,000
1882	1,644,000	3,753,000

Source: US Congress, *Report of the Commission [on trade with Latin America]*

For those Americans interested in foreign trade all this was humiliating enough — the chronic negative balance of trade was frequently perceived as a humiliation, even a national disgrace. But a perusal of the US trade position with regard to one of the larger South American countries such as Argentina could not have left anyone in doubt that the time for action had come. Argentine imports in 1882 were valued at $62 million; consisted mainly of cotton goods, woollen fabrics and iron manufactures; and were imported from Britain (33% of the total), France (20%) and Germany (7%), with the US share amounting to 8%.

Argentine exports were valued at $62 million; consisted mainly of wool, hides and agricultural produce; and were exported to France (27% of the total), Belgium (23%), Britain and Germany (7% each), with the US share amounting to 12%. In the 20 years between 1863 and 1882 Britain and France significantly increased their share of Argentina's booming external trade, while the American export offensive which might have been expected in the light of the rapid growth of the US economy during this time gained little momentum. Although US exports to Argentina doubled within the period and reached an aggregate of $40 million, British exports reached $254 million in the same period and French exports even reached $313 million, almost eight times the volume of US exports.

The implications of this lamentable state of affairs had been serious enough to move the interested parties — the business community and politicians — to energetic action in the interests of trade. There was little mystery about the reasons for the lack-lustre performance as the members of the commission had already realized during their tour of American business centres. Their report, published in October 1885 following an an extensive fact-finding tour in Latin America, laid bare the deficiencies and failures of US trade policy.

The commission reported that American exporters did not seem to know the tastes of their potential Latin American customers. They did not study consumer habits, as apparently their European competitors did, and simply supplied the products successful on the domestic market to the same quality and in the same packaging. Whereas British and French merchants had developed the packaging of their products to a fine art, the Americans entirely ignored this, in their view trifling, matter.

The report highlighted the shortsightedness of this approach with a simple example. It pointed out that the common carrier of the Latin American interior was either a native who took a package on his back, or a mule which carried a load in a pannier. A carrier was able to carry a package weighing from 100–125 lb weight, and a mule twice as much. So if the export goods were to reach their customers in the Andes, the Pampas or the Amazonian jungle, they needed to be in packages weighing no more than 125 pounds weight. And if mules were to be used, the goods had to be divided in two equal parts, so that they could be hung on either side of the saddle. The British and French sent their goods to Latin America in light-weight boxes made of strong wood and secured with metal straps. But the Americans sent theirs in bulky and heavy packing cases which, apart from being cumbersome, would tear easily. As a result loss of goods by breakage was so great that Latin American merchants came to the conclusion that they could not afford to buy goods from the United States.[8]

Among the other obstacles to the expansion of trade listed in the report was the absence of American banks in Latin America. Almost all merchandise shipped to the region from the United States was paid for by bills of exchange drawn on London accounts, which meant, annoyingly, that British banks took a large share of the profits of any commercial dealings. In any case, the Latin Americans preferred to buy from the British, French and the other Europeans because they granted them generous terms of credit, whereas the stingy Americans almost invariably insisted on cash payments, often enough for fear that they would lose their hard-earned dollars in the next local revolution. The report also noted the absence of American consular agents in the region with a knowledge of commercial matters or who could even speak Spanish.

But the main obstacle to an expansion of US trade with Latin America was the lack of transport lines. There were in fact only four steamship lines connecting the United States with Central and South America: the Pacific Mail, which plied between New York and Colón and between San Francisco and Panama City; the Brazilian Line, which plied between New York and Rio de Janeiro; a private line managed by the firm Boulton, Bliss and Dallett, which plied between New York and Venezuela; and a single steamer chartered to ply between New York and Central America. Thus the only Latin American countries which American citizens could reach on ships flying their own flag were Brazil, Venezuela and Panama (which was then part of Colombia). Should they want to visit other parts of the region, they had to board British or French ships. To get from New Orleans to Venezuela, the commission itself had to travel via Havana and Saint Thomas on foreign-owned ships.

The American ports were full of 'tramps', British ships willing to sail wherever a cargo had to be carried and underbidding their American rivals. In 1884 the total tonnage of American ships engaged in export trade amounted to 1.2 million, while the British built 1 million tons of new ships in that year alone. And these were large and fast iron steamers, unlike the old, wooden and decaying American ships. As the commission observed, while the Americans were building railways to link the 'land ocean' between New York, Baltimore, Philadelphia and San Francisco, the British were building ships. The figures bear this out. The British railway network totalled 13,300 miles in 1865 and 19,200 miles in 1885. The American network, on the other hand, already totalled 35,000 miles in 1865, and had nearly quadrupled to 128,400 miles by 1885. The situation was reversed in shipbuilding. British steamship tonnage in the 50-ton plus category amounted to 4.4 million, which made the British merchant fleet the world's largest by far. American tonnage in this category amounted to a mere 0.7 million. This explains why American ships carried only 16% of US exports, while British ships carried the lion's share of 65%.

There were several reasons which accounted for the underdevelopment of the American merchant fleet. One of the most important was that the federal government, faithful to the liberal creed that within capitalism any enterprise which responds to market forces will prosper, had left merchant shipping to the private sector. Instead of using state subsidies to encourage the development of shipping lines to Latin America, as the British and French governments did very generously (and a few American politicians like James G. Blaine advocated), the US government actually discouraged any initiative in this direction. For instance, it paid very little to the shippers for transporting the mail and even compelled them to transport the letters and parcels from the post office to their ships at their own expense, which often cost more than the money received for rendering the service.

In lamenting the lack of means of communication and transport as the principal obstacles in the way of increased trade, the commission also pointed to the remedy. It recommended, among other things, the establishment of four mail-steamer lines to Latin America, one from the north-eastern ports to the east coast of South America down to Argentina, a second from the same ports to the east coast of Central America, a third from New Orleans to the east coast of Central America, and a fourth from San Francisco to the west coasts of Central and South America.

The commission also urged the government to increase consular representation, at least in the continent's major ports. Furthermore, the quality of the officials employed should be improved. To be transferred to diplomatic or consular service in Latin America was widely considered more of a punishment than an honour. So to provide the consular officials with an incentive to become more actively involved than the civil service routine demanded, the commission suggested that they should engage in trade, act as agents for American companies and share in the profits made by their clients. (This recommendation, also articulated in other quarters, was not taken up by the government at the time.)

The commission also called for a kind of training in marketing for American exporters and for the establishment of agencies in the major cities of Latin America to promote American products. Manufacturers should 'send down agents or drummers who are able to speak the Spanish language to introduce their products to the attention of the people and educate them in their use'.[9]

And finally, the commission strongly urged the establishment of extensive banking and financial facilities, and the negotiation of trade agreements and reciprocal tariff concessions with the Latin American countries. These two recommendations were made especially with an eye to improving not just commercial relations but economic relations in general. For the situation regarding the export of capital was not much rosier than the export of goods.

Prior to the victory of the United States in the Spanish–Cuban–American War of 1898, US investments in Latin America were negligible. Although American capital was already active in Mexico, Cuba and Chile a few years after the proclamation of the Monroe Doctrine, the scale of the investments and returns was small. Hardly anything changed over the next 60 years. In 1880 it was estimated that the value of direct US investments in Latin America came to no more than $100 million. By comparison, British investments on the southern continent amounted to over £123 million in government bonds and over £56 million in economic enterprises, including railways, public utilities, mines, banks, insurance companies, real estate, shipping lines and so on. Total US investment in Latin America increased to $250 million by 1890 and to $320 million by 1897, with the list of enterprises including mines, railways, telephone exchanges, submarine cable, timber, sugar and banana plantations, asphalt, petroleum, public utilities, river transport and ranch lands.

These investments were spread unevenly across the continent. In 1890 over half, and in 1897 nearly two-thirds, of investment was in neighbouring Mexico. But since the Díaz regime encouraged foreign investment, the Americans were not unduly concerned by this degree of concentration. Nor did they fear for their interests in Cuba, the second most important area for investment, after that country's 'independence' from Spain in the aftermath of the 1898 war had been achieved at the price of more or less direct political control by the United States (by means of the notorious Platt Amendment, which circumscribed national sovereignty). Yet despite the generally favourable climate for investment in these two countries, American investors invariably raised a hue and cry over any sign, however tentative, of revolutionary unrest or even just of nationalistic attempts by the locals to run their own country.

Just as US investments were geographically concentrated in a few advantageous countries of Latin America, they largely flowed only into sectors which complemented the domestic economy within the context of the international division of labour, rather than competed with it. This rule of thumb applied less to the sugar industry: Americans were involved in the production of cane sugar in Cuba, and found themselves in direct competition with the beet sugar growers in the United States, a situation which led to endless wrangles over the import of sugar from American-owned mills in Cuba. But the complementarity of investments certainly applied in the case of the production of bananas and other subtropical fruits, which found eager buyers on the growing US market. The Americans built railways in Latin America not to provide the continent with the necessary infrastructure to take off into the industrial age, but above all to serve their own interests — to transport bananas, lemons, oranges, coffee, cocoa, rubber and other products from the inland plantations to the ports.

Around 1880, then, the volume of US exports of goods and capital to Latin America was still very small. It was the activities of American politicians and entrepreneurs in the following years which 'opened' Latin America to the United States. James G. Blaine, the secretary state appointed by President Garfield in 1881, had ambitious plans for multilateral commercial agreements. But these initially came to nothing because he had to clear his desk after President Garfield had been murdered on 2 July 1881, and his successor, Chester A. Arthur, appointed Frederick T. Frelinghuysen as secretary of state. Unlike Blaine, Frelinghuysen preferred separate bilateral agreements. During his term of office bilateral reciprocity treaties were agreed with Mexico, Cuba, Puerto Rico, the British West Indies, the Dominican Republic, El Salvador and Colombia. But he declined to deal with the larger South American countries of Argentina, Brazil and Chile, for in these cases he would have have had to negotiate on wool imports, a move which would have probably stirred the powerful US wool lobby.

Even without these agreements US trade with Latin America was showing a marked upward trend in the 1880s, with the volume of US exports to Latin America increasing steadily throughout the decade. The composition of exports also changed. In their trade with Argentina, for example, the Americans used to buy hides and wood and sell timber, cotton, cloth, rice and metals; now they were also selling petroleum, farming machinery and manufactured goods. American industry had begun its advance southwards.

The First Pan-American Conference

Although at the state department for only six months in 1881, Blaine was instrumental in determining the direction of US Latin American policy in the following years. His ambition was to convene an inter-American conference whose primary aims would be to contribute to the resolution of regional Latin American conflicts (such as the Nitrate War which had been raging between Chile, Peru and Bolivia since 1879) and to remove at a stroke all barriers to regional trade. Although Blaine invoked the legacy of Simón Bolívar in support of his pan-American dream, his pan-Americanism differed considerably from Bolívar's, not least in that in Blaine's imagination the whole project would be under US direction.

The first pan-American congress had been convened at the initiative of Bolívar in Panama in 1826, two years after the decisive battle of Ayacucho which broke the remaining Spanish resistance in the wars of independence. Bolívar envisaged the eventual formation of 'one single nation', a 'confederation of Latin American nations' which would ensure that the new world would be 'governed as one great republic'.[10] He did not invite the United States to the congress, partly so as not to antagonize Britain (which sent an observer), but primarily because US participation did not fit into his plans for *Latin* American union: 'To us the Americans of the north are strangers. That is why I would never agree to them being invited to participate in our efforts to arrange our American affairs', he wrote in 1825.[11] And in any case the proposed confederation would strive for unity, mutual defence of the new republics and the liberation of Cuba and Puerto Rico from the Spanish yoke, objectives which could not easily be harmonized with those of US foreign policy.

But the Americans were invited to the Panama congress anyway. The responsibility for this is attributed to Francisco de Paula Santander, the vice-president of Colombia, who acted on his own initiative in the absence of President Bolívar. But Washington's response was far from enthusiastic. Only the indefatigable expansionist Henry Clay, secretary of state since 1825, argued for acceptance. President Adams, however, suspicious even of the word 'confederation', sensed a danger of the United States becoming involved in the kind of entangling alliance which it had hitherto so carefully tried to avoid. But Clay persuaded him that the gathering in Panama would merely have diplomatic character and would not prejudice US sovereignty. He requested the appropriation of the necessary funds to send a delegation to Panama in an address to the House of Representatives on 15 March 1826.

But as it turned out, this speech and the nomination as delegates of Richard C. Anderson, the ambassador in Colombia, and John Sergeant, a lawyer from Pennsylvania, exhausted the 'participation' of the United States in the First Pan-American Conference. Clay's request sparked off a five-month-long debate in Congress and in the press over whether or not the United States should be represented in Panama. When both houses of Congress finally voted the necessary funds to send a delegation in March and April 1826, it was already too late. The two delegates would not be able to reach Panama in time for the opening of the congress on 22 June. Anderson left Bogotá only ten days earlier and in fact never arrived at the venue: he died on 24 July in Cartagena of yellow fever. Sergeant refused to leave for Panama during the hot months, and did not leave the United States until the end of the year, by which time the congress had long since been adjourned. (It had ended with the adoption by the four states represented — Central America, Colombia, Mexico and Peru — of a 'treaty on the perpetual union, league and confederation', a document of little practical value.) So Clay's instructions to the delegates, which stated that the United States did not intend to change its neutrality between Spain and the new Latin American states and would resist any attempt by the latter to liberate Cuba, were never transmitted to the Latin Americans.[12]

In the words of one historian, at Panama 'the marriage of the two Americas ended in divorce before there was even a honeymoon ... Uncle Sam left the Spanish American bride waiting at the church'.[13] Since leading Latin Americans like Bolívar could hardly be accused of showing the kind of interest in the northern republic implied by this metaphor, it does not reflect the Panama fiasco entirely accurately. But there can be no doubt that the cause of closer inter-American relations was set back by decades, until Blaine rediscovered pan-Americanism, albeit of US provenance, in 1881.

Blaine launched his pan-American movement not out of platonic love for the southern neighbours, but for very concrete reasons. Among these were the great increase in US economic output, and the consequent need to expand foreign trade to sell the surplus products; the firmly entrenched position of the United States' European competitors in Latin America; and the regional conflicts which threatened the conditions for a potential increase of US commercial activity in the south. Blaine proposed to invite all Latin American governments to a conference in Washington in November 1881 to discuss the prevention of war, the preservation of peace and, if possible, the creation of machinery for solving existing regional disputes. But the assassination of President Garfield upset all his plans.

The new secretary of state, Frederick T. Frelinghuysen, disagreed fundamentally with Blaine's approach. He discourteously withdrew the invitations to the conference almost immediately he assumed office. In his view the inevitable diplomatic embarrassment was the lesser of two evils. He did not relish the idea of the United States subordinating its hemispheric policies to a supra-national grouping in which it would have, along with much weaker countries, only one vote.

Eight years later, Blaine gained an unexpected opportunity to put his pan-American ideas into practice when he was appointed secretary of state for a second time in the administration of President Harrison. In the meantime the course for the advance of US industry into Latin America had been set. And the multilateral approach abandoned by Frelinghuysen had been revived in 1886, when a subcommittee of the Senate foreign affairs committee debated the reissuing of invitations to an inter-American conference. (In the course of these discussions Solon O. Thacher, a member of the 1884 congressional commission, had paraphrased the Americans' imperialist consensus as 'As never before in our history does future growth, peace and order depend on us finding more consumers'.)[14] In July 1888 Thomas F. Bayard, the secretary of state under President Cleveland, formally invited the Latin American governments to a meeting in the following year for the purpose of discussing the state of inter-American relations.

A business initiative supporting official diplomacy also came to fruition just in time for the launch of Blaine's active Latin America policy. This was the establishment of the Latin American Commercial Union in New York in March 1889. President Harrison, as interested as Blaine in finding new markets for American products, especially agricultural products, did not hesitate to convey his best wishes to the new organization for the success of its export drive.

After years of preparation, the First International Conference of American States — or Pan-American Conference, as it was popularly known — was opened with great ceremony on 2 October 1889. The representatives — the United States and 17 Latin American countries (only the Dominican Republic did not attend) — set themselves a wide-ranging agenda. Among the topics for discussion and negotiation where the arbitration of disputes; bilateral reciprocity treaties; the construction of an intercontinental railway; the improvement of lines of trade between ports; a sanitary code for the protection of public health; uniform systems of customs and port dues; the establishment of a common monetary unit; conventions on trademarks, patents and copyrights; a common system of weights and measures; a common code of civil and commercial law; a treaty concerning the extradition of criminals; and the establishment of an international bank. The ambitious plans proposed primarily by the United States to link together, if not integrate, North, Central and South America, above all at the economic level, were debated in 15 standing committees, which met over 70 times. The inter-American dialogue dragged on for six months of, at times, tough negotiations, until 19 April 1890.

But before the conference could start its deliberations, the delegates were taken on an excursion. The composition of the ten-member US delegation, which comprised one career diplomat and nine representatives of big business (including the steel baron Andrew Carnegie), had already left little doubt about the overwhelming importance which the American business world and its political supporters attached to the conference. The travel arrangements only underlined the point. To impress upon their guests the size and wealth of their country, the planners from the state department sent the delegates on a 6,000-mile journey in a luxury train of six pullman cars costing $150,000. Official Washington stood on the platform to see off the Latin American guests, who were huddled in greatcoats presented to them for protection against the crisp autumn weather. In the course of their travels the delegates alighted at nearly all major industrial and commercial centres east of the Mississippi. They may well have been swept off their feet by what they saw; but, as it turned out, it made them no more willing to yield to US interests. Least of all the Argentine delegation which, having pointedly declined the invitation to the excursion, persistently tried to subvert US strategy once the conference finally got down to business on 18 November.

For the Americans the main objective of the conference was the creation of an inter-American customs union. But they got nowhere with this idea. For one thing, many Latin American delegates found Blaine's vision of a hemispheric customs union, with no duties internally and a common tariff barrier to the outside world, all too reminiscent of the German Customs Union (*Zollverein*). They feared that just as this had paved the way for the establishment of the German empire under Prussian domination, so a customs union between North and South America could prove to be the first step towards an American commonwealth of nations under US domination. Most delegates were also protective enough of their countries' recently achieved and hard-won independence to reject the kind of restrictions of national sovereignty which a customs union would inevitably entail. The Latin Americans objected to the US plan on practical grounds as well. A number of their countries, the non-industrialized ones in particular, depended to a large extent on the collection of customs dues to finance their government budgets. These countries had rejected proposals which would effectively deprive them of one of their few sources of income, for they could hardly impose new taxes (to compensate for the loss of customs revenue) on the little which the peasants produced for subsistence.

The US political establishment also showed remarkable insensitivity by debating and deciding tariff increases on imports of raw materials from Latin America at the very time that delegates were gathering to attend a regional conference whose primary objective was after all to be the removal of barriers to trade. As the delegates arrived in Washington, Congress was debating the imposition of higher tariffs on hides and wool from Argentina; and while they enjoyed themselves in Kentucky, the secretary of the treasury confirmed a duty on Mexican lead so prohibitive it was tantamount to an import ban.

The conference committee on customs union roundly rejected the US proposition as 'impracticable'. It considered the establishment of a free-trade zone, but dismissed this as only a theoretical possibility. It recommended instead the negotiation of separate reciprocal treaties — the only thing which the Latin Americans were willing to concede — which would take into consideration the special situation and interests of each country.[15] Fifteen countries declared their willingness in principle to negotiate such treaties. Chile and Argentina, piqued by Congress's deliberations on wool, their main export product, rejected even this. Subsequently the United States signed reciprocity treaties with Brazil (in January 1891), Guatemala and El Salvador (December 1891), Nicaragua (March 1892) and Honduras (April 1892).

The project for an inter-American bank fared little better than the proposal for a customs union. The US representatives employed all their gifts of persuasion to try to convince their guests how regional trade could be stimulated to the benefit and prosperity of both Americas if the monopoly held by London on credit lines were broken and the dependence on the British financial markets overcome. But it was patently obvious to the Latin Americans that the establishment of a regional bank would really only benefit US financial and commercial interests. Reflecting their suspicions, the committee on banking issued a vague recommendation on 'the granting of liberal concessions to facilitate inter-American banking' and the desirability of pursuing the matter further.[16] It would take another 69 years for this project to become reality: in May 1959 the Organization of American States (OAS/OEA) accepted a recommendation of its economic committee and set up the Inter-American Development Bank (IDB).

Not much came of the plan for an inter-American arbitration treaty either. Blaine had proposed obligatory arbitration of all disputes regarding diplomatic privileges, territorial limits, indemnification, rights of navigation and the inter-pretation and implementation of treaties. But for many Latin Americans the danger of the United States bringing pressure to bear in a dispute seemed too great. Most implacably opposed were the Chileans, who suspected behind the proposal an intention to establish a permanent court of justice dominated by the United States. Blaine pleaded with the delegates to adopt his plan, claiming that it was based on the principles of 'American international law'.[17] But his efforts were largely in vain. On 9 April 1890 only 7 of the 17 Latin American republics represented in Washington (Argentina, Bolivia, Brazil, Colombia, Guatemala and Venezuela) joined the United States in signing the arbitration treaty.

Yet another US project which had little chance of gaining the acceptance of the southern neighbours was the creation of an inter-American monetary union. The United States sought to persuade the Latin Americans to adopt bimetallism, that is, a currency system based on both gold and silver. This would have suited the American farmers and silver producers in particular, and they had the backing of the state department. But the Latin Americans had nothing to gain from the proposal. Quite the opposite. They could expect strong reactions from their European trading partners, who opposed such a monetary system. The commit-tee on monetary conventions gave an ambivalent recommendation, accepting the proposal in principle but urging further discussion at a special conference.[18] Called by Blaine in Washington on 7 January 1891, this conference assigned the study of the US proposals to a five-member commission. Its report, which in effect rejected the plan, was adopted unanimously by the full conference in due course.

The report which gave the American plan such an emphatic rebuff had been prepared by the Cuban poet, journalist and diplomat José Martí, who took part in the conference as a representative of Uruguay. Uniquely prescient among political leaders, Martí recognized the signs of the times and sought to alert the Latin American countries to encroachment from the north. Acceptance of projects like monetary union would hasten the day on which Latin America would become a victim of US hegemony, which was already visible on the horizon, he argued. Tellingly he summarized his prediction of future dependency and oppression as 'Whoever says economic union says political union. The nation that buys, commands. The nation that sells, serves'.[19] The link between economic and political dominance could hardly be put more succinctly. Predict-ing the rise of American imperialism, emerging at the time of the Washington conferences but undetected by many of his contemporaries, Martí urged Latin American countries 'to distribute their commerce among a number of countries' — to diversify, as we would say today.[20]

The Commercial Bureau of American Republics and the Pan-American Union

The only concrete result of the First Pan-American Conference was the establishment of an international commercial bureau. On 14 April 1890 — later celebrated as Pan-American Day, the birthday of the inter-American system — the conference accepted, by 14 votes to 0 with no abstentions, a recommendation from the committee on customs regulations that the participating countries should form the International Union of American Republics. Its primary purpose would be to furnish member countries with commercial statistics and other useful information. Care of all translations, publications and correspondence pertaining to the work of the union was discharged to a permanent secretariat, to be called the Commercial Bureau of the American Republics, which would also publish an information bulletin.[21]

The Commercial Bureau was set up in November 1890, and, needless to say, based in Washington, so that its work could be closely supervised by the state department. The conference had allocated an annual budget of $36,000 for its operation, a decidedly meagre amount in view of its wide-ranging remit to inform the business communities north and south of the Rio Grande about commercial and economic customs, laws and regulations. The US government had agreed to advance the funds to cover the expenses of the bureau in its first year of operation, but from the second year onwards each member country would contribute to the running costs in proportion to its population: thus Nicaragua, with a population of 0.4 millions, would contribute $150, and the United States, with a population of 25 millions, $19,000. So the Americans also held the purse strings. But most important of all, they provided the director of the bureau, who headed a staff of ten, including three translators for English, Portuguese and Spanish.

The bureau's first director was William E. Curtis, a member of the 1884 congressional commission, and widely regarded in the United States as a model pan-American, although he lacked the key qualifications for this accolade — knowledge of Spanish and knowledge of the region. He had offended many Latin Americans with the publication of *The Capitals of Spanish America*, based on a very brief tour of some of them. At the insistence of the Argentine delegation his title at the Washington conference had been toned down from chief secretary to executive officer. But Blaine appointed Curtis as director of the bureau despite his highly questionable credentials, thereby providing yet another illustration of how little US politicians were prepared to take account of Latin American sensitivities.

Under its American directors the bureau quickly developed into a news and information source for the US government bureaucracy on all aspects of Latin American commerce. In violation of its statutes, which required the dissemination of economic information to diplomats, chambers of commerce and authorized persons regardless of nationality, the bureau almost exclusively serviced US business interests. Not surprisingly, it soon had a reputation as a colonial office and was the cause of rising Latin American dissatisfaction.

But whatever reservations the Latin American governments may have had, all of them, except the Chilean and Dominican, agreed to join the International Union of American Republics and the bureau. Apparently reasons of principle did not guide the two which stayed outside the club; or perhaps they eventually decided they had little choice but to pay tribute to pan-Americanism à la Blaine. In any case the Dominican Republic joined the union in 1892, and Chile followed suit in 1899. Cuba and Panama joined soon after having acquired 'independent' status in the early 1900s with the active support of the United States. More or less the whole family of American nations was now united within the International Union of American Republics.

Soon after the secretaries, book-keepers, translators, messengers and porters started their employment at the bureau, Latin American voices began to demand the transformation of this *North American* commercial bureau into a *pan-American* one, as originally intended by the Washington conference. President Cleveland's secretary of state, Richard Olney, was unable to avoid inviting the Latin Americans to discuss the future of the bureau, and diplomatic representatives from 13 countries gathered in Washington in April 1896. The meeting appointed a committee of five to consider how the scope of the bureau might be enlarged. Since these tasks were initially restricted to producing the *Bulletin of the Bureau of American Republics*, taking stock did not take too much time, and the committee produced its report within two months. The reconvened meeting adopted the report, which largely met Latin American demands, in June 1896. In future the activities of the bureau would be extended from the mere collection and dissemination of commercial statistics and information mainly for the benefit of US economic interests to the study of all subjects relating to the economic life and growth of the American republics. Furthermore, the direction of the bureau would be broadened and internationalized by the creation of a permanent executive board of five members, which would meet once a month to supervise and direct the administration of the bureau. This institutional correction had a blemish, however, in that the US secretary of state would ex officio be the chair of the board; the Latin Americans could draw lots to fill the four other posts.

The organization and activities of the bureau would be on the agenda of regional conferences for years to come, and each successive conference marginally enlarged its functions. A meeting in March 1899 gave the executive board the authority to appoint and dismiss officials of the bureau. The Third Pan-American Conference, held in Rio de Janeiro in July–August 1906, made the bureau into a permanent committee of the conference. To reflect the broader scope of the growing organization, the Fourth Pan-American Conference, held in Buenos Aires in August 1910, decided to change the bureau's name to Pan-American Union. (This title had been coined by the *New York Evening Post* in its reports of the 1890 conference.) Meanwhile Andrew Carnegie, a member of the US delegation to the First Pan-American Conference, had been magnanimous enough to donate a building to provide the 'oldest international regional organization in the world', as it liked to call itself, with an appropriate headquarters.

The Latin American delegates at the Buenos Aires conference wanted more than the rather symbolic concession of the name change, which of course cost the United States nothing. They wanted to have a say in the Pan-American Union. Specifically, some of them argued that true pan-Americanism could not be reconciled with the US secretary of state's ex officio presidency of the governing board of the union. But they could not yet successfully press their demand to change the presidency into an elective office. For the time being the US secretary of state, perceived by the majority of delegates as the most authoritative among them, remained as the permanent head of the union. In his absence, the most senior Latin American diplomat in Washington — where, as if self-evident, the Pan-American Union was based — would be allowed to deputize for him and chair meetings.

A major problem arose at this time because Latin America's diplomatic representatives in Washington were asked to play two roles which were anything but identical and at times impossible to harmonize. On the one hand they were ambassadors of their country, which involved little more than acting as a messenger between the US and their own governments. On the other hand they were representatives of their country in the Pan-American Union, which often involved dealing with the US government as an opponent rather than a partner. Under these circumstances it should not come as a surprise that many Latin American diplomats, who as ambassadors had to maintain good bilateral relations with the Americans, took care not to offend the US government in the international forum. A further complication arose from the fact that countries which did not have diplomatic relations with Washington could not be represented in the Pan-American Union (although it was decided at the Buenos Aires conference that such countries could each designate a member to act as its representative). This meant that the US president had the power to exclude a disliked government or diplomat from the work of the union by the simple means of refusing recognition or accreditation.

At the Fifth Pan-American Conference, held in Santiago de Chile in March–May 1923, the Costa Rican delegation launched a new initiative to make the union more representative, to 'panamericanize' it, as it were. It proposed a change in the statutes to the effect that in future each country would be free to appoint whomever it wished as conference delegate, whether its ambassador in Washington or someone else. This should have been a matter of course, but the United States was nevertheless able to block the proposal. With 14 delegations threatening to withdraw from the union, the Americans made one concession: they agreed to change the presidency of the union into an elective office. In future the US secretary of state would not be appointed president of the Pan-American Union, he would be elected to this office. Some Latin Americans hoped that this rule change would increase their influence in hemispheric affairs, but it would make little difference politically.

Little changed in 1948 either, when the OAS was established as the successor to the Pan-American Union. Although the Latin Americans were granted formal rights and co-determination within the new organization, the US version of panamericanism remained dominant. For example, at the instigation of the

Kennedy administration, the consultative conference of OAS foreign ministers, meeting in Punta del Este, Uruguay, in January 1962, declared Marxism irreconcilable with the inter-American system and on this basis expelled Cuba from the OAS. The Cuban leader, Fidel Castro, responded by describing the OAS as the US department of colonial affairs. He wanted to draw attention, as the critics of the Commercial Bureau of American Republics and the Pan-American Union had done before him, not so much to the political submissiveness of the Latin Americans but more to the fact that the United States, with its economic power and its imperialist policy towards Latin America, would dominate any organization no matter how avowedly pan-American.

The southward expansion of American industry

Although the formal results of the First Pan-American Conference were meagre indeed, it proved very successful from a psychological standpoint, rousing American capital out of its passivity in foreign-trade matters and stimulating the industrial conquest of the southern continent. While the pan-American conferences of the first half of this century became gatherings primarily for the benefit of US investors, the Washington conference had been a forum *par excellence* for US commercial interests. And in the eyes of many Americans it was high time that the exporters gained some official backing for their efforts in Latin America, since, it was widely argued, the US economy was in danger of collapsing under its own growth.

The fortuitous combination of abundant and above all varied resources and raw materials, a highly organized skilled labour force (including many well qualified immigrants), and a strong capital equipment base (the value of manufacturing capital nearly doubled in the 1900s, from $9.8 billion to $18.4 billion, and was estimated at $44.5 billion in 1920) with which the United States was uniquely endowed produced a phenomenal growth of the economy in the 15 years after the Spanish–Cuban–American War. While the US population increased by only 30% in this period, production in various agricultural and industrial branches soared, largely as a result of massive improvements in productivity. Between 1898 and 1913 production of wheat increased by 70%, cotton by 58%, coal by 90%, steel by 131%, copper by 89% and cement by a staggering 406%. Although production overall did not grow by as much as production in specific sectors of the economy, it grew rapidly enough to raise the question as to what the US economy would do with all its goods once the domestic market had been saturated. Productivity per person-hour rose by about five percentage points every five years at the turn of the century, from 50.7% in 1895 to 55.6% in 1900, 59.9% in 1905 and 64.4% in 1910 (1929 = 100%). Notable in this context was the fact that, thanks to extensive mechanization, productivity actually rose faster in the agricultural sector than in the industrial sector, and had reached 90.0 on the above index in 1910. Small wonder, then, that above all the farmers became increasingly concerned that one day they would be buried under their own harvests.

The national economy expanded at such a pace in these years that the search for external markets became ever more urgent. The gross national product — the total value of goods and services produced by the US economy — averaged $7.4 billion (at current prices) between 1869 and 1878, $11.2 billion over the next decade, $13.1 billion in 1890 and $13.9 billion in 1895 (the last figure reflecting the impact of the economic recession of 1893–97). But once the recession had been overcome and the 'splendid little war' in Cuba had provided a new impetus for economic activity, the gross national product grew rapidly, by nearly half to $18.7 billion in 1900, $25.1 billion in 1905, and $35.3 billion in 1910. So in the two decades straddling the turn of the century, the output of the US economy nearly tripled, expanding by an average rate of nearly 5.1% per year. With inflation taken into account, the growth rate still remained an impressive 4.2% per year (from $52.7 billion in 1890 to $120.1 billion in 1910 at constant 1958 prices). Furthermore, between 1907 and 1911 on average $5 billion of the gross national product was saved, much of which was available for use as overseas investment.

The problem facing the US economy — how to turn the added value into profit — moved Elihu Root, secretary of state under President Theodore Roosevelt, to rearticulate the traditional notion of expansionism. In November 1906 he declared that since 1897 'the people of the United States have for the first time accumulated a surplus of capital beyond the requirements of internal development'. That surplus was increasing with extraordinary rapidity:

> Our surplus energy [he continued] is beginning to look beyond our own borders, throughout the world, to find opportunities for the profitable use of our surplus capital, foreign markets for our manufactures, foreign mines to be developed, foreign bridges and railroads and public works to be built, foreign rivers to be turned into electric power and light.[22]

How fortuitous that just as America was ready for it, great opportunities for commercial and industrial expansion to the south offered themselves. Root waxed lyrical about a 'newly awakened' Latin America, a 'vast continent' inviting the attention of American business. And even more fortuitously, the economic mentalities of the people of the two continents 'are complementary to each other ... Where we accumulate, they spend'.[23]

America's manufacturers, merchants and investors had not sat still since the days of Blaine (praised, incidentally, as one of the pioneers of southward expansion by Root). They moved into Latin America with a conscious, concerted effort. In 1894 a New York steamship company opened a regular trade route between the docks of Manhattan and the Pacific coast of South America. Two years later, with business flourishing, the line increased its fleet and a second company entered the field. The railway companies also began to invest heavily in railway construction in Latin America, where, unlike in the United States itself, the transport system was still underdeveloped. Although efforts concentrated on Mexico and its largely untapped market, the railway companies looked beyond the southern neighbour as well: for instance, in Costa Rica a consortium from Denver financed an important railway, and in Colombia an American-owned company built and operated a line along the Atlantic coast.

Entrepreneurs from the southern states were particularly hopeful that the commercial expansion to Latin America would alleviate their region's economic problems. To increase the appeal of their products for their southern neighbours, they organized a number of industrial expositions in the mid-1890s. The largest and most publicized of these was the Atlanta Exposition of 1895, which President Cleveland and several members of his cabinet found time to visit. The secretary of state, Walter Q. Gresham, had previously instructed all US ambassadors in South America to assist its organizer, J.W. Avery, in whichever way they could during his visit to the region to drum up interest in the exhibition. Another means used to stimulate the economic expansion to Latin America was the setting up of commercial museums, intended in effect to provide the business community with the ideological requisites for its foreign ventures. Once again members of the US foreign-policy establishment were present at the formal opening of such a museum in Philadelphia in June 1897.

But the most publicized and concerted movement for the development of foreign, especially Latin American, markets began with the formation of the National Association of Manufacturers (NAM). Founded, with the encouragement of Governor McKinley of Ohio (within two years to become president of the United States), by a group of recession-damaged capitalists gathered in Cincinnati in January 1895, this organization was a direct response to the economic malaise of the time. In one of the circulars sent out after the convention to influence industrialists and politicians, the NAM noted bluntly that 'The trade centres of Central and South America are natural markets for American products'.[24] Armed with this certainty of purpose inspired by the notion of manifest destiny, the American business community set out to capture and control the markets of the south. Among its first activities, the NAM in early 1896 established its first sample warehouse, in Caracas, the Venezuelan capital, and sponsored a party of businessmen for a visit to Argentina, Uruguay and Brazil to inspect market conditions in those countries and investigate the opportunities for increasing trade.

The success of the commercial expansion soon became apparent in the trade statistics. The value of US exports to Latin America had increased from a very modest $13 million in 1821 to $20 million in 1850, $65 million in 1875 to a still very modest $90 million in 1895. But from then onwards exports soared, doubling in the following decade and reaching $263 million in 1910. Sales nearly tripled within the space of 15 years, so the description 'export offensive' would not seem out of place (see Table 2.3). The figures reveal that despite all the great efforts the expansion took a few years to gather momentum, largely because the after-effects of the 1893–97 recession were still felt until the turn of the century. They also show a degree of geographical concentration, with the nearest neighbours Cuba and Mexico accounting for up to 40–50% of US exports throughout this period (a figure which by 1910 showed signs of falling, however). And while US companies were able to double their exports to Cuba almost immediately after the victorious Spanish–Cuban–American War of 1898, they had difficulty breaking the British trading monopoly in the large Brazilian market, with sales to that country remaining level until 1905 and rising only moderately in the next five years.

In general the American exporters had only limited success in the eastern half of South America, where the British and the Germans called the tune. And on the west coast there was initially a distinct north–south divide. The further that market observers like Lincoln Hutchinson, a special agent of the department of commerce and labour, travelled south from Guatemala, the shorter their reports about existing commercial relations, although the trend was definitely up.

Table 2.3
US exports to Latin America, 1896–1910
(in millions of US dollars)

	total	Cuba	Mexico	Brazil	others
1896	93	8	19	14	52
1897	94	8	19	12	51
1898	90	10	21	13	46
1899	106	19	25	12	50
1900	132	26	35	12	59
1901	135	26	36	12	61
1902	132	27	40	10	55
1903	133	22	42	11	58
1904	155	27	46	11	71
1905	177	38	46	11	82
1906	181	48	58	15	105
1907	249	49	66	19	115
1908	242	47	56	19	120
1909	224	44	50	18	122
1910	263	53	58	23	129

Source: *Historical Statistics of the United States*

For example, only 9% of Chile's imports in 1904 originated in the United States. The value of US exports to Chile ($4.8 million) lagged far behind that of Britain ($16.2 million) and Germany ($11.6 million). By this time the Americans had overtaken their French competitors, however, and between 1904 and 1906 they were able to nearly double sales to Chile to $8.7 million, threatening the position of Germany, which had traditionally close ties to that country. Future prospects also seemed promising, in particular the outlook for sales of mining machinery required by the Chileans. The upward trend could already be detected in the development of iron and steel exports, which more than doubled between 1897–1900 and 1901–03.

Reports from neighbouring Bolivia revealed a similar situation, with trade relations still underdeveloped at the beginning of the century. Germany (19.6% of the total) and Britain (16.8%) accounted for just over a third of Bolivian imports, with the United States (7.4%) sharing the remainder with Peru, Chile and other countries. In Peru the situation seemed somewhat more positive, with US exports to that country shooting up by 166.1% between 1895–99 and 1900–04. As far as the sales of iron and steel goods were concerned, the Americans had already left the German competitors behind and only the British remained to be overtaken, something which had already happened further north in Colombia and Ecuador. This sector appeared to indicate the trend for the future development of US trade with Latin America.

Railway construction in Bolivia, Peru, Ecuador and Colombia offered American business interests an opportunity to achieve two of their objectives simultaneously. For one thing, locomotives, carriages, track and other railway materials could be exported in large quantities, as the iron and steel producers realized very quickly and to their gain. For another, the construction of railway lines — and roads, in which US firms were also involved — alleviated the widely lamented lack of transport facilities and opened up the unexploited interiors of the Latin American countries.

With its wealth in raw materials, Bolivia provided an ideal field for investment, according to American observers. Huge quantities of tin, silver, copper, gold, bismuth and antimony were just waiting to be dug out of the ground and carted off to American factories. The exploitation of rubber and cocoa also offered great opportunities for investment. The Americans had already made their presence felt in Peru, where firms like the Cerro de Pasco Mining Company, the Inca Mining and Rubber Company and the Pacific Company had invested $25 million by 1904.

Apart from yielding very high profits, the extractive industries, in which US investments in Peru and other countries would be concentrated for many years to come, also helped to alleviate a disadvantage acutely felt by American exporters. As Hutchinson observed, 'American sales are handicaped by the lack of American capital investments'.[25] It was clear that exports could not expand significantly as long as investments in the infrastructure and the industrialization of Latin American countries (even if only in the form of economic enclaves) remained limited. In turn, investments in areas such as railway construction also stimulated demand for exports of railway equipment, spare parts and other goods.

This applied above all to those investments which affected the economic structures of the 'host' countries in such a way that they brought about changes in their social structures. From the turn of the century this was above all the case in Central America. The flow of dollars from the north proved increasingly a curse for the countries of the land bridge between North and South America. Under its influence the national economies became distorted by monocultural production, which mercilessly exposed the peoples of the region to the vagaries of the world market. The preponderance of the United States in the economy and trade of Honduras, for instance, was evident as early as 1905. In that year Honduras bought 72% of its imports from the north and sold 83% of its exports there. As in the other Central American countries, with the exception of El Salvador, the United States had supplanted the European powers which were still contesting the markets further south. In 1894 the United States became Costa Rica's largest importer with a share of 34.6%, overtaking Britain. Eleven years later its share significantly exceeded that of Britain, Germany and France combined. The Americans achieved their market dominance despite the barrier created by the mountains between the Atlantic and Pacific coasts, which, from their point of view, divided these countries into two distinct economic zones between which communication was very difficult. But as long as the interoceanic canal in Central America remained a figment of the engineers' imagination, the goods 'made in USA' had to be transported into the interior in ox carts or on the backs of pack animals. With success, as the export statistics showed.

The statistics also reveal the extent to which even then the economies of Central America had been distorted by the prevailing division of labour with the industrial countries, especially the United States. Foodstuffs, above all flour, were high on the list of imports of each of the five countries, swallowing up a very large share of foreign exchange. Things had been different in the recent past. Before German chemists developed aniline and other cheaper synthetic dyes, the Central American countries had supplied the European textile industries with prized cochineal and indigo dyes, while agricultural production was successful and diversified enough to feed the population. Some decades after the collapse of the dye industry, coffee took its place with a vengeance. The Europeans' and Americans' thirst for coffee seemed unquenchable, and everywhere valuable agricultural land was converted into coffee plantations without regard for the social costs. As the large estates usurped the fertile valleys and squeezed out the production of foodstuffs for domestic consumption, the subsistence farmers were forced to retreat to the mountains where they raised beans, maize and wheat on semi-barren plots, producing too much to starve and not enough to live.

Early in the century banana enclaves also made their appearance in Honduras, Guatemala and Costa Rica. US concerns took over the railway lines built by local capital (to take coffee to the ports) and built others to carry the products of their own plantations exclusively. The United Fruit Company swallowed up its competitors in the production and sale of bananas to become Central America's largest landowner, while its affiliates cornered rail and sea transport. It took over the ports and set up its own customs and police. American companies monopolized the electricity, postal and telegraph services, and politics, 'a no less important public service: in Honduras a mule cost more than a deputy, and throughout Central America US ambassadors [did] more presiding than presidents'.[26] The US dollar in effect became the national currency of Central America.

The United States and Cuba

Economically the United States had become the colossus of the north casting its shadow over Latin America by 1890 at the latest; politically it had yet to become the dominant power in the hemisphere. The Americans really flexed their political muscle for the first time in 1895, when they intervened in the long-standing conflict over the border between British Guiana and Venezuela. At issue in this dispute was not just a piece of tropical rainforest, but control of the mouth of the Orinoco river. The German explorer Robert Schomburgk, a cartographer in British service, had claimed the delta for Britain in 1841.

Convulsed in domestic revolutionary upheaval, the Venezuelans had at first no option but to acquiesce in this colonialist encroachment. But in 1876 the government appealed to Washington for moral support in the controversy. In response the US government, in 1882 and again in 1887, proposed arbitration of the dispute, which in the meantime had led to a serious deterioration in Anglo–Venezuelan relations. But the British could still afford to reject US mediation.

By 1895, however, the Americans had resolved the worst of their economic problems and had built themselves an effective navy. They could now stand up to the old mother country. President Cleveland decided to end the controversy, by force if need be.

In a strongly worded diplomatic note the secretary of state, Richard Olney, on 20 July 1895 informed the British government that the issue at stake was nothing less than the recognition or violation of the Monroe Doctrine. Declaring that vital US interests would be affected by the outcome of the conflict, he went on to make the memorable megalomaniac statement that 'Today the United States is practically sovereign on this continent, and its fiat is law upon the subjects to which it confines its interposition'.[27] The threatening gesture had the desired effect. The British government backed down and met the US demand to submit the dispute to arbitration, thereby also recognizing in effect the US claim to control in its back yard. In October 1899 an international arbitration commission awarded most of the disputed territory to Britain, although it preserved Venezuelan control of the Orinoco delta.

The Americans were not really very interested in north-eastern South America; their real obsession since the early days of the republic had, of course, been Cuba. And now that they had passed their first test as a major power in Venezuela, possession of the pearl of the Antilles seemed at last within reach. The vast importance of Cuba for the United States was considered self-evident by most Americans as early as the beginning of the nineteenth century. John Quincy Adams wrote in 1823 that 'it is scarcely possible to resist the conviction that to annex Cuba to our federal republic will be indispensable to the continuance and integrity of the union itself'.[28] The Louisiana Purchase had led to that of Florida, and both pointed with unerring certainty to the eventual acquisition of Cuba and Puerto Rico, if only because the two islands — Cuba even visible from Florida — were natural appendages of the United States. Again, in the words of Adams, 'there are laws of political, as well as of physical gravitation; and if an apple, severed by the tempest from its native tree, cannot choose but to fall to the ground, [so] Cuba can gravitate only towards the North American union'.[29] It was not a question of whether the United States would acquire Cuba, but rather of when, how and under what conditions.

As far as the expansionists were concerned, the American people were unanimous in their desire for Cuba. In a report submitted to the Senate foreign affairs committee on 24 January 1859, John Slidell, the man who had tried to persuade the Mexicans to sell part of their territory, argued that the United States could claim 'on this hemisphere the same privilege' that the European powers exercised everywhere else in the world. 'The law of our national existence is growth', he declared. 'We cannot, if we would, disobey it. The tendency of the age is the expansion of the great powers of the world.'[30] (He had in any case persuaded himself, against all the evidence, that 'an immense majority of the people of Cuba are not only in favour, but ardently desirous' of annexation to the United States.)[31] Needless to say, the Americans had not the slightest intention of setting themselves against the spirit of the age; but as yet they had to content themselves with waiting for the laws of 'political gravitation' to work in their favour. Until such time, American visitors to Havana would have to breathe 'ardent prayers that their next visit should be hailed by the stars-and-stripes floating from the Moro fortress' at the harbour entrance.[32]

For many years US administrations argued in support of the status quo in Cuba, a delaying tactic which seemed the best means of protecting the opportunity for annexation when the time was ripe. On 20 November 1822 the US ambassador in Madrid, John Forsyth, wrote to Adams, then secretary of state, that it would probably be best to leave Cuba in the hands of Spain, if only to prevent its transfer to another colonial power which might then abolish slavery on the island and thus endanger the peace and prosperity of the southern states.[33] This fear, that the emancipation of the Cuban slaves might spark off an uprising by the slaves of the southern states, would remain a major preoccupation of US Cuba policy until the 1850s. Adams mentioned two other concerns in his reply to Forsyth: the disruptions to US commerce caused by Cuban-based pirates and the British government's efforts to obtain the island (according to confidential information he had received, the British had been lobbying the Spanish court for two years).[34] Possession of Cuba would allow the British to command the inlets to both the Gulf of Mexico and the Caribbean, a prospect which filled the American politicians with dread, since in case of war Britain would be able to blockade the mouth of the Mississippi and deprive the (then) western states of their access to foreign markets.

The danger that Britain might emerge as the real winner in the struggle for Cuba loomed already in 1823, when France and Spain went to war. France also had to be considered as a possible usurper of Cuba, as had Mexico and Colombia, which by expelling the Spanish from their remaining colonial possessions would have hoped to dispel the threat of Cuba being used as a base for the reconquest of the Latin American republics. To guard against the possibility of any such transfers, US secretaries of state time and again declared themselves in favour of the island remaining in Spanish hands. According to Henry Clay in 1825, the United States was 'satisfied with the present condition of the islands' as long as the Cuban ports remained open to American trade (which they did).[35] Martin Van Buren wrote to the Madrid ambassador, C.P Van Ness, that 'motives of state policy render it more desirable to us that [Cuba] should remain subject to Spain' for the foreseeable future.[36] And James Buchanan also warned in 1848 that 'we should be compelled to resist the acquisition of Cuba by any powerful maritime state with all the means which providence has placed at our command'.[37]

By this time the Americans had begun to shift their position, however, and had decided to join the other interested parties in bidding for Cuba. The time for alternatives for Cuba's future had apparently passed. The apple that Adams still saw hanging firmly in the Spanish colonial tree at last seemed ripe enough to fall to the United States. Since independence (tantamount to the creation of a 'black republic') or transfer to another power were discounted on grounds of national security, annexation by the United States was the only option. 'Purchase by negotiation seems to be the only practicable course', according to Buchanan, although certain quarters called for a swift military action to seize Cuba and the Mexican peninsula of Yucatán.[38]

Employing the power of money against the impoverished colonial power, simply to buy Cuba from Spain, almost became an obsession with the Americans. The bankers and politicians had calculated the economic value of Cuba almost to the cent before Buchanan transmitted an offer of $50 million, to be doubled if necessary, as compensation to Spain for handing over the island to the United States. He must have been dismayed when the Spanish brusquely rejected his financial advances, the more so since he had already confidently predicted that Cuba would 'speedily be americanized, as Louisiana has been'.[39] This would have to wait.

The expansionists and the capitalists with Cuban interests next tried a rebellion against Spanish colonial rule, a rebellion they 'commissioned' hardened adventurers to carry out. The economic interests were headed by the New York firm of Drake Brothers, which owned one of the island's most profitable sugar plantations; the United States Mail Steamship Company, which had diversified interests in shipping, sugar production and slave labour; and the Illinois Central Railroad, which had plans to bring Cuban sugar to the Chicago market and export wheat and meat to the Caribbean. The most eager expansionists within the political establishment were three senators, Stephen A. Douglas of Illinois, George N. Sanders of Kentucky and George Law of New York, who called themselves the 'Young Americans' (after Ralph Waldo Emerson's *Young America*, in which he depicted the United States as the land of the future). Supplied by the expansionists with arms and money, the filibustering adventurer Narciso López and his men — modelling themselves on Garibaldi's army, they wore red shirts — made three attempts to launch an armed insurgency in Cuba between 1849 and 1851. The landings failed to have any impact, however, and on 28 August 1851 the entire band was captured by the Spanish. Four days later López was publicly garrotted in Havana.

Three years later the expansionists in Congress clamoured for war with Spain when the port authorities in Havana, on 28 February 1854, seized the US vessel *Black Warrior* on a technical charge of violating port regulations. The least that should be demanded for this outrageous action was an indemnity of $300,000, it was argued. The US ambassador in Madrid, Pierre Soulé, did indeed present a claim for damages on behalf of his government, as well as a 48-hour ultimatum. But the Spanish called the Americans' bluff. Only a year later did they agree to apologize for the incident and pay compensation.

Meanwhile the US government made another attempt, the last as it turned out, to purchase Cuba from the Spanish. Soulé had already been instructed at the time of the *Black Warrior* affair to make a fresh offer of $130 million. When this was rejected, he was instructed some months later to arrange a meeting with the ambassadors in Paris and London, John Y. Mason and James Buchanan, in the Belgian coastal resort of Ostend for the purpose of shaping a new policy on the acquisition of Cuba. The meeting took place on 9 October, and its outcome was the remarkable 'Ostend Manifesto'. Not intended for public consumption, the document was leaked by a diplomat and published in the press. In it the three ambassadors opined, having declared US possession of Cuba indispensable for the security of slavery in the southern states, that the government should make every effort to purchase the island. Should Spain refuse to sell, 'then by every law, human and divine, we should be justified in wresting it from Spain if we possess the power'.[40] But that was definitely not yet the case in 1854. So of necessity the expansion plans had to be postponed.

The 'splendid little war' with Spain

By 1898 the Americans had sufficient economic, political and military clout to throw the Spanish out of Cuba. They did so in a war which, with some justification, entered the history books as the 'splendid little war' (a phrase of John M. Hay, the secretary of state). It was 'little' in that it lasted all of 113 days and in that, apart from the soldiers who lost their lives, it did not cost the United States very much. Its aftermath was truly 'splendid' in that for the next 60 years Cuba became one of the most profitable of the United States' economic fiefs. Both John Hobson and Vladimir Ilyich Lenin, the most influential theorists of imperialism, whose analyses on the whole differed considerably, rightly characterized the 1898 war as a classic example of an imperialist war.

Works dealing with this conflict, particularly American ones, usually call it the 'Spanish–American War of 1898', a name which reflects ignorance of and contempt for the Cuban involvement. It implies that the Cubans were merely bystanders or unfortunate victims, and that the United States bore the burden of the final expulsion of Spanish colonialism from Latin America. The Cubans themselves refer to the Spanish–Cuban–American War. And rightly so, because they had been engaged in a bitter struggle for independence with the colonial power for decades. The dominant creoles (descendants of European settlers) opposed Spanish rule for a variety of reasons. They wanted to abolish the arbitrary taxes on imports and exports imposed by the colonial government, which favoured the Spanish traders; more generally, they wanted to loosen the tax screw which held back the island's economic development. They also preferred to turn the black slaves, who had to be fed for the whole year but were not fully employed during the 'dead time' (*tiempo muerto*) between the sugar harvests, into cheaper 'free' wage labourers. And finally, they aspired to political rights and administrative autonomy commensurate with their economic status.

The Cubans declared war on the colonial power 30 years before the American intervention. On 10 October 1868 the sugar-mill owner Carlos Manuel de Céspedes, acting in consultation with influential friends, freed his slaves, proclaimed Cuba's independence and assumed the presidency of the new republic. The insurgents (*insurrectos*) fought their first battle at Yara in the south-east and soon afterwards occupied the nearby city of Bayamo. (Cuba's national anthem, the Bayamesa, was composed at this time by Pedro Figueredo, who was still writing the lyrics on horseback as the liberation army entered his home town.) The unequal struggle between the rebels and the Spanish army raged for ten years, particularly in Oriente province. The Spaniards' scorched-earth policy caused untold damage, but only increased the rebels' resolve. The war was brought to an end with the convention of El Zanjón in 1878, in which the Spanish government promised administrative reforms.

For radical freedom fighters like José Martí, the outcome constituted a cowardly capitulation by the bourgeoisie within the revolution's leadership and a betrayal of the people. Deported by the Spanish, Martí began to organize the revolutionary forces in the United States, mainly in New York but also among the immigrant workers on the tobacco plantations in Florida. He was able to unite them in the Cuban Revolutionary Party, established on 5 January 1892. In January 1893 the legendary Dominican general Máximo Gómez was formally appointed as military chief of all the men in arms. In the Manifesto of Montecristi, the programme of the new revolutionary war drafted by Martí, the rebels formulated their aim: to free Cuba, and thereby the Antilles and the whole continent, from foreign rule. Having overcome various setbacks, they finally set sail from Hispaniola in a small boat and landed on the stony beach of La Playita, at the easternmost point of the island, on 11 April 1895. The second war for a free Cuba had begun.

Martí realized that the cause was caught in a race against time. The insurgents would have to secure victory quickly so as to prevent an intervention by the United States and renewed colonization. He did not feel wholly powerless in a confrontation between the Cuban dwarf and the American giant — 'my sling is that of David', he wrote — but knew that the unequal struggle would inevitably end in defeat.[41] Martí himself did not see the end of the war. The 'president', as his comrades-in-arms called him, and the 'apostle', as posterity would reverently call him, was killed on 19 May at the battle of Dos Ríos, at the confluence of the Contramaestre and Cauto rivers.

The second war of liberation proved as unequal a struggle as the first — towards the end the Spanish deployed 250,000 soldiers to defend their colonial regime — and even more bitterly fought. Gómez tried to achieve victory with the same scorched-earth methods used by the Spanish in the 1868–78 war. His men burned or destroyed everything the enemy needed to live and fight — sugar cane, warehouses, bridges, railways. In this way he hoped to raise the financial cost of the war to a point where the Spanish would decide to abandon the island to cut their losses. What even the most optimistic among the freedom fighters, dressed in rags and armed only with machetes but fierce fighters, had not dared hope actually happened. The heavily outnumbered guerilla army led by Antonio Maceo, the black general, advanced far into the west, passing Havana and reaching Pinar del Río province by early 1896. In doing so it overcame the supposedly impenetrable fortified lines (*trochas*) constructed across the island by the Spanish. These and other military successes showed that the insurgents were capable of defeating the Spanish and driving them from the island by themselves.

The notorious Spanish commander, General Valeriano Weyler y Nicolau, vilified as the 'butcher', escalated the struggle to total war. Unlike Gómez, who for obvious reasons tried as best as possible to spare the civilian population, Weyler tormented it relentlessly. To cut the guerillas off from the people and the land, he introduced a policy of 'concentration' (*reconcentación*), under which the transport of food from one place to another was forbidden, all cattle were to be brought to the towns 'protected' by Spanish troops, and the rural population was given eight days to move to fortified towns or to designated concentration camps. As a result, tens of thousands of hungry, sick and homeless men, women and children crowded the streets of all the major towns. Thousands fell victim to starvation and rampant disease. But the concentration policy failed in its objective of isolating the guerillas.

As the Spanish used ever more brutal means to preserve their colonial power, the insurgents increasingly gained the sympathies of American and world public opinion. But expressions of solidarity with the Cuban revolution were not enough. The insurgents needed weapons. And to obtain weapons from the United States they had first to be granted the status of a belligerent party. In February 1896 the Senate supported recognition of Cuban belligerency and the House of Representatives adopted a similar resolution (which, however, reserved the right to intervene in Cuba to protect American life and property). After a further two months of hard debate, both houses of Congress on 6 April approved, with only a few objections, the recognition of the Cuban independence movement as a belligerent. At the same time the senators and representatives called on President Cleveland to extend his good offices to Spain to effect peace on the basis of Cuban independence.

But Cleveland pretended not to hear, and ignored the appeal from Capitol Hill. This was hardly surprising, since the administration had already shown its lack of interest in the fate of the Cuban people on several occasions. It was only interested in Cuba's economic potential. Olney, for example, declined to be informed about the situation on the island by representatives of the independence movement, which to him were just 'bandits'. Instead he preferred to hear the views of an American planter, Edwin F. Atkins, the owner of the Soledad sugar cane plantation at Cienfuegos, one of the world's largest. (Atkins later boasted that one of his reports was embodied almost verbatim in one of Olney's reports to Congress.)[42] The administration also feared that the (white) Cubans, incapable of governing themselves, would not be able to prevent domination by the island's blacks, with all the negative consequences for American interests that that would entail. Although it was at pains to stress that its policy towards Cuba was one of 'neutrality', it in fact openly discriminated against the insurgents. President Cleveland had already shown his true colours in June 1895, when he ordered an end to all aid for the Cubans. Now, a year later, he simply ignored the Congress resolution supporting the independence movement.

Little changed under President McKinley, who succeeded Cleveland in March 1897. His administration's Cuban policy was even more explicitly subordinated to US economic interests. After two years of chaos on the island and a vain wait for reforms which might have revived the economy, these interests apparently called for forcing the hand of the colonial power. So from the end of 1897 onwards, confrontation between Spain and the United States was in the air. When the war threatened to affect American citizens in Matanzas province, the US consul, Fitzhugh Lee, asked Washington to dispatch a warship to Cuban waters. In response the armoured cruiser *Maine* was moved to Key West, only a few miles from Havana, on 15 December. It was ready to set course for the Cuban capital as soon as it received the codewords 'two dollars' from Lee. As it turned out, the coded signal from Havana was never required.

On 24 January 1898, President McKinley decided to send the *Maine* on a friendly visit to Havana, ostensibly as a gesture of support for the reforms being implemented by the Spanish. That this was a highly provocative act was clear to all concerned. With the *Maine* anchored in Havana harbour, an unexpected opportunity arose to escalate the carefully orchestrated confrontation between the two countries. Insurgents in Havana intercepted a private communication from the Spanish ambassador in Washington, Enrique Dupuy de Lôme, in which he carelessly called the president 'weak and catering to the rabble, besides [being] a low politician'.[43] The letter was passed on to the *New York Journal*, one of the newspapers published by the press baron William Randolph Hearst, a fervent supporter of the expansionists. A gloating Hearst published the fateful letter in the columns of his yellow press on 9 February under the headline 'The worst insult to the United States in its history'. The sense of outrage which swept the country provided the best possible psychological background to the administration's plans to move even faster on its collision course with Spain.

On 15 February, six days after the highly embarrassing revelation of the contents of de Lôme's letter (which led to his immediate resignation), Lee sat in his office writing a dispatch on the disastrous consequences of the affair for the Spanish government. At 9.38 in the evening he heard a massive explosion followed by a series of smaller explosions from the sea. Rushing to his window, Lee saw, as did thousands of locals, the burning *Maine* sink into the water. The disaster, which killed 264 seamen and 2 officers, was considered an accident by most experts: a US naval court of inquiry into the sinking explicitly excluded the possibility of fixing responsibility for the explosion on any person or persons. But an outraged American public had little doubt that Spanish agents were to blame. That Spain could not possibly have any interest in provoking a war with the United States was a consideration perhaps discussed in more educated circles, but certainly not in the popular press. The sensationalist Hearst papers fuelled anti-Spanish feelings with the slogan 'Remember the *Maine*, to hell with Spain!'

On 9 March, even before the court of inquiry had submitted its report on the incident, Congress approved without dissent a defence — read: war — appropriation of $50 million. The Spanish government then transmitted a serious proposal to Washington for an armistice on 9 April. But it was already too late. Two days later a warmongering President McKinley willingly yielded to the general hysteria and in a message to Congress demanded that the United States secure peace in Cuba by a 'forcible intervention'.[44] Events followed a predictable course. On 20 April, Congress adopted a joint resolution recognizing Cuban independence, demanding the withdrawal of Spanish troops, authorizing the president to deploy the armed forces in support of these demands, and, in the so-called Teller Amendment, disclaiming any disposition or intention by the United States of gaining sovereignty, jurisdiction or control over Cuba. On 22 April, McKinley ordered a naval blockade of the island. On 24 April, Spain responded by formally declaring war on the United States.

The first priority of the US army and navy was to neutralize, in a joint operation, the Spanish fleet — consisting of four cruisers and three destroyers — based in the eastern port of Santiago de Cuba and protected by land batteries. While the navy successfully bottled up the Spanish flotilla on 29 May, the army was in no position to capture the harbour and the city. In fact an expeditionary force of volunteers and regulars under General William Shafter was still being assembled, trained and equipped in Florida. It sailed from Tampa on 14 June and arrived off Santiago on 20 June.

One of the first exchanges of the war, at Las Guásimas, was a militarily pointless exercise which, moreover, involved heavy casualties. (Theodore Roosevelt, the commander of the Rough Riders, the first volunteer US cavalry regiment, made a name for himself here.) Following this and similar setbacks the American soldiers and officers began to accuse their Cuban allies of cowardice and to blame them for their own military failures. The accusations quickly took on racist overtones, not surprising in view of the many southerners in the US forces and the large number of blacks in the Cuban liberation army. The contemptuous term 'nigger' was frequently heard.

While the Cubans might put up with these scurrilous insults, their patience was stretched when they were not allowed to take part, even symbolically, in the occupation of Santiago following its surrender on 17 July. For three years the insurgents had fought the Spanish in a bitter and bloody self-sacrificing struggle, inflicting such tremendous damage on them that victory seemed imminent. But Shafter — a grossly overweight man who, clad in a woollen uniform singularly inappropriate for the hot tropical climate, always seemed nearer to physical collapse than to reaching a clear decision — forbade all armed insurgents to enter the city, let alone celebrate the victory over the colonial power as an ally at the side of the Americans. Forced to wait outside the city, the Cubans could see how the Americans raised the stars-and-stripes over the governor's palace and hear how they played the star-spangled banner as if the victory was theirs alone. That same day the commander of the Cuban army in the east, Major-General Calixto García, resigned his post and leaving the address Campos de Cuba Libre ('fields of free Cuba') sent Shafter a stinging letter of protest.[45] But to no avail. The Cubans were demoted to extras on the political stage of their own country, while the American generals and politicians took the lead roles.

Cuba's political leaders also found themselves pushed aside when a US–Spanish peace commission sat down to negotiations in Paris on 1 October. Terms were quickly agreed, or rather dictated, since Spanish resistance to the American demands had in effect been broken with the devastating defeat of Santiago. Under the Treaty of Paris signed on 10 December 1898, Spain ceded Puerto Rico and adjacent islands, Guam and the Philippines to the United States, and relinquished all claims of sovereignty over Cuba. Unlike the other territories, Cuba did not become a US colony, primarily because annexation would have meant assuming Cuba's debts of $400 million but also because it would have constituted a violation of the Teller Amendment.

So upon the formal termination of the Spanish–Cuban–American War with the exchange of ratification documents and a proclamation issued by President McKinley on 11 April 1899, a provisional US military government was constituted in Cuba pending national independence. Resigned to the fact that they would be defenceless against future reprisals by the occupation army, the insurgents knew they had no choice but to give up their arms and leave the maintenance of order to the 45,000 American soldiers stationed on the island. The military government brought some benefits after years of war. The second military governor, General Leonard Wood, for instance, did much to improve the education system and initiated health measures which resulted in the eradication of yellow fever. But strikes and protests by workers against the miserable working conditions, particularly the ten- or eleven-hour working day, were ruthlessly suppressed by the military and the police.

America's inveterate imperialists found the transitional military government, whose term would end with the inauguration of a Cuban government, anything but a satisfactory arrangement. They fulminated against the terms of the Treaty of Paris and the Teller Amendment (with its lamentable concession of a sovereign Cuba), which in their view tied the United States' hands. Among the most vociferous critics of the Teller resolution, which he called 'foolish', was Senator Orville H. Platt of Connecticut, the chair of the Senate committee for relations with Cuba. Recognizing the prevailing anti-imperialist mood, he began to devise schemes to ensure that the United States would remain in Cuba while formally withdrawing from it. For it had become clear that withdrawal had to come, as those critics who decried withdrawal as a crime and demanded immediate annexation lost ground to those who warned against the annexation of Cuba on the grounds that it would lead to a rebellion, as it had done in the Philippines.

First, then, a Cuban government had to be installed. To provide it with a constitutional basis the Americans arranged for the election of a constituent assembly which would not only *frame* but also *adopt* a constitution. This summary procedure — producing a 'bastard constitution', as the *New York Times* put it — had the inestimable advantage of excluding illiterates, blacks and radicals from the constitutional process while retaining a semblance of democracy.[46] The 32 members of the assembly duly gathered in Havana on 5 November 1900 under the supervision of the military governor. They completed the final draft of the constitution on 30 January 1901, adopted it on 11 February, and signed it on 21 February. This document brought the much-discussed americanization of Cuba nearer to reality. Cuba's constitution was closely modelled on that of the United States, and provided for a president and vice-president, a bicameral congress composed of a senate and a house of representatives, and a supreme court. To show their American mentors that they had learnt the (albeit modest) lesson in democratic government, the Cubans modelled their new parliament building, a few steps from the Parque Central in Havana, on the

Capitol in Washington.

This still did not satisfy the annexationists and imperialists. They wanted to put a much tighter rein on the Cubans. First Elihu Root, the secretary of war, suggested that the United States should secure naval bases and a right to intervene in Cuba. Then, on 25 February 1901, Platt introduced the notorious amendment named after him — a 'dreadful document' in the words of *The State*, a contemporary newspaper — as a rider to the US army appropriation bill.[47] In clauses one and two this amendment impaired Cuba's sovereignty and its right to contract foreign debts. But that was not all. Clause three read:

> The Cuban government consents that the United States may exercise the right to intervene for the preservation of Cuban independence, the maintenance of a government adequate for the protection of life, property, and individual liberty, and for discharging the obligations with respect to Cuba imposed by the Treaty of Paris on the United States, now to be assumed and undertaken by the government of Cuba.

Clause seven read: 'The government of Cuba will sell or lease to the United States land necessary for coaling or naval stations at certain specified points'. To add insult to injury, this travesty of the promised sovereignty of the new republic was to be inserted into the Cuban constitution.[48]

On 27 February the Platt Amendment was carried unchanged in the Senate by 43 votes to 20, with 42 Republicans and 1 independent, the zealots of the imperialist cause, voting in favour and 16 Democrats, 2 Populists and 2 independents voting against. In the House of Representatives the army appropriation bill and its amendment were debated for only two hours on 1 March, and approved by a majority of 161 to 137. In his second inaugural address on 4 March President McKinley could indicate his satisfaction with the work of Congress, declaring that it expressed what 'the legislative branch of the government deems essential to the best interests of Cuba and the United States'.[49]

The Cubans, with the exception of those few who from the beginning had pushed for annexation, thought quite differently. They reacted with utter dismay to the enactment of the Platt Amendment. A tide of protest swept the country. Havana was the scene of a huge torchlight procession on the night of 2 March, the day that Wood introduced the notorious amendment for adoption by the constituent assembly. What most Cubans, especially the veterans of the independence struggle, felt about US imperialist encroachment was expressed eloquently by Juan Gualberto Gómez, the delegate from Santiago and secretary of the committee appointed to prepare an answer to the United States, in his report to the assembly on 26 March:

> For the United States to reserve to itself the power to determine when our independence is threatened, and when, therefore, it should intervene to preserve it, is equivalent to handing over the keys to your house to someone so that he can enter it at any time, whenever the desire seizes him, day or night, whether with good or evil design.[50]

The Americans did their best to cajole the incensed Cubans. For example,

Root — the real author of the Platt Amendment — tried to persuade a Cuban delegation visiting Washington on 25 April that the amendment gave the Monroe Doctrine teeth and was the most effective means of keeping the European powers out of the Caribbean.[51] But he failed to convince.

In the end, all protest against the dictate from Washington was in vain. The carrot having failed, the McKinley administration brought out the stick and made it clear to the Cubans that they had no choice in the matter, since the alternative was continued military rule. No doubt feeling as if they were handing over their money to a man holding a knife at their throat, a majority of the members of the constituent assembly submitted to the inevitable on 28 May and agreed to insert the Platt Amendment into Cuba's constitution. The deed was formally done on 12 June.

The only element still missing for the proclamation of Cuban 'independence' and the termination of US military rule was a president. After the legendary Máximo Gómez turned down an offer to crown his heroic career with the presidency, the conservative Tomás Estrada Palma was put forward as a candidate. No opposition candidates stood and the voters stayed away in droves. Estrada Palma, the victor in the quasi-election, was sworn in as the first president of the quasi-republic on 20 May 1902. In his inaugural address he praised the United States and its role in Cuba in more glowing terms than the American imperialists themselves would have dared, even implying that US policies were the greatest philanthropy.[52]

Whatever future policies the United States would pursue in Latin America — whether it chose to establish finance protectorates, confiscate customs revenue, refuse diplomatic recognition to undesirable regimes, or intervene openly — Cuba was the prototype for American neo-colonialism.

Gómez would be proved right very quickly. Soon after the Americans had ended their military rule in Cuba on 20 May 1902 and incorporated the Platt Amendment into a bilateral treaty on 22 May 1903, they leased, on the basis of clause seven of the amendment, land around Guantánamo for a naval station at an annual rent of $2,000. Now they had a foot in the door. Over the next two decades they 'entered the house' on a number of occasions, intervening in Cuba's internal affairs with military force whenever the banks, the utility companies or the sugar companies considered it warranted.

The first such occasion was in 1906, when a revolt followed the re-election of Estrada Palma, who pleaded with the Americans to take over the government. Acceding to his request, the administration sent General Charles E. Magoon to take charge of a provisional government on 13 October. He ruled the island for three years with such a loose hand that the reserves of the national treasury fell from $13 million to a deficit of $12 million. When race riots broke out against the government of General José Miguel Gómez in 1912, American troops were landed on Cuban soil for a third time. And the United States intervened for a fourth time in 1917, when the re-election of President Mario García Menocal was disputed between liberals and conservatives. When Menocal found himself once again secure in power with the help of American bayonets, he agreed to the the presence of 2,000 US marines sent by Washington to protect American sugar interests in Cuba. Most of the marines were withdrawn in August 1919, but two companies remained stationed in Camagüey until February 1922.

The fact that no more American soldiers were to land in Cuba until 1933 did not mean that the United States left the island to its own devices and to its 'independence'. Occasional armed intervention whenever the fires of rebellion threatened to engulf American property was replaced by permanent political regulation. The arrival of General Enoch H. Crowder on 10 March 1919 on board a US destroyer — it remained anchored in Havana harbour during his entire stay, for moral effect, as it were — marked a new chapter in the United States' Cuban policy. Military occupation was replaced by the 'civil occupation' of an army of financial and other 'advisers'. This was found to be an equally efficient means of making the Cuban government pliable to US economic interests. In case of emergency the big stick of the Platt Amendment could always be resorted to.

Cuba: the ripe and sweet fruit

The quick reaction of the business community to the adoption of the Platt Amendment in Washington and Havana gave an indication of the real purpose of this constitutional instrument. On 1 August 1901 *The Nation* reported the enlargement of the capital stock of the American Sugar Refining Company, commonly known as the Sugar Trust, and noted that this foreshadowed its intention to acquire properties in Cuba for the production of sugar.453At closer inspection the *right of intervention* turned out to be a form of insurance for the *protection of investment*. Big business could afford to celebrate, since the climate in Cuba had finally been made suitable for investment. Trade and commerce also prospered. With the Platt Amendment and the Guantánamo naval base (the 'key' to the Caribbean and the Gulf of Mexico) the United States had not only secured free entry in Cuba but also unhindered access to the Cuban market. Before the 1898 war Britain and Germany had been the United States' main competitors for this lucrative market, which they tried to develop with aggressive policies. But during the period of military occupation the transitional govern-ment simply decreed tariff reductions on US imports to Cuba to keep out unwanted foreign competition.

At the time when the outrage over the proposed insertion of the Platt Amendment into the Cuban constitution reached its climax, in the spring of 1901, Root and other US politicians had given the Cubans assurances that once a stable government was established under the 'protection' of the Platt Amendment, Cuba would be granted trade concessions. Reciprocity was generously offered to sweeten the bitter pill of the Platt Amendment. To overcome the opposition of the formidable domestic beet-sugar lobby to the lowering of tariffs on Cuban cane sugar, a vast propaganda campaign in favour of reciprocity was launched before Congress opened its session in December 1901. It made out that reciproc-ity, promoted by Cuba's well-meaning friends in Washington, would serve solely the welfare of the Cuban people. But its sponsors were entrepreneurs with major economic interests on the island, such as Edwin F. Atkins and Henry O.

Havemeyer, spokesmen of the Sugar Trust, who had anything but philanthropic feelings for the Cubans and envisaged in fact the americanization of the Cuban economy. To complete the scandal, the military governor used Cuban state funds to send out tens of thousands of 'information' circulars to opinion formers. And the mill owners and other interested parties even sent their people onto the streets of Havana to demonstrate in favour of a reciprocal trade agreement.

The campaign achieved its aim, as the events of the following months would show. One of Theodore Roosevelt's first official acts as president — he succeeded the assassinated McKinley on 14 September 1901 — was to send a message to Congress pointing out that the issue of reciprocity with Cuba should be solved for 'reasons of morality'.[54] But the beet-sugar lobby had successfully organized congressional resistance to a trade agreement, and a bill on the matter was shelved in the Senate. In the autumn of 1902 the administration nevertheless sent General Tasker H. Bliss to Havana to negotiate a treaty. The Cuban negotiators had clearly taken to kowtowing to the Yankees with some alacrity, because it took only two meetings to reach agreement on US conditions. The treaty was signed on 11 December 1902. But it still took another year, and a special session of Congress called by President Roosevelt, before the legislators finally ratified the agreement on 17 December 1903.

The reciprocal trade agreement was the economic complement to the Platt Amendment. Under its provisions, US tariffs on some Cuban exports (primarily sugar and tobacco) were reduced by 20%, and Cuban tariffs on US imports were reduced by between 20 and 40%; the preferences agreed in his extraordinary treaty could not be extended to other countries, unlike those traditionally known as the most-favoured-nation clause; and the preferences themselves could not be changed, only the level of tariffs. The long-term effects of this unequal treaty on the Cuban economy were disastrous. It prevented both industrialization and agricultural diversification, and intensified the island's structural dependence because it was forced to export unrefined sugar almost exclusively to the United States and import all capital goods, most finished products and many raw materials and foodstuffs from there.

However, it would take considerable time before the Americans could reap the treaty's benefits. For one thing, it proved impossible to cut from one day to the next the traditional links between Cuba and the former colonial power, Spain. In 1905 the journalist Charles M. Pepper, sent to Cuba by the department of commerce and labour to investigate trade conditions in Cuba and the export opportunities for American industries, found to his displeasure that the Spanish still controlled a major share of Cuba's foreign trade. This was hardly surprising, since they still maintained large commercial houses in Cuba and extended generous terms of credit to importers. Furthermore, the Spaniards constituted the great majority of the foreign-born inhabitants of Cuba, thousands of Spanish seasonal workers came to the island every year, and the number of Spanish emigrants from Andalusia and other poor regions rose dramatically in the 1900s (from 9,000 in 1902 to 15,000 in 1903, 24,000 in 1904 and 48,000 in 1905). All of these groups brought their preference for Spanish-made goods with them.

Meanwhile a few thousand Americans had also settled in Cuba, who among other things were useful as 'missionaries of American goods', in Pepper's words.[55] The American Club of Habana also did its best to promote US products and advance US commercial interests. An early result of these efforts had been, Pepper reported, the penetration of the Cuban boot and shoe market by American manufacturers who had studied 'the peculiarities of the Cuban foot ... and adapted their lasts to the narrow toe and high instep common in Cuba'.[56] The shoe market set the pattern: eventually the Americans would displace their foreign competitors in all areas of Cuba's foreign trade. Partly as a result of the economic restructuring on the sugar island, US exports to Cuba quadrupled from $10 million to $43 million in the seven years following the 'splendid little war'; between 1905 and 1915 the value of exports nearly doubled again, to $76 million. During the First World War, when the European suppliers more or less disappeared from the scene, US trade with Cuba soared: exports rose to $165 million in 1916, $196 million in 1917, $227 million in 1918, $278 million in 1919 and a staggering $515 million in 1920, only to fall again because of the collapse of sugar prices. The US share of Cuban imports rose from 45% in 1902–06 to 65% in 1922–26. Overall, bilateral trade increased fivefold in the 25 years from 1904 to 1928, and around 1920 trade with Cuba accounted for almost a tenth of all US foreign trade.

But for some Americans who knew Cuba these export successes were still not enough. Among them was General James H. Wilson, the military governor of Matanzas and Santa Clara provinces during the first occupation. Wilson recognized the inestimable value of Cuba for the United States and called for a 'commercial union between Cuba and the United States, or, in other words, reciprocal free trade between the two countries under a common tariff against other countries'. He stated with brutal directness that the realization of his proposal would constitute 'a fair compensation for our altruistic work [in] voluntarily assuming the obligation of defending Cuba'. Providing a classic illustration of the notion of 'enlightened' imperialism, he claimed that commercial union would give all the economic advantages of annexation without the political disadvantages, such as military and administrative costs. In a commercial union, he argued almost in so many words, the Americans need not concern themselves with alleviating poverty and suppressing revolutions; instead they could imbibe the sugar-sweet economic profits of what President Gómez had called the 'cup of gold'.[57]

Pressing Cuba into a commercial union was tantamount to annexation in the limited sense, since its situation, once overshadowed by the star-spangled banner, would hardly have been distinguishable from that of a US state. The only difference might be that the share of blacks in the population exceeded what Wilson considered acceptable. But he offered a remedy to improve the population balance in favour of whites, namely the migration to the tropical island of 'northern farmers who ... suffer from rheumatism induced by exposure to the cold of winter'.[58] While concentrating his attention on Cuba, Wilson also ventured to raise the possibility of the eventual inclusion of Mexico and Canada in his commercial union; ideally he would have tied all of Latin America irrevocably to the United States in this way. It is important to note that Wilson was not a peripheral imperialist dreamer. He had been considered for the post of military governor of Cuba at the beginning of the occupation and was regarded as one of the spiritual fathers of the Platt Amendment. His views on Cuba carried weight.

In the case of Cuba the United States demonstrated to the established European colonial powers how instruments like the Platt Amendment and the reciprocal trade agreement sufficed to establish total economic domination over a country of the periphery, to a point where it was little more than a satellite. Direct US investment in Cuba had amounted to a mere $50 million in 1896. After the 1898 war investors swarmed to the sugar island, and the value of US capital investments was estimated at $115–120 million in 1906, $220 million in 1913, and $919 million on the eve of the depression in 1929. The latter figure was equivalent to 26.5% of all US investments in Latin America, which put Cuba top of the list both in absolute terms and on a per-head basis. According to contemporary estimates, US investment in Cuba amounted to around $400 per head of population, seven times the Latin American average.

The lion's share of US investments flowed into the sugar and tobacco sectors, which in 1905 accounted for half of all investments, with railways and roads accounting for a quarter (see Table 2.4). And since the railways' main function was to link the sugar-growing areas to the ports, the dominance of sugar investments was even greater than suggested by the official figures.

Table 2.4
US direct investment in Cuba, by economic sector, 1911 and 1924/5
(US$ million, book value)

	1911		1924/5	
	amount	%	amount	%
sugar	50	24.4	750	55.1
railways	25	12.1	110	8.0
public services	20	9.7	100	7.4
commerce	–	–	30	2.2
mining	25	12.1	35	2.6
others	55	26.8	235	17.3
debt servicing	30	14.6	110	8.0
total	205		1360	

N.B. Figures may not add up due to rounding

Source: Fabian, *Der kubanische Entwicklungsweg*

Once Cuba had been brought under the military and political 'protection' of the United States, Americans bought land and sugar mills wherever they could. They invariably got what they wanted, usually at a ridiculously low price and often even at the expense of veterans from the liberation war who had been settled on state lands and now had to make way for the voracious companies from the north. Atkins, for instance, acquired land in the Escambray region. The Rionda family acquired the Francisco sugar mill in 1899 and the Washington mill in 1910. The Hawley group appeared on the scene in 1899, organized the Cuban–American Sugar Company and acquired two mills in Matanzas. United Fruit — always at hand when there was a quick buck to be made — used some of the excess profits accumulated from its Central American banana business since the 1880s to buy its way into Cuban sugar, acquiring a mill near Nipe in 1901. By 1905, US citizens owned 29 sugar mills, whose production amounted to 21% of Cuba's total sugar crop; and by 1919, US-owned mills accounted for 35% of total sugar production.

This concentrated investment in the sugar sector had the effect of expanding an already overblown monoculture, with all its undesirable social implications, and strangling all other economic, and especially agricultural, activities. The highly productive new companies drove the small mills out of business and the subsistence farmer off the land: of the 2,000 small mills in operation in 1860, none survived Cuban 'independence'; and where farmers in Camagüey and Oriente provinces had grown vegetables and fruit, cane sugar was now planted as far as the eye could see. Within the space of a few decades the Cuban economy had been completely transformed. Sugar was processed in 165 large mills (*centrales*). During and after the First World War the price of sugar soared to previously unknown levels, the industry boomed, huge amounts of money were made. But as the American businessmen toasted the success of the sugar business with exotic cocktails in Havana's expensive clubs, the rural population starved. Deprived of their own land to grow their own food, the people simply could not afford to buy the expensive imported foods. So by tying Cuba's principal export crop to the American market and by keeping the marketing conditions under its control, the US government gained a more enduring influence in Cuba than that based on the Platt Amendment.

The struggle for the Panama Canal

When in the summer of 1898 the US battleship *Oregon*, anchored off the Pacific coast, was ordered to join the American fleet on the Cuban war front, it took 68 days to circumnavigate Cape Horn, steam up the east coast of South America and reach its battle-station in the Caribbean. The trip would have taken a third of the time if the current Panama Canal had existed. No clearer dramatic evidence could be adduced to demonstrate the strategic necessity of a passageway across the Central American isthmus.

Since the middle of the century the Americans had been preoccupied with domestic matters, first the civil war and then the economic crisis, and had done little to consolidate their position and extend their influence in Central America. Their claims and interests were enshrined in the Clayton–Bulwer Treaty of 1850, in which Britain and the United States undertook not to attempt to gain sole control over a future interoceanic canal, and the Bidlack–Mallarino Treaty of 1846, in which Colombia granted the United States transit rights across its province of Panama in return for a (fairly meaningless) guarantee of neutrality and respect for its sovereignty. The latter treaty had been negotiated at the initiative of the Colombians, who had become so suspicious of the imperialist machinations of the British in the southern Caribbean that they had asked the big northern neighbour for protection. The US chargé d'affaires in Nicaragua, Elijah Hise, had also concluded a treaty with the government of that country in June 1849, which granted the United States an exclusive transit right across the isthmus and the right to build canals, road and railways in Nicaragua, in return for a similar guarantee of protection contained in the 1846 treaty. In fact Hise had no authority to negotiate such a treaty, and a second treaty was concluded later in 1849. Soon to be overtaken by the Clayton–Bulwer Treaty, however, it was never submitted to Congress for ratification.

In the meantime the notorious American filibuster William Walker had decided to take the initiative in promoting US interests on the isthmus, specifically those of the Accessory Transit Company. Skillfully exploiting the civil war in Nicaragua to their own ends, Walker and his fellow adventurers established control over the divided country in the summer of 1855, and Walker set himself up as dictator. President Pierce issued a proclamation in which he distanced himself from the invasion; but Walker's endeavours could not have been that unwelcome, since the president's subsequent reception of a representative of the dictator amounted to virtual recognition of the regime. Walker was overthrown in 1857, and his private politicking and military campaigning eventually undid him. He died in front of a Honduran firing squad in September 1860.

Under the terms of the Bidlack–Mallarino Treaty the Americans landed troops for the first time in Central America in April 1856, to restore order during the so-called 'watermelon war' between black Panamanians and passengers and employees of the Panama Railroad opened a year earlier. The Americans were 'forced' to intervene again in October 1860, May 1861 and March 1865. Troops were landed in Panama on four more occasions between 1873 and 1902. Each expedition was ostensibly aimed at the protection of American lives and property, but also intended to keep open potential transit routes across the isthmus.

In the meantime the United States had also become active on a political level with a view to shortening the cumbersome sea route from the east to the west coast by two thirds. After the French engineer Ferdinand de Lesseps had been granted the rights to build a canal in Panama in 1878 and had begun the construction, President Hayes boldly stated the US position: 'It is the policy of this country to build a canal under American control'. And to give the claim geographical backing, he made a large semicircle with his index finger on a map behind him and described the interoceanic canal as 'part of the US coastline'.[59] He might as well have declared Mexico, Guatemala, Honduras, El Salvador, Nicaragua, Costa Rica and Panama part of the union at the same time. With these aggressive undertones the new American offensive in Central America was launched. In the same vein the secretary of state, James G. Blaine, tried the following year to secure British consent to a modification of the Clayton–Bulwer Treaty. But this was declined, and the Americans had to live with the detested canal treaty until the turn of the century.

Two events and developments strengthened the Americans' determination to build their canal: the annexation of Hawaii in July 1898, and, linked to it, the proclamation of the 'open-door' policy in September 1899. With the transcontinental domestic expansion ended at the Pacific and the essential dispositions made to turn Latin America economically and politically into the United States' back yard, the time seemed ripe to extend American imperialism beyond the western hemisphere and the Philippines. The government could also exploit the favourable strategic situation created by the victory in the war with Spain and the acquisition of a chain of island bases across to Asia. On 6 September 1899 the secretary of state, John M. Hay, asked the European powers and Japan to pledge themselves to recognize the principle of the 'open door', that is, free and equal economic access to China (which had been allocated a passive role as a mass market for American products). The open door was the American form of the British free-trade policy of the nineteenth century. Both policies sought ostensibly to foster equality of opportunity, but in effect they favoured the strongest capital interests, the British in the last century and the American since the First World War.

But without a Central American canal under US control the door to Hawaii and the China trade would be only half open. So the Americans set out to kick it open. Hay pressured the British into concluding a new canal treaty, the so-called Hay–Pauncefote Treaty, signed on 5 February 1900. This superseded the Clayton–Bulwer Treaty in that the British no longer insisted on joint construction and ownership of a future canal and in fact renounced this right altogether. Ratification of the treaty was not smooth, however. The Senate rejected the concession to the British, agreed by the anglophile Hay, that the United States would not be allowed to fortify the canal. Roosevelt, the self-proclaimed expansionist and the Republican candidate for the vice-presidency in the 1900 elections, became the objectors' champion. Hay had to renegotiate the treaty. The British had more than enough problems with the Germans and Russians in Europe to involve themselves in a dispute with the Americans over an interoceanic canal, and conceded all demands. The second Hay–Pauncefote Treaty, signed on 18 November 1901, gave the United States a free hand to construct, maintain and control a canal linking the Atlantic and the Pacific, and of course granted it the right to fortify the canal.

The legal and political obstacles had thus been removed; only the natural obstacles remained. Congress still had to choose between the two favoured routes for the isthmian canal, across southern Nicaragua or across Panama. The Nicaraguan route was traditionally considered the 'American' option, and the Panamanian route the 'French'. The congressional commission on the isthmian canal, known as the second Walker Commission, formally recommended the Nicaraguan route on 16 November 1901, not least because the New Panama Canal Company, the successor to the failed de Lesseps venture, demanded the exorbitant sum of $109 million for its holdings and franchises. Allowing for this demand, the commission had calculated that the Nicaragua route would be $63 million cheaper than the Panama route.

After the preliminary decision had been taken in favour of Nicaragua, two men appeared on the scene who proved instrumental in converting the US government to the Panama option after all. One was the New York lawyer William

Nelson Cromwell, US representative of the New Panama Canal Company and a partner in it, a director of the Panama Railroad Company, and since 1897 proprietor of a press office disseminating anti-Nicaraguan propaganda. Acting as the agent of the Panama Syndicate, which included among others the financier J.P. Morgan, Cromwell arranged for New Panama Canal to lower its price from $109 million to $40 million, thereby making the Panama route marginally cheaper than the Nicaraguan. The Walker Commission immediately changed its position, and on 18 January 1902 declared that under the changed circumstances the Panama route was the better option.

But the Panama Syndicate had not reached its goal yet. Consent to the commission's recommendation had still to be obtained from Congress, where the Nicaragua lobby could count on formidable support. At this juncture a second man appeared on the scene, the Frenchman Philippe Bunau-Varilla, who had been chief engineer on the de Lesseps project and had played a central role in the formation of the New Panama Canal Company. Reaching Washington in late January 1902, he joined Cromwell and Mark Hanna (a senator from Ohio, sponsor of McKinley and one of Roosevelt's advisers) in pushing for a reversal of the preliminary decision in favour of the Nicaraguan route. A bill to this effect, introduced by William P. Hepburn of Iowa, had been passed by the House of Representatives by 308 votes to 2 just as Bunau-Varilla arrived in Washington. So attention shifted to the Senate, where John C. Spooner of Wisconsin introduced a pro-Panama amendment to the Hepburn bill which instructed President Roosevelt to buy the New Panama Canal claims for $40 million and purchase the Panama route from the Colombians; only if this failed should he enter into negotiations with the Nicaraguans.

The Panama Syndicate received unexpected support from a natural phenomenon, the eruption of Mont Pelée on the island of Martinique on 8 May 1902. Supporters of the Panama option had frequently pointed to the risks involved in the Nicaraguan route because of volcanic activity in the region. And at the precise moment that the two factions squared off in the US legislature, hot lava spewed out of Mont Pelée, ran down the valley and covered the city of Saint Pierre, killing 26,000 people. Strictly speaking this had nothing to do with Nicaragua. But Bunau-Varilla remembered that the Nicaraguan government had some years earlier issued a postage stamp showing Lake Managua and a lava-belching volcano. He bought out the Washington dealers' supply of the stamp. Hanna distributed copies to every senator, and arranged for the publication in The *Sun* newspaper of a report of a major volcanic eruption in Nicaragua. The report was pure invention, but the immediate denial by the Nicaraguan government made little impression. To what extent the escapade influenced the senators may be arguable, but they passed Spooner's amendment on 28 June 1902. The Panama route had won the day.

Freely disposing of Colombian territory in planning the Panama canal, the Americans had made only a perfunctory effort to discover the Colombians' views on the matter. They took the trouble to gain the consent for the transfer of sovereignty required under international law only once Congress had created a *fait accompli* and the practical preparations for construction of the canal had been set in motion. The Colombian government, whose negotiating position improved somewhat after the settlement of a bloody three-year civil war between liberals and conservatives in November 1902, refused to sign an initial proposal for an unconditional concession to the United States. Only after a good deal of armtwisting in negotiations with the Colombian chargé d'affaires, Tomás Herrán, did Hay get what he wanted. The Hay–Herrán Convention of 22 January 1903 gave the United States a 99-year lease, unilaterally extendible, on a canal zone six miles wide, in return for a payment of $10 million and an annual fee of $250,000. Colombia would not receive any part of the money paid to the New Panama Canal Company.

Although the pact explicitly confirmed Colombian sovereignty over the canal zone, the Colombians were outraged when its contents became public, with anger being directed particularly at the unfortunate Herrán. The US Senate ratified the Hay–Herrán pact in March 1903, and despite its initial reaction the Colombian Senate was widely expected to do the same. But the extent of opposition to the treaty, even with its sovereignty clause, soon became clear. For weeks the Senate adjourned itself to avoid having to take a decision. And when it finally sat on 20 June, a whole range of issues was debated — except the one on everyone's mind. The Senate rejected the treaty provisionally on 12 August, adding a few conditions which left the door open for further negotiations. On 31 October it adjourned without having taken a final vote.

To the dismay of the Americans, the government refused to put pressure on the recalcitrant legislators. On 7 April, in no uncertain terms, Hay informed the Colombian government via the ambassador in Bogotá, A.M. Beaupré, that the treaty would have to be accepted as given; two months later he warned that the US Congress, faced with a rejection of the treaty by the Colombian Senate, might be forced to take actions which 'every friend of Colombia would regret'; and this was followed in early August by a demand for acceptance stripped of the usual diplomatic niceties.[60] President Roosevelt also raged against the intransigent Colombians. He compared them to 'a group of Sicilian or Calabrian bandits. You could no more make an agreement with the Colombian rulers than you could nail currant jelly to a wall'. He even called them 'contemptible little creatures' and a 'corrupt pithecoid community'.[61] Although he toyed with the idea of forcibly seizing Panama, a prepared message to Congress to this effect was never sent.

The cunning Bunau-Varilla, in collusion with Hay, solved Roosevelt's dilemma for him. Over the years, several Panamanian separatist movements had taken up arms against the distant central goverment. (The mountainous jungles in eastern Panama were so dense that at this time an American could reach Panama more easily by steamer from New York than a Colombian could by horse from Bogotá.) Why, Bunau-Varilla asked himself, could the separatists not join forces with the railroad and canal interests to stage a secessionary revolution; and why could the United States, invoking the 1846 Bidlack–Mallarino Treaty, not intervene in support of the insurgents? When he learned on 30 October that the battleship *Nashville* was leaving Jamaica for an unspecified destination, he correctly guessed on the basis of confidential inquiries in Washington that it was heading for Colón, the port at the northern entrance of the future canal. The countdown to revolution had begun.

As the zero hour approached, the US assistant secretary of state, Francis B. Loomis, cabled the consulates in Panama City and Colón at 3:40 in the afternoon of 3 November with the request to keep the department fully informed of the uprising which had broken out on the isthmus. Clearly Loomis was jumping the gun, because the consul in Panama City, John Ehrman, reported at 8:15 that evening: 'No uprising yet. Reported will be in the night. Situation critical'.[62] President Roosevelt would subsequently vehemently deny any direct US involvement in the Panamanian revolution. Doubtless a case of the stronger the denial, the more likely the veracity of the accusation: later he would boast that 'I took the isthmus'.[63]

Whatever the extent of US involvement, the Panamanian protégés achieved their goal in an operetta-like coup. The superintendent of the Panama Railroad, Colonel James R. Shaler, talked two Colombian generals into taking the luxury train from Colón to Panama City, assuring them that their troops would soon follow. But they could not, since all the locomotives and carriages had already been moved to the Pacific side of the isthmus. The troops were stuck in Colón. They were united with their less than glorious commanders when all were packed aboard a British steamer for the return to Colombia. Smug American observers would later peddle the anecdote that the 'revolution' had succeeded at the cost of the deaths of a Chinese citizen (trapped in some desultory shelling), a mule and, according to some reports, a dog.

More notable was the uncharacteristic situation of the United States, more familiar with supporting counter-revolutions, for once aiding the revolutionaries. But it was to be a short-lived change. When the Americans learned that Panamanian troops were preparing to land at Colón to claim the city, they stopped them. But they were quick to recognize the new government, doing so on 6 November in the interests of 'civilization', according to President Roosevelt.[64] On the same day Bunau-Varilla — occasionally called Felipe to conceal the foreign influence — was appointed as Panama's ambassador to Washington. In a letter to Hay this devoted servant of US hegemony took it upon himself to express in painfully excessive rhetorical flourishes the deep gratitude of the Panamanian people to the United States, the 'mother of the American nations', the 'liberator and educator of nations', the 'eagle which has spread its protective wings over our republic, thereby sanctifying it'.[65]

In his strongly economically motivated exuberance Bunau-Varilla was prepared to leave more to the claws of the eagle than might have been considered absolutely necessary. On 13 November, when he presented his credentials to President Roosevelt, Hay handed him a draft text of a canal treaty comparable to the Hay–Herrán Convention. Forestalling the two members of the Panamanian governing junta who were on their way to Washington to negotiate a treaty, Bunau-Varilla worked all night and all day to 'revise' Hay's paper. Not in his wildest dreams could the secretary of state have hoped that the representative of Panama in the United States would solemnly offer to turn the recently independent state into a US protectorate. But the Hay–Bunau–Varilla Treaty, signed on 18 November and in effect from 26 February 1904, did exactly that. It granted to the United States control of a canal zone ten miles wide *in perpetuity* and with *full sovereignty*, including the right of fortification and tax and customs immunity for US citizens. In return the United States guaranteed Panama's independence and agreed to pay $10 million and an annual fee of $250,000.

The two Panamanian emissaries arrived in Washington three hours after the signing ceremony and were unable to prevent the worst. One of them reportedly nearly fainted when Bunau-Varilla showed them the treaty. But all they could do was put a brave diplomatic face on the treachery. They had no choice, since it was either a matter of being conquered by the Americans or reconquered by the Colombians. The Panamanians accepted their political 'fate' and joined in the celebrations for the opening of the Panama Canal on 15 August 1914. Even so, 'the treaty that no Panamanian signed', the apt title of a documentary made in Panama on the affair, would remain a festering wound in US–Panamanian relations for the next six decades.

Notes

1. Quoted in Williams 1959 p. 28.
2. Address to the National Council of Foreign Trade, 6 May 1914, quoted in Williams, op. cit., p. 84.
3. US Congress 1886 p. 1.
4. Ibid., pp. 6 and 9.
5. Ibid., p. 4.
6. Ibid.
7. Ibid., p. 20.
8. See ibid., p. 10ff.
9. Ibid., p. 9.
10. Letter to a Jamaican gentleman, 6 September 1815, quoted in Burr and Hussey (eds.) 1955 p. 26.
11. Letter to Francisco de Paula Santander, 30 May 1825, quoted in Lawrezki 1981 p. 280.
12. Instructions to US delegates to Congress of Panama, 18 May 1826, quoted in Gantenbein (ed.) 1950 p. 497ff.
13. Whitaker 1954 p. 41.
14. Evidence to subcommittee of the Senate foreign relations committee, 20 April 1886, quoted in Wehler 1974 p. 85.
15. Report of the majority of the committee on customs union, First Pan–American Conference, 28 February 1890, quoted in US Congress 1890 p. 104.
16. Report of the majority of the committee on banking, First Pan–American Conference, 8 April 1890, quoted in US Congress 1890 p. 837.
17. Address to the First Pan American Conference, 19 April 1890, quoted in Gantenbein (ed.), op. cit., p. 58.
18. See report of the committee on monetary convention, First Pan–American Conference, 12 March 1890, quoted in US Congress 1890 p. 625.
19. Martí 1975 p. 372.
20. Ibid., p. 373.
21. See US Congress 1890 p. 409.
22. Address to the Trans-Mississippi Commercial Congress, 20 November, 1906 quoted in US Congress 1960 p. 2.

23. Ibid., p. 4.

24. Quoted in LaFeber 1963 p. 194.

25. Hutchinson 1906a p. 103.

26. Galeano 1973 p. 121.

27. Letter to Thomas F. Bayard, 20 July 1895, quoted in Gantenbein (ed.), op. cit., p.348.

28. Letter to Hugh Nelson, 28 April 1823, quoted Gantenbein (ed.), op. cit., p. 425.

29. Ibid., p. 426.

30. Report to the Senate foreign relations committee, 24 January 1859, quoted in US Congress 1859 p. 9.

31. Ibid., p. 13.

32. Ibid., p. 17.

33. Letter to Adams, 20 November 1822, quoted in US Congress 1852 p. 4.

34. Letter to Forsyth, 17 December 1822, quoted US Congress 1852 p. 5.

35. Letter to A.H. Everett, 27 April 1825, quoted in US Congress 1852 p. 17.

36. Letter to C.P. Van Ness, 13 October 1830, quoted in US Congress 1852 p. 27.

37. Letter to Romulus M. Saunders, 17 June 1848, quoted in Gantenbein (ed.), op. cit., p. 429.

38. Quoted in Slidell, report to the Senate foreign relations committee, published in US Congress 1859 p. 10.

39. Letter to Romulus M. Saunders, 17 June 1848, quoted in Gantenbein (ed.), op. cit., p. 429.

40. Quoted in Morris 1976 p. 259.

41. Letter to Manuel Mercado, 15 May 1895, quoted in Kirk 1983 p. 170.

42. See Foner 1972 p. 182.

43. Letter to José Canalejas, 6 December 1898, quoted in Foner, op. cit., p. 232.

44. Message to Congress, 11 April 1901, quoted in Gantenbein (ed.), op. cit., p. 474.

45. Letter to Shafter, 17 July 1898, quoted in Foner, op. cit., p. 369ff.

46. Editorial in the *New York Times*, 6 August 1900, quoted in Foner, op. cit., p. 541.

47. Editorial in *The State*, 3 June 1901, quoted in Foner, op. cit., p. 574.

48. Treaty of Relations between the United States and Cuba, signed 22 May 1903, quoted in Gantenbein (ed.), op. cit., pp. 488–91.

49. Inaugural address, 4 March 1901, quoted in US Congress 1969 p. 181.

50. Report to the constitutional convention, 26 March 1901, quoted in Foner, op. cit., p. 605.

51. Discussion with representatives of the constitutional convention, 25 April 1901, quoted in Foner, op. cit., p. 615ff.

52. Inaugural address, 20 May 1902, quoted in Foner, op. cit., p. 665.

53. Report in *The Nation*, 1 August 1901, quoted in Foner, op. cit., p. 629.

54. Annual message to Congress, 3 December 1901, quoted in Gantenbein (ed.), op. cit., p. 487.

55. Pepper 1906 p. 36.

56. Ibid., p. 22.

57. Address to American Society of Political and Economic Science, November 1906 [no specific date], quoted in US Congress 1909 p. 16.

58. Ibid., p. 17.

59. Message to Senate, 8 March 1880, quoted in Miner ??? p. 21.

60. Cable to A. M. Beaupré, 9 June 1903, quoted in Miner, op. cit., p. 285.

61. Letter to Hay, 14 July 1903, quoted in LaFeber 1978 pp. 36 and 23; and Miner, op. cit., p. 308.

62. Cable to Loomis, 2 November 1903, quoted in Miner, op. cit., p. 363.

63. Quoted in Bemis 1943 p. 150.

64. See cable from Hay to Ehrman, 6 November 1903, quoted in Miner, op. cit., p. 373.

65. Cable to Hay, 7 November 1903, quoted in Miner, op. cit., p. 376.

3. Dollar imperialism

The Roosevelt Corollary and Drago Doctrine

Economically weak and politically unstable, the Latin American countries, particularly those in the Caribbean, found themselves at the mercy of the European powers around the turn of the century. Condemned in the international division of labour to become suppliers of foodstuffs and raw materials, they inevitably also became heavily indebted. The Europeans used the collection of outstanding debts, as well as claims by their citizens for loss of property incurred during the frequent civil wars, as excuses for intervening in the internal affairs of the Caribbean countries.

Venezuela, then considered a prime example of internal political disorder and financial mismanagement, became the Europeans' first victim in 1902. In this case the primary reason for armed intervention was claims by foreign nationals and companies, including the powerful German trading firm Diskonto Gesellschaft, arising from the civil war which had been raging in the country since 1898. But President Cipriano Castro rebuffed all efforts to obtain redress. Under the Monroe Doctrine, the German government should have pursued the matter by diplomatic means. But President Roosevelt virtually invited the use of military force to punish the recalcitrant Venezuelans when he indicated that the United States would remain passive in such an eventuality. In his annual message to Congress on 3 December 1901 he declared that the Monroe Doctrine 'has nothing to do with commercial relations of any American power ... We do not guarantee any state against punishment if it misconducts itself, provided that punishment does not take the form of acquisition of territory by any non-American power'.[1] It should not have come as a surprise to the Americans when Germany, Britain and Italy (which were also involved in claims) imposed a naval blockade of Venezuelan ports on 20 December 1902, thus taking recourse to the international law of the jungle in order to extort compensation.

This high-handed armed intervention outraged all of Latin America. Indignation reached hysterical proportions in Buenos Aires. But unlike many of his compatriots, Argentina's foreign minister, Luis María Drago, kept a cool head. On 29 December he submitted a note to the US government in which, in summary, he argued that the use of armed force by the European creditor countries against debtor countries in order to force fulfilment of a financial commitment constituted a violation of national sovereignty and should therefore be rejected.[2] With this contention, which became known as the Drago Doctrine, Drago did not intend to provide the Latin American debtors with a means of evading their financial obligations. Rather, he intended to supplement the Monroe Doctrine by adding an economic dimension to it and putting it on a multilateral basis. But that was unlikely to be acceptable to the US government, for which the Monroe Doctrine was nothing if not a key unilateral, *national* policy. Washington's reaction was predictably cool, a rebuff in all but name. The secretary of state, John M. Hay, replied enigmatically that he could express 'neither agreement nor disagreement' with Drago's proposal.[3]

But that did not mean that the administration wanted to remain inactive or let this sensitive political and legal matter rest. There were ample grounds for an active policy. For one thing, early in 1904 the International Court of Justice in The Hague ruled that the European powers' intervention in Venezuela was justified, a decision which would only encourage the victors in the case to embark on further military adventures in Latin America. (In 1895 Henry Cabot Lodge, one of Roosevelt's closest associates, had already warned that Latin America might become a playground for the European powers, 'another Africa'.)[4] For another, the conditions in the Caribbean, particularly the financial bankruptcy of the Dominican Republic, gave the Americans specific cause for concern that the Venezuelan affair would be repeated. They did not want it to come to that.

On 26 February 1904, President Roosevelt wrote to the journalist William Bayard Hale that his attitude toward the 'weak and chaotic people south of us' was based on the theory that 'it is our duty, when it becomes absolutely inevitable, to police these countries in the interest of order and civilization'.[5] And on 20 May, at a dinner to celebrate the second anniversary of Cuban 'independence', his friend and adviser Elihu Root, who had recently resigned as secretary of war, read out a message giving a first warning to the Latin American countries and indirectly also to the European powers that henceforth the United States would no longer tolerate disorder and mismanagement in the south: it would consider 'brutal wrongdoing' or 'impotence' sufficient grounds for 'intervention by some civilized nation or another'.[6] Since for years Roosevelt had been unfolding the banner of civilization at every appropriate and inappropriate moment as if it were owned by the United States and identical to the stars-and-stripes, even the most benighted listener would have realized which 'civilized nation' would create order out of chaos in Latin America.

Seven months later, on 6 December 1904, in his annual message to Congress, Roosevelt became the second president after Polk in 1845 to add a corollary to the Monroe Doctrine. The Roosevelt Corollary held, in essence, that 'in the western hemisphere the adherence of the United States to the Monroe Doctrine may force the United States, however reluctantly, in flagrant cases of such wrongdoing or impotence, to the exercise of an international police power'. As far as responsible countries were concerned, like Cuba, which 'with the aid of the Platt Amendment ... had shown progress in stable and just civilization', Roosevelt magnanimously conceded that US interference in their internal affairs 'would be at an end'. In conclusion he underlined — hardly necessary in the light of his general philanthropic rhetoric — that he was acting not only in the interest of the United States but also 'in the interest of humanity at large'.[7]

The Roosevelt Corollary, widely regarded as the administration's most important foreign-policy measure, would, like almost no other, sour relations between the United States and Latin America for decades to come. It went well beyond what had been intended by Monroe. During his visit to Latin America as secretary of state in 1906 and on numerous other occasions Root would argue that the corollary — which was mainly his work — was not one of dominance, aggression or might but of equal friendship. He would still assert in 1914 that with the exception of the Polk Doctrine there had been no other change or extension of the Monroe Doctrine since it was first promulgated.[8] But the purpose of the Roosevelt Corollary, as of the Polk Doctrine before it, was in fact to provide a crude expedient to justify US aggression.

Ostensibly intended to check the disintegration of Latin American states and encroachments by European powers, in reality the corollary meant nothing less than the United States claiming for itself an exclusive right to intervention. Roosevelt thus wrote the prologue to American interventionism in Latin America. That at least is how the Latin Americans saw it, who at the time branded his rhetorical excess as the 'doctrine of the big stick' and later as the 'politics of the garrotte'. All Latin American analyses of the corollary — and there were many — agreed that this amendment to the Monroe Doctrine, whatever its benefits, went far beyond the politically acceptable.

The Third Pan-American Conference, held in Rio de Janeiro in July–August 1906, provided an initial focus for the concerted expression of Latin American resentment and criticism of Roosevelt's interventionist philosophy. But the diplomats failed to persuade the Americans of the benefits of alternative interpretations of international law. The US government rejected the Drago Doctrine (just as they had previously rejected the proposals by Carlos Calvo, the Argentine jurist and historian, that territories of sovereign states be inviolable and that foreigners be subject to the legislation and courts of the country in which they resided). With especially the Argentine delegation holding to the Drago Doctrine, a stalemate ensued, which was eventually broken with an agreement to refer discussion of the matter — in any case deemed too delicate to be resolved within an inter-American framework — to the forthcoming Hague conference. This had the result the Americans hoped for. The agreement adopted by the Second Hague Peace Conference on 18 October 1907 merely restricted the collection of outstanding debts by force, thus effectively denaturing the original Drago Doctrine.

In the meantime the principal concern of the US government continued to be the protection of the American investors who were swarming southwards. Even though the aggressive tone was occasionally lowered by stressing 'protective imperialism' or the aspect of 'self-protection' in the Monroe Doctrine, in essence the degree of independence allowed to a Latin American country became dependent on the amount of dollars invested there: the smaller the investment, the greater the possibility of maintaining sovereignty. For the Americans the sovereignty of other countries was not so much a value in itself as an aspect of a government's friendly relations with the United States. Those Latin American countries which willingly ceded part of their sovereignty to US economic interests were allowed to enjoy the remainder of their rights with less interference than those which refused to compromise their sovereign rights. Not surprisingly, this ideological presumption by the Americans became a source of never-ending controversy and contributed in no small means to the rise of Latin American nationalism and yankeephobia which subsequent US administrations found such an irritant.

In the United States the debate on the pros and cons of direct interventions in Latin America dragged on for three decades. As late as 1927 President Coolidge was still declaring that 'the person and property of a citizen are part of the general domain of the nation, even when abroad'.[9] This thesis — the essence of what became known as the Evart Doctrine — which claimed legal immunity for US citizens and their business activities in Latin America, in violation of the national sovereignty of the affected countries, was forcefully expounded in the following year. Addressing the Sixth Pan-American Conference in Havana in January–February 1928, the US delegate, Charles Evans Hughes, once again asserted that when a government could not provide adequate protection for the life and property of foreigners, then 'under such circumstances another government has the right I will not say to intervene, but to interpose in a temporary manner to protect the lives and interests of its nationals'.[10] The semantic juggling did little to placate the Latin Americans.

A gradual change of heart occurred only after the Hoover administration took office in January 1929. It signaled a moderation of the right to intervention with the publication of the Clark Memorandum on the Monroe Doctrine in March 1930. Prepared 18 months earlier by J. Reuben Clark, an undersecretary of state under Coolidge, this document rejected the view that the Roosevelt Corollary was 'justified by the terms of the Monroe Doctrine', while at the same time upholding the view that it was 'justified by the terms of the application of the doctrine of self-preservation'.[11]

Regardless of all the theoretical clarifications, the United States had by this time invoked the 'right' of intervention on several occasions. Implicitly or explicitly following the Roosevelt Corollary, it reduced five Latin American countries to financial protectorates in the 1910s and 20s. 'Dollar imperialism' succeeded traditional imperialism. That did not mean, however, that economic power and financial pressure replaced armed force, as suggested by the slogan 'dollars for bullets'. Rather, whenever they saw fit, successive US administrations interwove dollars with bullets in such a way as to maintain control at all times over the Latin American domains they had arrogated to themselves.

Haiti: 20 years a US protectorate

Apart from the Dominican Republic, which experienced the first US intervention of the type portended in the Roosevelt Corollary, neighbouring Haiti suffered most and above all longest from dollar imperialism. Over a period of decades, above all during the 20 years between 1915 and 1934, US policy towards Haiti would be characterized by the pursuit of interlinked selfish political and financial interests and the almost total neglect of the national interests of the Haitian people.

As early as 1847 the United States had attempted to obtain Môle Saint Nicolas on the north-west coast for use as a naval base, which would have ensured control of the Windward Passage, one of the major access routes to the Caribbean. But the Haitian government refused to discuss any cession of land, even after the Americans sent a sizeable fleet to Port-au-Prince, the capital, in 1891. Expansionist desires on this part of the *mare nostrum* had to be postponed for the time being.

They were revived 24 years later, when the National City Bank of New York sought to consolidate its shareholding in the Haitian national bank, which was entrusted with the administration of the national treasury. Not for the first time, and certainly not for the last, US diplomats and politicians became active on behalf of the bankers. To protect the latter's investments, the department of state made direct overtures to the Haitian government on six occasions in 1914 and 1915 to obtain control of the customs houses, the main source of revenue for the government. When the Haitians turned down the proposals, which they quite rightly considered an infringement of national sovereignty, the Americans resorted to a well tried desperado tactic. On 17 December 1914 a contingent of US marines landed in Port-au-Prince, marched in broad daylight on the Banque Nationale, forced the opening of the vaults at gunpoint, seized $500,000 and carried it aboard the gunboat *Machias*. The stolen money was taken to New York and handed over to the National City Bank. But this attempt — repeated elsewhere on numerous occasions — to make the Haitian government more amenable to a surrender of sovereignty failed to have the desired effect.

When the European creditors (mainly France, Germany and Britain) which held investments in Haitian banking, commerce, transport and utilities threatened to intervene to seize customs revenues, the Americans made up their minds to send in the marines properly. Fortuitously, a revolution provided them with the awaited opportunity and an excuse to intervene ahead of the European rivals. Vibrun Guillaume Sam, who had come to power on 5 March 1915 in a palace coup, was overthrown on 27 July and had to seek refuge in the French embassy. But before leaving the presidential palace he ordered a general massacre of political prisoners. The following day an enraged mob dragged him from the embassy and literally tore him to pieces in the street. At this point the US warship *Washington* entered the harbour of Port-au-Prince.

The American officers forced the Haitian parliament to postpone the election of a successor to Guillaume until they had canvassed the situation, that is to say, until they had found a presidential candidate acceptable to the banks and the state department. They found him in Philippe Dartiguenave. Only after Admiral W. B. Caperton had assured himself that Dartiguenave was willing to accept Washington's terms did he allow the Assembly to vote for a new president. To underline US interest in the outcome of the election on 15 August, marines guarded the doors of the chamber and Caperton's chief-of-staff circulated among the deputies. Dartiguenave was duly elected president.

Two days later the US chargé d'affaires, Robert Beale Davis, submitted to the Haitian government a draft treaty regulating relations between Haiti and United States. Not even the pliable Dartiguenave would agree to put his name to this treaty, however, which went much further than previous drafts and would have reduced him to the role of Washington's agent. So the Americans again turned the screws. From 21 August to 2 September they took over the country's ten largest customs offices, which left the government in the precarious situation of not being able to pay civil servants. They also extended their military control from the capital and a few strategic points outside to the whole country. And on 3 September they formally declared martial law. This massive show of force had the desired effect. On 16 September Dartiguenave agreed to almost everything demanded of him.

The treaty signed by Dartiguenave made Haiti for all practical purposes a US protectorate. Under its provisions the Haitian government agreed to appoint a 'general receiver' designated by Washington to control customs collection and to manage the country's finances (the latter task being delegated to a financial adviser appointed by the receiver). The general receiver would dispense all customs revenue in the following order: towards the payment of his salary and those of his assistants and employees, the expenses of the receivership, interest payments on Haiti's external debt, and the maintenance of the new national US-supervised constabulary. The meagre remainder would be passed on to the Haitian government 'for the purposes of current expenses'. Furthermore, the government agreed to contract new loans or lower tariffs only with 'the previous agreement of the president of the United States'. It agreed not to alienate any of its territory to another power or 'do anything else that might impair [Haiti's] independence'. And it granted the United States the right to 'lend an efficient aid for the preservation of Haitian independence', a euphemism for permission to intervene at will in the country's affairs.[12]

But that was not all. On 28 March 1917 the Americans pushed through an additional protocol which extended the duration of the treaty to 20 years and required the Haitian government to take out a loan of $40 million as part of the reorganization of the national finances. The revenues to secure this loan would still be collected by US-nominated officials even after the expiration of the 1915 treaty. Moreover, in July 1920 the American financial adviser submitted to 'his' government in Port-au-Prince a treaty which would give the National City Bank a near-monopoly over Haiti's finances. When the Haitians protested, blackmail was again resorted to. Civil servants' salaries were withheld until the government accepted the terms and signed the agreement.

In the meantime a new constitution had been adopted on 18 June 1918, 'under the eyes of the American marines', which in effect made the administrations in Port-au-Prince into puppets of the US occupation authorities.[13] At the behest of the model democrats from Washington, parliament was abolished and replaced by a council of state exercising, under US supervision, legislative authority; to complete the constitutional farce, the president was allowed to appoint the council's members, who in turn were allowed to elect the president. And to make absolutely certain that nothing could happen in Haiti's domestic political scene against their wishes, the Americans insisted on an agreement, signed on 24 August 1918, that all draft legislation would be submitted to and approved by the US embassy before being discussed by the council of state.

From early 1921 onwards the highest-ranking American diplomat in Haiti carried the title 'high commissioner', a term frequently used for proconsuls of the British empire. In celebration of this honour the first high commissioner, General John H. Russell of the US Marine Corps, established court-martial for civilians for the crime of lese-majesty. On 26 May 1921 he issued an order banning speeches and writings which 'reflect adversely upon the US forces in Haiti, or tend to stir up agitation' against US officials, the president of Haiti or the government; offenders would be 'brought to trial before a military tribunal'.[14] Criticizing the occupation or the government was now expressly prohibited.

Twenty years of foreign rule brought some obvious material and social benefits, in terms of containing epidemics and corruption. But even the employment programmes, for instance, proved highly controversial and fuelled local resentment against the Americans. The use of forced labour in the construction of an important road link between Port-au-Prince and Cap Haitien in the north constituted perhaps the greatest single indictment of the US occupation. The marine officer in charge of this project revived the obsolete Haitian institution of the 'road law' (*corvée*), according to which all adult males were compelled to work for a certain number of days per year on the repair or construction of public roads. Using methods reminiscent of the slave raids of past centuries, the marines dragged able-bodied Haitians from their families, huts and farms, and forced them to toil on the roads for months at a time in often faraway places. Those who tried to escape were shot.

Over 3,000 Haitians were killed by the marines during the 20 years of occupation. This fact, as well as the politically humiliating circumstance that under the 1915 treaty the United States controlled almost every aspect of Haiti's government (through the general receiver, financial experts, construction engineers, police commanders and others), and the often blatant racial prejudice exhibited towards the black Haitians by the marines (especially the southerners in their ranks), led to frequent anti-American outbursts. In 1929 the disturbances became so widespread that the Americans had to increase the size of the occupying army in order to maintain (their) order.

Faced with the unprecedented outbursts of anti-American feeling, Congress authorized, at the request of President Hoover, the sending of a commission to study conditions in Haiti and review US policies. The commission — headed by W. Cameron Forbes, and comprising Henry P. Fletcher, Elie Vezina, James Kerney and William Allen White — toured Haiti in the spring of 1930. Wherever it went, the commission was greeted, to its self-confessed surprise, by anti-American demonstrations and demands for an end to US occupation. Having gathered its evidence, also from discussions with opposition groups, it had little option but to recommend the 'haitianization' of the country's government and services.[15] This was accepted by President Hoover and his successor, Franklin D.

Roosevelt, who ordered the withdrawal of the marines. The last contingent left Haiti in August 1934, ending a 19-year-long military occupation. US financial control outlasted the first indications of the new 'good neighbour' policy, however, and remained for another seven years.

The marines in Nicaragua

The operation to suppress all revolutionary movements damaging US economic interests in Nicaragua lasted for 25 years. It began in 1909, when a coup brought down the Liberal president, José Santos Zelaya. The Liberals, unlike their Conservative adversaries, pursued a policy of locking the country into the capitalist world market. In line with this approach President Zelaya had explored possibilities of co-operation with the Europeans as well as the Americans during the planning of the interoceanic canal through Nicaragua. This transgression, considered very serious indeed by the Americans, as well as his frequent meddling in the affairs of the neighbouring Central American republics, had made this dictator a highly unpopular figure in Washington.

The Americans also mistrusted Zelaya because his government contracted unusually large loans in Europe, thereby raising the spectre of European intervention in the hemisphere in case Nicaragua defaulted on payments. This prospect made American capital and its political frontmen fear for US investments, which although not spectacularly large in absolute terms, were still very extensive. Thus, four American fruit companies owned 475,000 acres of banana and other fruit plantations; ten companies were engaged in mining operations; various firms had several million dollars invested in the forestry sector; and significant shares of the utilities and commercial sectors of the economy were in American hands. Towards the end of the 1920s, the United States bought 70% of Nicaragua's exports and supplied 75% of its imports.

To break the power of Zelaya, who opposed the efforts of US business interests to extend their influence in Nicaragua, the Americans quite predictably availed themselves of the services of the right-wing opposition, which had been planning a revolution. Civil war broke out when the Conservatives proclaimed General Juan J. Estrada as interim president in Bluefields, on the east coast, on 8 October 1909. Relations between the rightful government and the United States deteriorated to breaking point when loyal troops arrested two American filibusters caught trying to dynamite a ship with Zelaya loyalists on board; having confessed, they were summarily tried by court-martial and executed. The US secretary of state, Philander C. Knox, used this as a pretext to break off diplomatic relations with the Zelaya regime, personally handing the Nicaraguan chargé d'affaires his passports.

As was almost invariably the case in Latin America, Zelaya could not hold on to the presidency without Washington's blessing. He resigned on 16 December in favour of one of his political supporters, José Madriz, in the hope that this would keep the Liberals in power. But the Americans were no more kindly disposed to the successor than they had been to Zelaya himself. They did everything to prevent the loyalist forces from pressing their military superiority over the conservative rebels. And once they intervened openly in his favour, Estrada took the offensive and was able to enter Managua, the capital, in August 1910 and take over the government. Zelaya fled the country on board a Mexican gunboat.

Estrada was disappointed in his hope that Washington would grant immediate diplomatic recognition of his regime and welcome him as an ally. The Americans shrewdly played for time, letting it be known that several conditions would have to be met, especially concerning financial matters, before recognition could be extended. They sent the US ambassador in Panama, Thomas G. Dawson, to Managua to underline their demand for the rehabilitation of the country's finances and above all for the payment of all legitimate foreign claims on the government (that is, those of the American banks). Dawson had a solid background in the management of the financial affairs of other countries, since it was he who in 1905 had successfully arranged for the transfer of control of the customs of the Dominican Republic to Washington and Wall Street. He 'negotiated' a series of agreements with Estrada and his closes associates, the so-called Dawson Agreement, signed on board an American battleship on 27 October 1910. The Estrada regime was now allowed to take office, having undertaken to include guarantees for the rights of foreigners in a new constitution, to obtain a loan with the help of the US government to stabilize the country's finances (in the interests of the American creditors), and to guarantee the loan by a certain share of the customs revenue collected.

This pact, more a straitjacket, was wisely kept secret. But the defeated Liberals obtained a copy of the treaty and published it. When the Nicaraguans realized that their country was being turned into a US protectorate, a storm of protest broke loose. Confronted by implacable opposition from the Liberals and even criticism from within the Conservative ranks, Estrada could not last. On 9 May 1911 he resigned in favour of his vice-president, Adolfo Díaz.

The United States now had a man at the helm in Nicaragua who had been of invaluable service to them in the removal of the detested Zelaya and who would prove more compliant than any politician before or after him. As an employee of the American-owned La Luz y Los Angeles Mining Company based in Bluefields, Díaz had received an annual salary of $1,000 until 1909; yet he had been able, drawing on resources unknown but presumably provided from north of the Rio Grande, to finance the overthrow of Zelaya to the tune of $600,000 and thus gain a key position in the Conservative Party. As Washington's man in Managua, he was perfectly willing to sell his country's sovereignty in exchange for the presidential title.

On 6 June 1911 Díaz accepted the notorious ominous Knox–Castrillo Convention, which provided for the floating of an American loan to Nicaragua of $15 million secured by US control over customs. The Nicaraguan government also pledged only to alter the customs duties with Washington's permission and to submit regular reports on the country's financial situation to the state department. Negotiations for the loan were conducted between the state department and the banking houses of Brown Brothers and J. and W. Seligman. Nicaragua, already counted among the 'banana republics' controlled by the United Fruit Company and Baccaro Brothers, also became known in financial circles as the 'Brown Brothers Republic', since this company, together with J. and W. Seligman, US Mortgage Trust and others, shared out the wealth and resources of the country among themselves.

But the state department had failed to reckon with the Senate, which refused to ratify the Knox–Castrillo agreement. So the banks had to make new arrangements for the highly lucrative deal. This was done within a few months, and on 1 September an agreement on a provisional loan of $1.5 million was ready for signature. In return the bankers received control of the customs revenue as well as the reorganized national bank. The loan contracts were approved by the Nicaraguan parliament on 9 October 1911, and two months later the US customs collector and two financial experts arrived in Managua to start work. The New York bankers had selected a man they could trust, Colonel Clifford D. Ham, who from then on laid claim to all Nicaraguan customs revenue on their behalf.

The first loan was followed by others with similar political implications. On 26 March 1912 the banks extended a supplementary loan to Nicaragua of $755,000 to finance a currency reform, followed by another loan of $1 million on 8 October 1913. The banks in return exercised their options to buy 51% of the shares of the state-owned railways and the Banco Nacional. Both the railways and the bank were presented with nine new directors, six appointed by the bankers, one by the state department, and two, more to make up the numbers than exercise any authority, by the Nicaraguan government.

The insistence by the Americans on control of the country's finances as a whole, with its emphasis on loans and customs receiverships, led critics as well as supporters to describe US policy in Nicaragua between 1911 and 1913 as as 'dollar diplomacy'. An accurate enough description, but only half the story. Unlike the pattern established in other countries of the region, in the case of Nicaragua the policy should also be characterized as 'gunboat diplomacy or 'bullet diplomacy'. For whenever there was unrest in the country or the local political leadership called for assistance, US warships would be ordered to Nicaraguan waters. When, for example, the bombing of the Loma fort in Managua — attributed to the Liberals — killed over 60 people on 31 May 1911, ships were ordered to patrol both the Atlantic and Pacific coasts. The upshot of this policy was that the United States would remain entangled in the internal affairs of this Central American country for years to come.

By late 1911, Díaz was no longer able to control the power struggles within his government and his party. On 11 December 1911 he more or less begged the great northern neighbour to carry out a 'friendly intervention ... to establish a constitutional government'. To signal his total submission to Washington, he also proposed the insertion of a clause in the new constitution which would give the United States a right to intervene in Nicaragua — another Platt Amendment, in other words.[16] The invitation to make Nicaragua officially into a US protectorate did not make Díaz any more popular at home of course, and actually made his position more precarious.

The factional struggles intensified over the following months and by the summer of 1912 the country seemed to be on the brink of another civil war. With the life and property of American citizens seemingly threatened, the secretary of the navy, George Meyer, on 14 August sent in 100 marines at the request of the embassy in Managua. For the next 13 years US troops held Nicaragua under their control, and their bayonets kept in power the successive Conservative governments, which dutifully sold the country out to foreign interests.

That the first detachment of troops would not be adequate to the task became clear after only a few days, as Liberal forces, allied with those of Díaz's Conservative opponent General Luis Mena, began to attack foreign property. Another 360 marines were sent in, with half of them taking up quarters in the Banco Nacional (on US territory, as it were). Soon afterwards another 2,700 marines were landed. As this superior force bombarded Managua, occupied Bluefields and took control of the key railway line from Managua to Granada, the insurgents lost ground. Mena and 700 of his men surrendered on 25 September. The commander of the Liberal forces, General Benjamín Zeledón, was killed by his own troops when he tried to flee from Masaya after marines had seized the Barranca fortress. The revolt against Díaz was finally suppressed with the capture of León on 6 October. On 2 November, Díaz was re-elected as president.

Nicaragua was more or less at peace with itself for the next five years. But only really because the US marines, having supervised the presidential election, stayed on. Until 1925 a minimum of 100 marines remained as a 'legation guard', a symbol of the American commitment to the existing order. In this sense the year 1912 marked a turning point in US Caribbean policy. Previously the deployment of marines had always been intended as a show of force or a deterrent. In Nicaragua they had gone into battle to suppress a revolution deemed to threaten American life and property. As far as the American bankers and investors were concerned, the US soldiers subsequently stationed permanently at strategic points in the capital and elsewhere stood guarantee for good business. With their intervention and support of the Díaz regime the Americans also achieved their primary goal, the exclusive right to construct an interoceanic canal across Nicaragua. The so-called Bryan–Chamorro Treaty, signed on 5 August 1914 but not ratified until 18 February 1916, provided this. In fact it provided much more, and made Nicaragua into nothing less than a US protectorate.

On 1 August 1925, after years of relative stability, the Americans could withdraw the marines from their semi-colony. But only a year later an outbreak of violence persuaded them to intervene anew. Towards the end of August 1926 the Freiberg Mahogany Company and the Bragmans Bluff Lumber Company sent a cable to Washington requesting the dispatch of a warship since property had been attacked by revolutionaries. In response, the US navy once again set course for Nicaragua. At first the *Galveston* was ordered to patrol the Atlantic coast. In early September the two firms sent another cable, this time requesting that the *Rochester* remain stationed off Bragmans Bluff indefinitely and urging the creation of 'neutral zones' and the use of military force, if necessary, to protect their interests. These requests were accepted, and neutral zones were established around Bluefields and El Bluff.

These and other appeals for help, accompanied occasionally by pointed references to the multi-million dollar investments at stake, once again led to a deep US military involvement in Nicaragua. In addition, the Americans' old ally Adolfo Díaz, who had returned to the presidency for a second term on 14 November 1926 after an absence of ten years, requested the intervention of US troops almost as soon as he was sworn in. His position was under threat because of the failure of a conference (held on board a US warship anchored off Corinto) of Liberals and Conservatives to agree on the formation of a coalition government. On 1 December the exiled Liberal leader, Juan Sacasa, landed at Puerto Cabezas and was inaugurated the same day as the president of Nicaragua by a small group of supporters. As his Liberal forces gained ground against those of Díaz, the Americans established further 'neutral zones' for the purpose of protecting US citizens in Rio Grande, Puerto Cabezas, Pearl Lagoon, Prinzapolka and Rama.

The neutrality affected by the United States should not be taken too literally. In January 1927 the state department agreed to the export of arms and ammunition to the Díaz regime on the grounds that otherwise the revolutionaries, who received weapons from abroad (mainly Mexico), would be at an advantage. A 'legation guard' of 175 marines arrived in Managua on 8 January to provide further support for Díaz. And two days later President Coolidge explained in his message to Congress that his administration had had to resort to renewed military action in Nicaragua because of the 'great investments in lumbering, mining, coffee growing, banana culture, shipping, and also in general mercantile and other collateral business'; the 'internal strife' jeopardized American interests, he warned.[17]

Since this could not be allowed, the size of the military force committed to protect US interests in Nicaragua was steadily increased. Between May 1927 and March 1928, 41 warships regularly operated off the coast of Nicaragua 'in connection with the conditions in the country', as the secretary of the navy, Curtis D. Wilbur, noted laconically.[18] And between 7 and 28 January 1927, 4,600 US troops were landed in Nicaragua. Ever since the Americans embarked on the creation of their 'informal' empire in the 1890s, they had tried to keep the financial costs as low as possible. But the deployment of the marines in Nicaragua proved decidedly expensive. The cost of the operation between May 1927 and April 1928 alone was calculated at $3.5 million, a sizeable sum in those days (particularly when compared to the $20–10 which Nicaraguan civil servants earned and which the government considered cutting by between 5% and 20% in July 1930).

In an attempt to bring the fighting to an end, President Coolidge decided to send a personal emissary to Nicaragua, General Henry L. Stimson, who had been secretary of war from 1911–13 in the Taft administration. His brief was to discuss the situation with the US ambassador and the commander of the US troops and to report back to Washington. On his arrival in Managua on 17 April 1927 Stimson immediately held meetings with President Díaz and other government officials as well as with various leaders of the Liberal opposition. According to official information released by the state department, Stimson reported that, 'without exception, everyone with whom he conferred stressed the absolute necessary for the supervision ... by the United States' of the elections due in 1928 if Nicaragua were to free itself from the scourge of chronic civil war. For in the past the party in power had used its dominant position to control and manipulate elections, with the result that 'the opposition, feeling that it could not have a fair chance, at times resorted to violence'.[19]

On 22 April President Díaz proposed a peace plan which provided for US supervision of the forthcoming elections, the organization of a new Nicaraguan police force under US command, Liberal participation in the government, a general amnesty, and — the key point — delivery of all arms into American custody. At a meeting with Stimson at Tipitapa on 4 May, representatives of Sacasa and General José Moncada demanded Díaz's immediate resignation but also accepted the US-sponsored plan for pacifying the country. On 11 May the commander-in-chief of the US forces in Nicaragua, Admiral Julian L. Latimer, appealed to all Nicaraguans to hand over their arms to his troops. The next day Moncada informed Stimson that he and 11 of his generals would lay down their arms, whereupon the other side agreed to do the same. In the following two weeks, the US marines received 11,600 rifles, 303 machine guns and 5.5 million cartridges.

One of Moncada's generals, Augusto César Sandino, refused to down arms and submit to foreign control and US occupation. From his base in the remote northern province of Nueva Segovia, where he could rely on strong popular support, he and a handful of followers launched the first modern guerilla war against the Americans and their allies in Nicaragua. Despite being overwhelmingly outnumbered, Sandino's forces were strong and mobile enough to inflict painful losses on the Americans. As US military records show, from June 1927 hardly a day passed without skirmishes.

A notorious example of the counterinsurgency methods employed by the Americans was the aerial bombing of the village of Ocotal on 16 July 1927. This operation was initially reported as an attack by 400 'bandits' on the heavily outnumbered marines stationed in the village, an attack which they repelled with the help of a detachment of five bomber planes called in from Managua. Suspicions were raised over this account partly because no estimates of enemy casualties were released, which was at variance with the usual practice of providing the kind of 'body counts' that became so infamous during the Vietnam War. Press reports of the operation told a very different story, namely of the killing of hundreds of men, women and children in a bomb attack on a Nicaraguan village. The matter was discussed in the Senate foreign relations committee in February 1928, but at the hearings the military commanders as well as Wilbur denied all knowledge of a massacre of innocent civilians and maintained that if there had been any civilian casualties during the US involvement in Nicaragua they could only have been victims of accidents. Even so, in a report to the Senate the following April, Wilbur openly referred to the bombing of villages suspected of harbouring guerilas. 'The village of Ciudad Antigua was bombed as a military measure against outlaws who were known ... to be using it as a base.' According to Curtis, civilians who came to grief during the operation would have been supporters or sympathizers of the rebels — not innocent at all, in other words.[20]

If all the official reports were to be believed, relations between the civilian population and the American soldiers were very cordial. General John A. Lejeune, the commander of the US marine corps, for instance, had observed that his men had been welcomed warmly by the people of Nicaragua; and Latimer had come to the conclusion that 75% of Nicaraguans strongly preferred the United States to take over the government and restore law and order.[21]

Meanwhile the Americans proceeded with their other plans for pacifying Nicaragua. Regarding the US supervision of elections, General Frank R. McCoy was appointed chief of the election commission for the presidential election on 4 November 1928 — won by Moncada — and a US navy captain acted in a similar capacity during the congressional elections held in 1930. But more importantly, the Americans set out to organize the new national guard, the key measure intended to ensure that they would not leave behind a military vacuum which might favour the opposition. On 8 May 1927, President Díaz formally asked the US government for assistance in this matter, specifically requesting Washington to designate an American officer to instruct and command the new armed police force.[22]This was immediately agreed to. A few days later a colonel of the US marines was appointed director of the Guardia Nacional, and the work of organization, enlistment and training could begin. The numerical strength of the Guardia was originally set at 1,200 men; but by October 1930 it already numbered 2,500 men.

The Americans had now consolidated their position in Nicaragua to such an extent that they could afford the luxury of leaving Nicaragua to the Nicaraguans. The boys could be brought home. The Hoover administration decided — against the advice of the Senate foreign relations committee and the US embassy in Managua — to withdraw the US forces from Nicaragua. The military recommended a gradual withdrawal, and this was accepted. The evacuation began on 21 August 1929, when the transport ship *Henderson* sailed from Corinto for New York with 750 men on board. By June 1930 only 1,000 US marines remained in the country to protect their fellow citizens and their business interests. By the time of the US presidential elections in November 1932 virtually all the marines had left. The last detachment was withdrawn on 2 January 1933.

The Guardia Nacional, now commanded by Anastasio Somoza, assumed effective political control and guaranteed that no one could challenge US domination of Nicaragua. As one of his first acts as commander, Somoza ordered the treacherous murder of Sandino in 1934, a plan carried out with the probable knowledge of the US ambassador, Arthur Bliss Lane. The death of Sandino and the suppression of the insurgency cleared the way for 46 years of dictatorship by the Somoza family. This dictatorship enjoyed the support, varying perhaps but in principle always unswerving, of eight US administrations.

The Mexican revolution and Wilson's policy of 'watchful waiting'

For more than a generation, from 1876 until 1911, Mexico — of which it was said after the land grab by the gringos in 1848, 'Poor Mexico, so far from God and so near to the United States' — was ruled with an iron hand by Porfírio Díaz, the mestizo from Oaxaca. The Díaz regime ruthlessly favoured the few rich at the expense of the poor masses. While Díaz forced the peasants into wage slavery and peonage on the large estates, and did nothing to prevent the inhuman treatment meted out to the Yaqui Indians (who had been unjustly dispossessed of their lands in Yucatán), he wooed investors from the north and welcomed them with open arms because they helped to turn his motto, 'prosperity at any price', into reality. That price included the reckless sale of land, mines and concessions to foreign, especially American, companies. (The proceeds of this jamboree were not even reinvested in domestic industries, but used to finance the huge government budget.) During this period, Mexico's *Gründerzeit*, the country rapidly became integrated into the world market. The Díaz era brought some economic progress, but no economic development.

In response to Díaz's tempting invitations America began to pour millions of dollars into Mexico. The railway companies were the first to answer the call to the promised land: by 1912 they had invested $560 million in railway construction and operation (the management of the Mexican national railways remained under American supervision until 1914). They were followed by the mining companies: by 1911 they had invested $250 million in the mining industry, and by 1913 they controlled 78% of mineral production. By 1912 some 15,000 American ranchers had settled south of the Rio Grande. By 1913 the rubber companies controlled 68% of rubber production. And last but not least, the oil companies and thousands of oil workers streamed southwards: by 1913 they controlled 58% of this key industry.

The Americans knew the value to them of Díaz, the dictator who had opened the door to their economic invasion. At a meeting in Juárez in October 1909, President Taft, Roosevelt's successor, fawned on the aging potentate and assured him of the admiration of the world for his great work. But by this time the senile Díaz was already politically as good as dead. Real power had long since passed to the clique of so-called 'scientists' (*científicos*) which he had encouraged and promoted. Just as the positivism of Auguste Comte served as a justification for the bourgeois order in Europe, the 'scientific government' claimed by this group of technocrats was supposed to legitimate the existing economic, social and political order benefiting the large landowners, the army and the clergy. Of course none of these groups, the pillars of *porfirismo*, had any interest in the abolition of Mexico's feudal society. But the landless peasants and penniless farmworkers, who had to endure a form of wage labour nearly as oppressive as the slavery at the time of the Spanish conquest certainly had a very strong interest in the abolition of peonage — as in fact most Mexicans, who often saw themselves as the Americans' 'economic slaves', had an interest in breaking their chains. It was inevitable that these economic and social contradictions come to a head. Some Americans, including President Taft, were right to be concerned at the prospect of Díaz's death and the fate of the millions of US dollars invested in Mexico.

Disaffection with the glaring social injustices and the sell-out of the country's valuable resources surfaced on several occasions before 1910. Although the strikes and uprisings staged by farmworkers in the south and mineworkers and millworkers in the north were isolated and uncoordinated, they raised general demands for bread and land, justice and liberty. Francisco Madero, a landowner and member of one of the country's richest families, which had clashed with the Díaz regime, emerged as a focus for the opposition in November 1910. Madero wanted to give the people both bread and freedom. But first the latter and then the former: his programme called for political and democratic rights, but said little about social rights. It was only after he made concessions, albeit very vague ones, on the land question that he received the crucial backing of Emiliano Zapata and Pancho Villa, whose guerilla armies operated in the south and north respectively. Díaz's days were numbered. He resigned on 25 May 1911 and went into exile in Europe. On 8 June, Madero — not born to the role of a people's tribune — entered Mexico City in triumph and was confirmed as president soon afterwards.

Madero swiftly lost popular support, however, partly because of the nepotism which tainted his administration from the beginning, but more importantly because he failed to implement his promise to return to the people their expropriated communal lands (*ejidos*). Towards the end of 1911 Zapata declared Madero a traitor to the Mexican revolution, and once again took up arms.

Fearful of their property and of possible imminent nationalizations, the Americans lost much sleep over the continuing unrest. The Taft administration warned its counterpart to ensure the protection of life and property of American citizens. (During the revolutionary upheaval, from 1910 until 1920, 397 American civilians and 64 soldiers lost their lives in Mexico.) But Madero lost control, and was overthrown and brutally murdered by counter-revolutionaries during ten days of fierce fighting in Mexico City in February 1913. Recognition of the new regime headed by General Victoriano Huerta, one of Díaz's henchmen and the leader of the counter-revolution, was strongly urged by the US ambassador, Henry Lane Wilson (who had intrigued against Madero and may have been implicated in his murder). But the outgoing Taft administration would grant only de facto recognition. The US government was in transition, and Taft, disgusted by Madero's murder, preferred to leave the difficult issue of Mexico to his successor in the White House, Woodrow Wilson, rather than commit him to one policy or another.

When President Wilson was inaugurated in March 1913, an 'idealist' entered office who would reputedly pursue US economic interests less aggressively than the dollar imperialists had. Imbued with the great American ideals of freedom and free enterprise, this trained lawyer and economist had an ambition to prepare America's back yard for democracy, just as he hoped eventually to secure democracy for the rest of the world. He wanted, in short, to teach the Latin Americans to elect responsible rulers in clean elections.

With regard to Mexico, Wilson decided to invoke a precedent set a few years earlier. At the instigation of Elihu Root, then secretary of state, the five countries of Central America had held a peace conference in 1907, in the wake of a regional war, at which they had agreed several conventions, including one which obliged the signatories not to recognize a government that had come to power by revolutionary means. On this basis the Wilson administration refused to recognize Huerta, who had come to power by means of an assassination. It went further and tried indirectly to precipitate the regime's demise by isolating it politically — not only because of revulsion at Huerta's usurpation of the Mexican presidency, but also because the new regime favoured British over American capital in the exploitation of the country's resources, especially in the oil industry. That at least is how Wilson and his secretary of state, William Jennings Bryan, saw it.

The Wilson administration thus deviated from the previous practice of making diplomatic recognition of a government dependent on its strength and probable permanence; instead it took up a moral and constitutional position. Hopes that this new recognition policy would promote a broader democratic legitimacy among Latin American governments and fewer US interventions in their internal affairs were soon dashed, however. For one thing, recognition by the United States, owing to overwhelming US economic and military power, was a matter of survival for every Latin American government; non-recognition could be an effective political weapon. For another, the policy laid itself open to abuse precisely because the United States arrogated to itself the right to decide which changes of power deserved the seal of legitimacy; non-recognition could not only deter the usual military coups but could also undermine genuine revolutions struggling to overthrow oppressive dictatorships whose 'legitimacy' more often than not relied on electoral fraud. In any case the new policy could certainly be regarded as a continuation of US interventionism by different means, and Wilson himself, though following his ideal of the 'new freedom', could certainly be regarded as one of the greatest interventionists of them all.

The Mexicans had no doubts on the issue. Regardless of their political allegiance — whether sympathetic to Huerta, to the 'constitutionalist coalition' (which the landowner and former senator Venustiano Carranza formed with Villa, Zapata and Alvaro Obregón) or to no particular party — all Mexicans indignantly rejected Wilson's attempt to prescribe them a government to his taste. The Mexicans had good cause to take offence, also because the US government did not apply its policy consistently. When Colonel Oscar Benavides seized power in Peru in 1914 in a violent coup, for instance, the administration turned a blind eye to the circumstances of his accession and, blithely abandoning its concern for democratic development, recognized his regime immediately.

Moreover, the policy of 'watchful waiting', as it was dubbed, until the Mexican regime democratized itself from within and thus earned US recognition, was not implemented passively. Rather, the administration intrigued actively against the Huerta regime and applied financial pressure to destabilize and strangle it. And when that failed it intervened directly in the fighting between Carranza's and Huerta's armies. On 4 February 1914 the US government lifted the arms embargo, originally enforced as a sign of neutrality in the civil war, to permit munitions to reach the constitutionalist forces.

Before this move could have an effect, what became known as the 'Tampico incident' changed the situation entirely. On 9 April Mexican officials arrested, on a spurious charge, a paymaster and crew members of the US warship *Dolphin* who had come ashore at Tampico to obtain supplies. Although the port commander immediately ordered their release and expressed his regret, the US government chose to turn this trifle into a major diplomatic incident. Admiral Henry T. Mayo demanded a formal apology and a 21-gun salute in honour of the US flag, which he wanted hoisted on Mexican soil. Huerta responded with a formal apology and the offer of a reciprocal salute. At this point secretary of state Bryan was prepared to drop the matter, but Wilson must have thought it furnished a good opportunity to transform his policy of watchful waiting into one of watchful acting, a move urged on him by the interventionists, with his predecessor Roosevelt in the forefront.

On 22 April the president obtained Congress's permission to use force to protect American interests. At this point US troops had in fact already landed on Mexican soil. To prevent the German steamship *Ypirango* from landing a consignment of 200 machine guns and 15 million rounds of ammunition for Huerta's forces, they shelled the port of Vera Cruz on 21 April and then landed and occupied the town (which they held until 23 November).

Although this incident united Mexican opinion behind Huerta, and brought the United States and Mexico close to war, it nevertheless marked the beginning of the end for Huerta. He was forced from office on 15 July and fled to Jamaica on board a German cruiser. A few weeks later, on 26 August, Carranza entered Mexico City. But hardly had he been sworn in as president when civil war broke out again, with Villa in the north and Zapata in the south resuming their social crusade to restore the land to the dispossessed peasants.

Carranza received the sought-after recognition from Washington as de facto president on 19 October, after having pledged his government to protect American lives and property. But it soon became clear that Carranza — who in the face of the advancing opposition had to flee the capital and rule from Vera Cruz — would not be able to keep this promise. In January 1916 the government invited the US mining companies to return to Mexico to restart operations in the mines they had abandoned some years earlier on the advice of Washington. Eighteen young engineers jumped at the chance and promptly set off for Chihuahua. They did not get very far. Their train was stopped by Villa's men, who abducted and murdered them at Santa Isabel on 10 January. Two months later Villa's men also raided the town of Columbus in New Mexico, killing 17 Americans and carrying away a large number of horses.

Calls for revenge swept the United States. On Capitol Hill the pressure for military intervention mounted. Once again the administration — already deeply involved in the civil war, having taken Carranza's side with the de facto recognition and the supply of arms to fight Villa and Zapata — abandoned watchful waiting and brought out the big stick from the foreign-policy cupboard. Wilson called on General John J. Pershing to head a punitive expedition of 15,000 men against Villa's 'bandits', with orders to pursue them through the Chihuahua desert and capture or destroy the guerilla army. (Pershing had proved himself a specialist in 'pacification' expeditions: as a young lieutenant in the US cavalry he had taken part in the Apache campaign in 1886, the massacre of the Sioux at Wounded Knee in 1890 and the 'liberation' and subjugation of Cuba in 1898; and he had commanded the campaigns against the Muslim Moros in Mindanao in the Philippines in 1901 and 1909–13, which ended with their defeat at the battle of Bagsak.)

The more this and other punitive expeditions violated Mexican sovereignty, the more they aroused the antagonism of the initially co-operative Carranza government. At Carrizal, US and Mexican forces actually encountered each other. Open warfare between the two countries was averted only narrowly, partly by Carranza's willingness to accede to a US demand for the release of 17 American soldiers imprisoned near Carrizal. As war with Germany became imminent and the United States had greater worries than a confrontation with its southern neighbour, Wilson finally ordered the withdrawal of the expeditionary force in early 1917. On 11 March 1917 Carranza was elected president of Mexico, and Washington now also extended de jure recognition to his government.

At this point US–Mexican relations would have been friendlier than at any time since 1909 but for the vexed question of compensation for losses suffered by American citizens during the revolutionary period. This unresolved issue would lead to numerous angry exchanges between the two governments for years to come. Bilateral relations were further soured due to certain provisions of the new constitution adopted by the Mexican Congress on 31 January 1917. Article 27, in particular, declared that the nation — the community — owned the country's water, land and mineral resources; foreigners would only be permitted to acquire land and exploit resources if they accepted the law of the land; enemies of the revolution would be expropriated; foreigners requesting their own governments for assistance in any conflicts with the Mexican authorities would forfeit their land, exploration rights or oil concessions. These stipulations were of course deeply offensive to the neocolonialist worldview of the Americans, who did not want to abide by Mexican laws, be treated as Mexicans or relinquish Washington's protection. The next collision between the United States and Mexico, the oil conflict of 1938, was inevitable.

The 'dance of the millions'

While the First World War greatly weakened the financial and economic strength of the major Entente powers, Britain and France, it gave a tremendous boost to the American economy. It may be true that the US economy would have expanded in any case to take up one of the top placings in the world economic league. But the material demands made of the United States during the war — it was primarily entrusted with providing logistical support — gave its economy an additional stimulus. The United States supplied the Entente with munitions, iron and steel, copper, brass, and large quantities of foodstuffs, especially wheat. Around a third of all US exports during the war years consisted of war material in the narrow sense, while a large share of the remaining two thirds consisted of agricultural products.

The agricultural sector, whose overproduction caused such concern at the turn of the century, was now producing even more, much more than the American people could consume themselves. Wheat acreage, for instance, expanded from an average 62 million acres in 1909–14 to 100 million acres by 1919. Other sectors of the economy also boomed. The big companies which had hitherto targetted their mass-produced goods primarily at the domestic market had to expand capacity year by year during the war to keep up with demand from abroad. Industrial output actually doubled between 1914 and 1919, with specific branches profiting greatly from the war effort: between 1913 and 1917 production in the motor industry increased fourfold, in the rubber industry threefold, in the oil-refining industry at least twofold, and in the steel industry by half.

This expansion and prosperity of the US economy were made possible by the fortuitous presence of the three key resources so typical of the United States: abundant raw materials, skilled labour and a strong capital equipment base. These factors, together with the economic gains provided by Taylorism, the conveyor belt and rationalization in general, brought about a rapid rise in productivity, which had remained at nearly the same level in the first decade of the twentieth century. By the end of the First World War the United States had become the world's richest country. It produced a quarter of the world's supply of wheat, half of iron and coal, three-fifths of aluminium, copper and cotton, two-thirds of oil, three-quarters of maize, and nine-tenths of all cars. It had overtaken Britain, once the 'workshop of the world', relying on its colonial empire and still the world's largest economy in 1913. The gap between the two countries grew rapidly, and by 1922 the national wealth of the United States was estimated at $320.8 billion, compared to Britain's $88.8 billion.

During the war a change occurred in the Americans' economic behaviour which would not be without consequences for the relations between the United States and Latin America. Instead of consuming everything they earned, to live from hand to mouth in other words, the Americans began to save — unlike the Latins, who were prevented from doing so for decades because of a lack of economic surpluses. US national income reached $45 billion in 1916, $14 billion of which was put aside as savings; these amounts increased to $61 billion and $22 billion respectively in 1918. This provided the perfect prerequisite for investing money abroad, which is precisely what the Americans turned to with alacrity in the wake of the expansion of trade.

It should here be borne in mind that the United States, once primarily an exporter of raw materials, established itself as a major exporter of finished products shortly before 1914 at the latest. And the Latin Americans could buy more of these goods because their own purchasing power had increased by 70% as a result of their products fetching much higher prices on the world markets. Partly left to their own devices by foreign investors, who were too involved with wars and depressions, the Latin American countries experienced considerable economic growth during this period. American exporters were the main beneficiaries: US exports to Latin America rose (apart from a slight decline in 1915) at a faster rate than with any other region of the world during and after the war (see Table 3.1). It should therefore not come as a surprise that in the period 1905–10 US politicians and business interests once again sought to hammer home the importance of foreign trade and the perceived link between exports and national prosperity. The word went out that the United States had a moral duty to the rest of the world to become a true export-oriented economy, and that all efforts should be concentrated on attaining that goal.

Table 3.1
US exports to Latin America, 1914–20
(in millions of US dollars)

	total	Cuba	Mexico	Brazil	others
1914	309	69	39	30	171
1915	275	76	34	26	139
1916	540	165	54	48	273
1917	744	196	111	66	371
1918	741	227	98	57	359
1919	1,004	278	131	115	480
1920	1,581	515	208	157	701

Source: *Historical Statistics of the United States*

The Latin Americans, however, wanted to enjoy and consolidate their newly founded relative prosperity, and tried to put obstacles in the way of US imports in the form of higher tariffs. But American investors, already on the lookout for new investment opportunities, could easily overcome these hurdles — in what was known as 'tariff hopping' — by transferring production to the destination countries. The widespread policy of import substitution, which Latin American countries had adopted to reduce their vulnerability to the vagaries of the world markets, actually assisted the Americans in developing larger and more secure markets for themselves.

The government also helped where it could. Under the guise of dollar diplomacy the politicians extended their protection to the investors, and the pan-American conferences in particular offered both sides appropriate forums to pursue their common economic interests. As secretary of trade in the 1920s, Herbert Hoover commissioned feasibility studies and estimates of Latin American resources for the benefit of investors. And with the Evart Doctrine the Coolidge administration provided a legally one-sided but nevertheless effective protection for investments.

Supported in this way, the export of capital southwards flourished. In 1914, on the eve of the First World War, the value of private US investments in Latin America stood at $1.7 billion, $2 billion less than British and only $500 million more than French investments. During the war the capital flow from the United States to Latin America increased significantly and paved the way for the major expansion of US investments in the region in the post-war years.

This development contributed to a fundamental change in the position of the United States in the international financial and economic system from a net *debtor* country to the world's largest *creditor*. In 1914 the US external debt amounted to $3–5 billion, while investments abroad were still limited. But even before the United States entered the war three years later, it had bought back

American securities owned abroad valued at $2–3 billion; in addition, private investors had advanced around $2 billion in credits overseas. In the course of the war the United States poured in total around $9 billion into Europe in the form of money and materials. Furthermore, by the time of the armistice trade between the United States and Europe showed a net overall balance in favour of the former of $11 billion — a further contributory factor to the rise of the United States as an economic and financial empire.

The United States overtook the other capital-exporting countries in particular in Latin America. Its share of foreign investment in the region rose from 17% of the total in 1914 to 40% in 1929; put in absolute figures, direct US investment in Latin America rose from $1.7 billion to $3.5 billion. This sum constituted 41% of all US investment abroad, an indication of the key role which the region so condescendingly described as America's back-yard played for US capital. In 1930 the United States had invested $4.9 billion in Europe, but nearly $5.4 billion in Latin America (see Table 3.2).

Table 3.2
US investment in Latin America, 1930
(in millions of US dollars)

	total	direct (%)	indirect (%)
Cuba	1,067	85	15
Mexico	811	85	15
Argentina	808	45	55
Chile	701	63	37
Brazil	557	38	62
Colombia	302	43	57
Venezuela	247	100	0
Peru	200	62	38
Bolivia	116	53	47
others	552	76	24
overall total	5,361	68	32

Source: Scroggs, 'The American Investment in Latin America'

Latin American countries did not attract direct and indirect investment in equal proportions. The differences between Argentina and Brazil on the one hand and Venezuela and Peru on the other, for instance, arose from the divergent economic structures of the respective countries, the former primarily agricultural and the latter mineral-rich. Cuba, an agricultural country which nevertheless attracted huge sums in direct investment, formed the only exception to this pattern, and this can be explained by the impact of the world war. As beet-sugar production collapsed in Europe, cane-sugar production in Cuba expanded. In addition, the repeal of US legislation which had protected the domestic beet industry through import quotas sent sugar prices spiraling upwards. The eagerness with which American investors sought a share of the spoils sparked off the orgy of spending and speculation that became known as the 'dance of the millions'.

Only the very few rich Cubans could indulge in the orgy; for the overwhelming majority of the people it brought more misery. As the Americans concentrated increasingly on monocultures in their investments in Cuba and the other Latin American countries, the Latin economies became increasingly vulnerable to fluctuations of commodity prices on the world markets. The bubble had to burst, and it did at the end of the 1920s. The region's internally generated, partly foreign-financed prosperity dissolved into nothing with the advent of the world economic crisis.

During the 1920s there also developed the phenomenon of decapitalization. This meant, in essence, that with the high returns on investments more money actually flowed out of Latin America in the form of profits than flowed in as new investment capital. To the Latin Americans this became a major source of irritation, not least because it did not equate with the official pronouncements on wealth creation emanating from Washington. So while the Americans did not tire of highlighting the social and economic benefits which their investments brought to the region, the Latin Americans did not tire of criticizing the negative impact of the net capital outflow on their economies. But their complaints went unheard. The hard economic reality was that the United States was now so deeply involved in Latin America that not even the depression of the 1930s and the Second World War could undermine its dominant position in the hemisphere.

The morning after the Wall Street crash on 25 October 1929, which marked the beginning of the world economic crisis of the 1930s, proved a rude awakening for the Latin Americans in particular. The existing structural disadvantages inherent in the unequal international division of labour between the United States as an exporter of manufactured products and Latin America as exporter of raw materials was now intensified by the dramatic downturn in economic activity, and the result was catastrophic.

From 1929 to 1930, the value of US exports to Latin America fell from $973 million to $686 million, a drop of 29.5%; and imports fell from $1,107 million to $780 million, a drop of 29.4%. In the space of one year exports fell back to the level of 1923 and imports even to the level of 1922. (It must have seemed cold comfort that exports were still 127% up and imports 79% up on the 1910–14 average.) Although all parts of the continent suffered under the dramatic slump in US foreign trade, Cuba, America's most important trading 'partner', was hardest hit; and Argentina, Brazil and Chile, the so-called ABC countries, were also disproportionately affected (see Table 3.3).

Not that the Latin Americans supplied fewer goods to the north in 1930 compared to the previous year. The volume of certain exports even increased. But export earnings plummeted because of the collapse of commodity prices, on which the monocultural Latin American economies hung by a thread. Coffee prices, for instance, fell from 18.7 cents a pound weight to just over 10 cents within a year. And although Brazil sold more coffee than ever before in 1930, the collapse of prices and the shrinkage of consumption forced it to burn 78 million sacks of coffee. The efforts of 200,000 people during five harvests had to go up in flames in order to counter that vicious economic cycle of high prices pushing production up, oversupply pushing first prices and then production down, and scarcity pushing prices up again. In the early 1930s the supply of raw materials on the world market exceeded demand to such an extent that producers had no hope of obtaining fair or stable prices.

Table 3.3
US trade with Latin America, 1922–30
(US$ million)

| | exports | | | imports | | |
	1922–26	1929	1930	1922–26	1929	1930
Mexico	129	134	116	158	118	80
Honduras	10	13	10	7	13	13
Nicaragua	6	7	5	3	6	4
Cuba	176	129	94	304	208	122
Dominican Rep.	14	14	9	7	9	7
Colombia	32	49	25	59	104	97
Venezuela	21	45	33	17	51	37
Argentina	124	210	130	89	118	72
Brazil	67	109	54	180	208	131
Uruguay	18	28	21	16	18	12
Chile	35	56	46	84	102	55
Peru	22	26	16	20	30	21

Source: Fourth Pan-American Commercial Conference

The pattern was repeated throughout the region: the fall in the value of exports was disproportionately greater than the fall in volume. The Central American countries befell the same fate as Brazil: in 1930 they actually exported 9% more coffee to the United States than in 1929, but earned 23% less. Cuba provided the most spectacular example: exports of sugar to the United States fell from 4.1 million tons in 1929 to 2.6 million in 1930, a drop of 37%; but they earned only $76 million in 1930, compared to $157 million in 1929, a drop of 52%. Mexico had to absorb major losses in earnings from sisal exports, Argentina from hides and maize, Chile and Peru from copper, and Uruguay from wool.

The collapse of export earnings of course had a dramatic affect on the purchasing power of the Latin American countries. Consequently the United States could no longer find buyers for its great export successes of the 1920s. In most countries car sales, for instance, did not recover from their peak of 1929 for many years. Matters might not have been so bad if the crisis had only required the middle and upper classes to tighten their belts. But in fact it was the poor masses who had to bear the brunt of the distortions in foreign trade and the depression. Impoverished peasants were evicted from their land and workers were thrown out of their jobs or had their wages slashed. The result was a wave of social unrest throughout the region, which was invariably ruthlessly suppressed by the armed forces. Increasingly the rich looked to the military to maintain their domination, and a series of strongmen emerged, such as Jorge Ubico in Guatemala (1931–44), Tiburcio Carias Andino in Honduras (1931–48) and Maximiliano Hernández Martínez in El Salvador (1931–44).

These dictators did not immediately become protégés of the United States, however. The Hoover administration, which took office in 1929, had made clear its intention to abandon dollar diplomacy and pursue a less aggressive Latin American policy than its predecessor. Although his presidency coincided with a period of considerable turmoil and political unrest in Latin America, President Hoover and his secretary of state, Henry L. Stimson, resisted the temptation to employ the big stick, if only because the costs were deemed too high. Instead, in an attempt to dissipate Latin fears concerning US policies and brush up Uncle Sam's image, Hoover embarked on a ten-week goodwill tour to several Latin American countries even before his inauguration. In his first address, at Ampalá, Honduras, on 26 November 1928, he embraced the ideal of the 'good neighbour' in inter-American relations, a theme he reiterated at each stage of the visit.

Had it not been for the tacit acceptance or friendly treatment of the Latin American strongmen and the steep increase in tariffs on Latin America's main exports adopted by Congress in the Smoot–Hawley Act of 1930, one might have been persuaded that the 'good neighbour policy' marked not just a new style and tone in US Latin American policy but a deliberate new departure.

Notes

1. Annual message to Congress, 3 December 1901, quoted in Gantenbein (ed.) 1950 p. 360.
2. Letter to Martín García Merou, 29 December 1902, quoted in Whitaker 1954 pp. 87–9.
3. Letter to Drago, 17 February 1903, quoted in Perkins 1933 p. 393.
4. Quoted in Whitaker, op. cit., p 92.
5. Letter to Hale, 26 February 1904, quoted in Munro 1964 p. 76.
6. Letter to Root, 20 May 1904, quoted in Munro, op. cit., p. 77.
7. Annual message to Congress, 6 December 1904, quoted in Gantenbein (ed.), op. cit., p. 361ff.
8. Address to the American Society of International Law, 22 April 1914, quoted in Whitaker, op. cit., p. 99.
9. Quoted in Aguilar 1968 p. 68.
10. Report in the *New York Times*, 19 February 1928, quoted in Aguilar, op. cit., p. 68.
11. Memorandum to Frank B. Kellogg, 17 December 1928, quoted in Gantenbein (ed.), op. cit., p. 406.
12. Treaty between the United States and Haiti concerning the Finances, Economic Development, and Tranquility of Haiti, signed 16 September 1915, quoted in Gantenbein (ed.), op. cit., pp. 916-19.
13. Nearing and Freeman 1925 p. 145.
14. Quoted in Nearing and Freeman, op. cit., p. 150.
15. US Department of State 1930 p. 20
16. Letter to Franklin M. Gunter, 21 December 1911, quoted in Munro, op. cit., p. 200.
17. Annual message to Congress, 10 January 1927, quoted in Gantenbein (ed.), op. cit., p. 624.
18. Report to the Senate, 17 April 1928, quoted in US Congress, *Operation of the Naval Service in Nicaragua*, p. 1.
19. US Department of State 1928 p. 47
20. Report to the Senate, 17 April 1928, quoted in US Congress 1928a p. 5ff.
21. See hearings of the Senate foreign relations committee, 11 and 18 February 1928, quoted in US Congress 1928 pp. 64 and 35
22. Letter to Coolidge, 8 May 1927, quoted in US Congress 1931 p. 21.

4. Under the imprint of the 'good neighbour' policy

Rhetoric and reality under Roosevelt

The inauguration of Franklin D. Roosevelt as president of the United States on 4 March 1933 paved the way for a change in the relations between the United States and Latin America. Unlike his relative Theodore, who at the beginning of the century had preferred to 'carry a big stick' rather than 'speak softly', which also formed part of his prescription for dealing with the southern neighbours, the new president talked to them in moderate tones and treated them as equals. He outlined the new departure, calling it the 'good neighbour' policy, in his inaugural address. Henceforth the United States would desist from the unilateral military interventions which had become so frequent since the Spanish–Cuban–American War (there had been 36 altogether since 1898); it would relinquish its administrative and financial control over Caribbean countries (the controversial dollar diplomacy) which had brought it a reputation of being no less rapacious in its exploitation of Latin America than the traditional imperialist powers; and it would respect the political traditions and the sovereignty of the sister republics.[1] A few weeks later, during the celebrations for Pan-American Day on 12 April, he spoke of his vision of an inter-American system 'of which confidence, friendship and goodwill would be cornerstones'.[2]

The Latin Americans could hardly believe their ears, so unprecedented were these sentiments, and awaited eagerly the first opportunity at which the Roosevelt administration could prove that its noble rhetoric was more than empty words. This arose at the Seventh Pan-American Conference, originally scheduled for early 1933 but postponed until December because of the general economic crisis and the tense international situation. To provide a visible expression of the new neighbourly relations, the secretary of state, Cordell Hull, decided to attend the gathering in Montevideo in person. On his way to Uruguay (by ship) he made a stopover in Rio de Janeiro to visit Brazil's president and foreign minister. And on arrival in Montevideo he broke with tradition and protocol by visiting the heads of the Latin American delegations rather than awaiting their courtesy calls, as had been the norm for the representative of the northern superpower in the past. This had a favourable effect on the atmosphere at the conference, which initially was anything but friendly — Hull described it as akin to 'a blue snow in January'.[3] Nevertheless, the US delegation found itself at the receiving end of some strongly worded criticism: the delegates from the Dominican Republic, which had endured occupation by the marines, and El Salvador, which had experienced non-recognition, denounced American interventionism; the delegate from Cuba, which was currently experiencing a milder form of intervention through being encircled by US warships, denounced American military intimidation; the delegates from Haiti and Nicaragua, which had both been subjected to US occupation and administration, denounced persistent American interference in the internal affairs of Latin American countries.

The US delegation found itself in a serious predicament. President Roosevelt had instructed it to make little more than fairly insubstantial placatory offers to the Latin Americans, such as financial support for a feasibility study on a pan-American highway and for the installation of beacons at South American airports for night flying. (Presumably he hoped that good-neighbourly relations could be bought on the cheap, for the time being at least.) The delegation was under no circumstances to engage in any discussion of the Monroe Doctrine or interventionism, which had for so long been the most vexed problem in inter-American relations. But in the face of this storm of Latin indignation, Hull realized that soothing diplomatic formulations would not be enough and avoidance of the real issues could not succeed.

The Americans were forced to concede that, like any other government, they would refrain from infringing the liberty, sovereignty and freedom of action of other countries. Hull pledged that 'no government need fear any interference on the the part of the United States under the Roosevelt administration'.[4] He also accepted a convention on inter-American relations which declared bluntly that 'No state has the right to intervene in the internal and external affairs of another'.[5] In their exuberance the Latin Americans appeared to overlook the fact that Hull had signed the document with the reservation that his government had certain treaty obligations which sanctioned its right to military intervention.

The rationale behind this two-faced policy is not difficult to fathom. The view of the 'enlightened' imperialists that military interventions were superfluous, costly and counterproductive had gained the upper hand in Washington some years earlier. It had become the received wisdom that overt intervention precipitated political reactions and unrest detrimental to business and economic stability. Hull too had argued this position for many years. But the reservation to the Montevideo convention was made with a specific case in mind: Cuba, currently in such political turmoil that the administration thought it wise not to forswear the big stick altogether.

The Cuban crisis of 1933–4

For better or, more likely, worse, Cuba was inextricably tied to the United States in 1933, when Roosevelt first proclaimed the good neighbour policy — economically because the American market absorbed 80% of its exports, and politically by the Platt Amendment. Economic upswings and downturns in the United States had immediate and usually more extreme effects on the island. Thus, it had benefited from the worldwide shortage of sugar during and after the First World War, and prices skyrocketed to delirious heights, to 10 cents a pound weight in March 1920, 13 cents in April and 20 cents in May. But when the price dropped sharply in the following months, to reach a low point of 4 cents a pound weight in December, the sugar boom (the 'dance of the millions') came to an abrupt end.

A price of 4 cents was still high, however, compared to the 1.4 cents a pound weight which Cuban sugar fetched in 1934. The world economic crisis which had broken in 1929 with devastating effects on the United States and other industrialized countries brought the monocultural Cuban economy to the point of near-collapse. The adoption of the Smoot–Hawley Tariff Act in June 1930, which imposed the highest tariff barriers in US history, effectively deprived Cuba of its only export market. By 1933 the value of Cuban exports to the United States had fallen from a high of $362 million in 1924 to $57 million. The country 'confronted ruin', as Sumner Wells, the assistant secretary of state, admitted.[6] Cuba's people suffered unprecedented misery. In 1933 unskilled sugar-mill workers earned as little as 30 cents a day. Cane cutters, who toiled in the fields under terrible conditions of heat, dust and vermin, had to make do with 15 cents a day, from which they had to live not only during the harvest but also in the off-season, the *tiempo muerto*.

Small wonder, then, that disaffection with the economic dependency on the United States increased steadily during the 1920s and the early 1930s. In the mid-1920s students and workers began to organize themselves against US crypto-colonial rule, against hunger and against the repressive policies of the current dictator, Gerardo Machado. Three months after the latter came to power, in August 1925, the student leader Julio Antonio Mella, the tobacco worker Carlos Baliño and a group of Havana trade unionists founded the Cuban Communist Party. The first national trade unions, including the key National Sugar Workers' Union (SNOIA), were also set up around this time. As the economic depression worsened and the political tyranny increased, these and other organizations took on Machado, who with good reason had been nicknamed the 'butcher', like his Spanish colonial predecessor Weyler, or contemptuously dismissed as the 'Mussolini of the tropics'. The dictator — a puppet whom the Americans let dance on the political stage of his country to the tune of big business — used hired assassins to remove Mella, his greatest rival, in January 1929. This failed to stem the wave of industrial unrest, however, and only strengthened the opposition movement to the point where Washington's officials began to fear for their puppet. A succession of strikes marked this period, with more than 200,000 workers taking part in a general strike in March 1930. By April 1933 President Roosevelt thought it advisable to dispatch a special envoy to Cuba.

This task fell to Welles, one of the state department's most able diplomats. Put in charge of the Latin American division in 1921, at the tender age of 28, he had subsequently headed several special missions to troubled Caribbean countries, acting as a troubleshooter, generally successfully. Although he resigned from the department in 1925, he was consulted frequently by Roosevelt on Latin American issues from 1927 onwards. As assistant secretary of state for Latin American affairs, a post he accepted in December 1933 (after his stint in Cuba), he became the architect of US Latin American policy during the Roosevelt era.

Welles rushed to Havana as a special ambassador to 'mediate', as the official announcement of his mission explained. He originally intended to try to keep Machado in office because he thought his removal would lead to chaos and the destruction of American property on the island. But he soon realized that conditions in Cuba had reached such a state of desperation that there was little to mediate between Machado and the opposition and that the only way out was the quietest and quickest possible removal of the dictator. In the eyes of the American sugar barons and bankers, too, a man who could not guarantee a climate conducive to business even by resorting to the most brutal repression had outlived his usefulness. (Machado's boast that 'under my administration no strike will last more than fifteen minutes' had proved all too hollow.)[7] Welles thus changed tack and began to prepare the ground for Machado's overthrow.

Power-hungry and money-grabbing dictators often show great tenacity in clinging to office, and Machado was no exception. Although he had accepted certain constitutional reforms and guarantees of human rights in the course of Welles' mediation efforts, he ordered a massacre of protesters in the streets of Havana on 7 August. It proved to be the turning point. A general strike gripped the city and spread rapidly throughout the country, threatening to paralyse the economy. Welles decided on a drastic solution. The next day he put an ultimatum to Machado, demanding his immediate resignation. He refused, but the arrival of 30 American warships in Havana and the threat of losing US diplomatic support helped to change his mind. A mutiny by the army's senior officer corps (which had been given the green light by Welles) proved the final blow and, on 12 August, Machado resigned and fled the country.

The next puppet was already on hand: Carlos Manuel de Céspedes, a former minister under Machado. He had no support among the Cuban people, but that did not particularly matter to Welles. The important thing was that he had the backing of all the groups which had taken part in the mediation conferences of the previous months. Céspedes was too weak politically to counter the accusation that the Americans had put him in the presidential palace. As far as most opposition groups were concerned, nothing had changed with regard to the country's dependence on the northern neighbour. One of the key opposition forces, the Revolutionary Student Directorate (*Directorio Estudiantil Revolucionario*), soon convinced disaffected non-commissioned officers in the army, who were demanding higher pay and other reforms, to broaden their rebellion into a coup. Céspedes was easily toppled on 5 September, after less than a month in office. He was replaced by a five-man junta, which a week later elected Ramón Grau San Martín, a widely respected biology professor, as president.

What Washington had granted its bloodthirsty protégé Machado until the bitter end, namely diplomatic recognition, was denied to Grau and his government. Despite Roosevelt's assurance six months earlier, almost to the day, that the United States wanted to be a good neighbour to the Latin American countries, the administration exhibited once again the might-is-right attitude typical of the Wilson and Harding days. Non-recognition was tantamount to blackmail and an indirect intervention in the internal affairs of Cuba, all the more effective because of that country's unique dependence on the United States. The administration justified this lapse into the old imperialist habits on the grounds that the Grau government was 'supported solely by university students, a few small groups … and the army' and 'clearly' did not possess 'the support and the approval of the people' of Cuba[8] — as if the US government had extended diplomatic recognition to Machado because of his immense popularity.

The reason behind the refusal of recognition was entirely different. The Grau government had taken office with a commitment to reform, its radical nationalist political programme including voting rights for women, advanced labour legislation, and nationalization of foreign property in key industries. The American business community always raised the alarm in Washington whenever such nationalist and reformist sentiments emerged in Latin America. It was doubly concerned now because they emerged in Cuba, the principal source of US sugar imports, an important export market for US goods and a major target for US investment.

The political establishment, so accustomed to serving business interests, was also concerned by developments in Cuba. Already during the early days of the sergeants' revolt Welles had recommended landing marines and occupying Havana to 'protect American lives and property', in the old interventionist phrase. But Roosevelt did not want to give the lie to his good neighbour policy quite so crassly. After consulting Hull, he rejected Welles' request for troops, but reiterated the refusal to recognize the Grau government. With the support of part of the army, Fulgencio Batista, a former sergeant who had played a prominent part in the September coup and was held in high regard by Welles, once again intervened in the power struggle. In face of twin pressures from inside and outside the country, Grau resigned on 18 January 1934 and Colonel Carlos Mendieta Montefur was nominated provisional president. Welles, who had left Cuba on 13 December 1933 to take up his new position in Washington, commented that Mendieta's government 'was welcomed with every possible sign of public approval from one end of the republic to the other'.[9] Soon after Mendieta's accession the Roosevelt administration discharged what it grandly called its moral obligation to extend recognition to his government.

Welles' interpretation was of course far removed from the reality of the situation, but at least it served the purpose of justifying the administration's Cuban policy. It also conveniently ignored the position of Batista, who had nevertheless established himself clearly as the country's new strongman although he did not hold any political office at this time. Behind the back of the official president he began systematically to roll back the social and political achievements of the popular movement of 1933.

As a sign of goodwill and good-neighbourliness towards Cuba, the US Congress in May 1934 passed the Jones–Costigan Sugar Control Act, which set up a favourable quota system for Cuban sugar. In return, however, Cuba was required to lift import duties on many US goods. This had the disadvantage from Cuba's point of view of stabilizing the country's economic dependency on the United States as well as its undiversified economic structure. For as long as the Cuban market would be inundated with manufactured goods from the north, a domestic industrial base could not develop.

The Jones–Costigan Act and a further reduction of sugar duties from 2 cents a pound weight to 0.9 cents a pound weight in June 1934 were not the only 'morning gifts' for the Mendieta government. The Americans also agreed to a treaty, signed by the two governments on 29 May 1934, which abrogated the hated Platt Amendment. Under the terms of the treaty the United States gave up its right to intervene in Cuba, and any restrictions on the Cuban government to contract foreign loans or enter into alliances with other countries were removed. But these concessions, which were also supposed to placate the Cuban opposition movement, had a catch. The United States retained its rights over the naval base at Guantánamo, a gateway to Cuba should a need for intervention arise in the future.

The good neighbour: other test cases in Latin America

Apart from crisis-torn Cuba, there were other countries in Latin America, particularly in Central America and the Caribbean, where the Roosevelt administration could and had to prove its commitment to the good neighbour policy. In July 1934 President Roosevelt embarked on his first foreign tour, a visit to three Caribbean countries, which attracted worldwide press coverage. His first stop on the goodwill tour was Haiti, perhaps a symbolic gesture, since in that country more than anywhere else the United States would have to mend its ways if it were serious about the non-interventionism. In Haiti the United States had practised dollar diplomacy more ruthlessly than anywhere else after the landing of the marines, the seizure of the customs offices and the declaration of martial law in 1915. The withdrawal of these occupation troops had been agreed by the Hoover administration in August 1933, with the haitianization of the national guard planned for October 1934 and the withdrawal of US troops a month later. Roosevelt decided to speed up the process. The last detachment of marines left Haiti in August 1934, three months ahead of schedule.

There was more to haitianize than the armed forces, however. The Americans would have to relinquish control of the customs services and the financial system before Haiti could be called even a partly sovereign state. In July 1935 the Haitian government secured an agreement which allowed it to buy back the Banque Nationale from the National City Bank of New York. But not least because Washington doubted the Haitians' ability to govern themselves and handle money, the small print ensured that in essence the Americans retained control over the country's finances. It would take another six years before the Roosevelt administration granted Haiti a few more sovereign rights. A further executive agreement signed on 13 September 1941 (which did not need the approval of the Haitian parliament) abolished the position of 'fiscal representative' or tax supervisor, and transferred the funds and property of his office to the Banque Nationale, which was at last allowed to exercise the functions of a national bank; it also transferred the right to set a government budget to the Haitian parliament.

There the concessions to Haiti's financial sovereignty ended. Once again, very little had in fact changed. Washington was entitled to nominate three US citizens as directors (with full voting rights) on the six-member board of the national bank. One of them would act as co-president, his duty being to 'represent the holders of the bonds of 1922 and 1923 and to coordinate and direct' the functions of the two vice-presidents, one of whom was charged with supervising and carrying out the fiscal functions of the bank and the other with its commercial functions. In other words, despite a semblance of sovereignty, the national bank remained under US control. Since, moreover, another clause of the agreement stipulated that the Haitian government would 'set aside in preference to any other other expenses' the sums necessary for the service of the existing debts to the US creditors, interest payments and the amortization of the debt had priority over all public expenditure. And to ensure that the financial control would be almost as total as during the era of crude dollar diplomacy, the agreement also stipulated that 'the public debt of Haiti should not be increased except by previous agreement between the [two] governments', that is, only with prior US approval.[10] When the Haitian government requested a credit of $500,000 from the Export–Import Bank in Washington in September 1942, it had first to obtain the US secretary of state's permission (which was magnanimously granted). This arrangement obtained until 1947.

The example of Haiti shows that under the good neighbour policy Washington had merely refined the means of intervening in the internal affairs of Latin American countries; it had certainly not abandoned interventionism. And several factors specific to Haiti made it easier to make such a tactical shift in this case. For one, despite all the American scepticism, the Haitian administration had been able to impose a degree of internal stability, which simply had not existed 20 years earlier. For another, the fear of European encroachment in the Caribbean and in particular in the Windward Passage between Cuba and Haiti (the only direct sea route between the North American east coast and the Panama Canal) had vanished, and hence Haiti was no longer such a crucial link in the defence of the canal's approaches.

With European influence in the hemisphere waning, the Roosevelt administration could also consider concessions to Panama. Like Cuba, Panama had been forced to grant — in the Hay–Bunau-Varilla Treaty of 1903 — the United States the right to intervene anywhere in the country whenever it perceived a threat to its interests and the canal. President Roosevelt used the opportunity offered by a visit of the Panamanian president, Harmodio Arias, in October 1933 to assure the Panamanian people that 'the most sympathetic consideration would be given to the removal of their just grievances', thus signalling the administration's willingness to discuss a revision of the controversial treaty.[11] Welles began negotiations for a new treaty — which he considered a key test case for the new policy — soon after his return from Cuba in December 1933. After two years of hard negotiations, what became known as the Hull–Alfaro Treaty was signed on 2 March 1936.

The Panamanians had hoped that the new era in inter-American relations would also herald a new chapter in the history of their country. But the treaty did not live up to the expectations raised by the earlier rhetoric. Most disappointingly, it did not bring the longed-for full sovereignty. While it explicitly ended the right of intervention outside the Canal Zone hitherto enjoyed by the United States, it also sanctioned the latter's right to hold military manoeuvres and establish military bases anywhere in the country. At least the annual fees for the use of the canal were increased from the laughable sum of $250,000 to $450,000.

In January 1934 the Roosevelt administration also ended the recognition policy which its predecessors had applied to Central America de jure since 1907 (and which it itself had applied de facto only a few months earlier in Cuba to install a more pliable government by more discreet means than the landing of troops). Treaties signed by the United States and the five Central American countries in December 1907 and February 1923 in effect obliged the signatories, and crucially of course the United States, to refuse recognition to any government in the region that had not gained power by constitutional means. President Hoover had honoured this commitment, known as the Tobar Doctrine, when he refused to give his blessing to a coup in Guatemala in December 1930. He followed a similar course in December 1931, when the elected president of El Salvador, Arturo Araujo, a reformer, was overthrown in a military coup and forced into exile nine months after taking office. Although the new ruler, General Maximiliano Hernández Martínez, was a lackey of the local oligarchy and unlikely to harm American property, his government was nevertheless denied diplomatic recognition. But when a year later several European governments began to normalize relations with El Salvador and some Central American governments were preparing, in violation of the 1923 treaty, to do the same, Washington must have considered that the non-recognition policy had been overtaken by events. In December 1934 the Roosevelt administration established friendly official relations with the regime. (Martínez, incidentally, gained considerable notoriety with his claim that 'killing an ant is a greater crime than killing a man, because a man is reincarnated after death while an ant dies once and for all', a pseudo-theosophist insight to which his 13-year reign of terror bore witness.)[12]

The abandonment of the non-recognition policy suited the new dictator emerging in neighbouring Nicaragua. Anastasio Somoza gained prompt recognition for his regime from the United States after he had ousted President Sacasa in June 1936. During the 20 years of authoritarian rule which followed the coup, successive US administrations meticulously avoided any intervention in the internal affairs of Nicaragua which might discomfort his regime.

The oil conflict with Mexico

The good neighbour policy was of course also extended to Mexico. In early 1937 the Mexican government asked for the abrogation of a clause in the Gadsden treaty — the Gadsden Purchase — of 1853 (which sealed the purchase of the Gila Valley in what is now Arizona) giving US troops transit rights across the Tehuantepec isthmus in south-eastern Mexico, thereby ensuring faster lines of communication between America's two coasts. The administration quickly agreed to the termination of this obscure clause restricting Mexican sovereignty, a hangover from the early days of American expansionism which in any case had lost its strategic significance with the opening of the Panama Canal.

A far sterner test of the spirit of the good neighbour policy was still to come. Under President Lázaro Cárdenas, who took office in December 1934, the Mexican government began a programme of nationalization of the country's mineral resources, particularly oil, on the basis of powers granted in the famous article 27 of the 1917 constitution. This move was a slap in the face for the American oil companies, which had invested around $100 million in Mexico to get the black gold out of the ground and refine it. It would also inevitably test the sincerity of the Roosevelt administration's commitment to the principle of non-intervention affirmed at the Montevideo conference in December 1933. Confrontation was in the air.

As the Mexican government became more assertive, so did the oilworkers. There had been widespread industrial unrest in the oil fields in 1935, with a major strike by oilworkers eventually settled through mediation by the government. This dispute had highlighted yet again the weakness of the labour movement, but the lesson was learnt. In early 1936 the 21 independent oilworkers' unions merged to form the Union of Oil Workers of the Mexican Republic (STPRM). Once sufficiently organized and united, in November 1936 the oilworkers presented their employers with an industry-wide draft labour contract which included demands for an eight-hour day, double pay for overtime work, strike pay, holiday pay, and housing, schools and accommodation for themselves and their families. The union also insisted on a closed shop, the inclusion of office staff within the union, and the right of workers to elect their own supervisors.

The oil companies, led by Sinclair (with a 25% share in production and a 40% share in refining) and Standard Oil of New Jersey, rejected the proposed contract out of hand. The situation was deadlocked. The union called a strike in May 1937, and, wary of a long struggle which it was not confident of winning, at the same time began legal proceedings to have the walkout declared an 'economic conflict' under the terms of the national labour code. This was accepted by the courts, and the dispute thereupon became the subject of compulsory arbitration by the Board of Arbitration and Conciliation. This body appointed a commission of experts to investigate the facts of the case and to make recommendations for a settlement. The three-member commission, comprising two senior civil servants and a respected economist (Jesús Silva Herzog), examined, with the help of over 100 assistants and researchers, the oil companies' books and sales contracts, the conditions on the world market, the industry's history, its technical problems and distribution system, relations between workers and employers — in short, all relevant aspects of the issue.

The commission's report, a document with strong anti-imperialist undertones, showed how the oil companies used a myriad of accounting tricks to avoid and evade taxes and how they made enormous profits in Mexico as compared with those they made in the United States. It submitted 40 recommendations to the board and concluded that the employers had sufficient resources to meet the workers' pay demands (totaling 26.3 million pesos, or \$7.2 million at current exchange rates). On 18 December the Board of Conciliation and Arbitration supported the commission's findings and its recommendations.

Hankering still after the good old imperialist times, the oil barons failed to see the writing on the wall. They arrogantly dismissed the commission's recommendations and launched a virulent anti-Mexican press campaign both at home and abroad. They also sought to destabilize the country's finances by using every means at their disposal to stimulate the demand for dollars and thereby deplete the reserves of the national bank and put pressure on the peso. A devaluation would then have become inevitable, a development which of course would have made it that much easier for the oil companies to meet an increased payroll in pesos.

As part of a dual strategy composed of subversive and legalistic elements, the oil companies also appealed to the Mexican supreme court. But for the first time their anti-government machinations failed to have the desired result. On 1 March 1938 the court upheld the award and ordered compliance with the board's ruling. The oil companies responded by declaring that they were unable to comply with the judgment (in a case which they themselves had brought). This not only fuelled Mexican resentment of the gringos but also put Mexican sovereignty fundamentally at issue. The companies adopted this hardline stance after they had belatedly recognized that they might no longer be able do as they pleased in Mexico or even lose financial and managerial control over their assets — or perhaps even be expropriated by the back door.

The Mexican government, intent on dispelling the suspicion that it might be powerless against big business, acted quickly and energetically. On the day that the oilworkers suspended work in protest at their employers' violation of Mexican law, 18 March, President Cárdenas announced in a nationwide radio broadcast his government's decision to nationalize the oil industry.

As was to be expected, the oil companies responded with long and bitter tirades against Mexico and even called for a boycott of Mexican goods. The barons' minimal goal was to obtain monetary compensation for the loss of their 'property', including the most obsolete production plant and the oil still in the ground. They also lobbied their government to send in the marines, in the time-honoured tradition, to punish the Mexicans' profaning of the holy of holies of the American way of life, private property. But the administration refused to bring the insubordinate Mexicans to their senses in this way. It upheld the principle of Montevideo, subsequently reaffirmed at a special inter-American conference in Buenos Aires in December 1936, that no American state had the right to intervene, militarily or otherwise, in the internal affairs of another state. It even acknowledged Mexico's right to nationalize foreign-owned assets, while insisting on full compensation. This the Mexican government readily agreed to in principle.

The negotiations between the two governments over the level of compensation to be paid to the oil companies dragged on for three years. For once, though, time was on Mexico's side. As the world situation grew more tense and the axis powers escalated their economic aggression against the United States, the Roosevelt administration became increasingly eager to come to an amicable settlement with Mexico. The administration recognized that the southern neighbour — all of Latin America, in fact — would have an important role to play as a supplier of raw materials to the United States in the seemingly unavoidable confrontation with Germany and Japan.

The oil companies had their own interests to consider, however, and were not as willing to make concessions. From 27 September 1941 Hull met their representatives on several occasions to persuade them that in this case specific economic interest would have to take a back seat to reasons of state, specifically the need for friendly relations with Mexico. But for the oil companies a more fundamental issue was at stake — the principle of property rights. They decided that they would rather leave the specific case of Mexico unsettled, even with the risk of losing their property altogether, than condone the violation of private property by accepting compensation. They feared above all the symbolic importance of the Mexican case as a precedent, which could have repercussions for all US investments in Latin America.

The two governments proceeded regardless and on 19 November 1941 agreed to appoint one expert each to determine the level of compensation to be paid to the oil companies. As a token of goodwill, the Mexicans deposited $9 million as a first payment. Then the unprovoked Japanese attack on Pearl Harbor on 7 December changed the situation completely. The oil barons were forced to gave in to hard political realities and finally agreed to a settlement. The experts eventually arrived at a figure of $29,137,700 and 84 cents as compensation for the expropriation, and on 29 September 1943 both governments agreed to this sum.

Thus one of the most explosive conflicts in inter-American relations was resolved peacefully after the US government and business community had considered it opportune, for a variety of reasons, to respect international law rather than act in the more traditional manner and violate it without hesitation. The Mexican expropriation controversy, and other issues in the 1930s, showed that while the good neighbour policy did not present a thorough overhaul of the old imperialist policy, it was more than empty words. Or to put it metaphorically, the US political establishment exchanged the big stick for the white glove in its relations with the Latin Americans without, however, thereby relinquishing its hold over the region.

Hull's free-trade philosophy

Roosevelt, Hull and their US Latin American experts did not advocate the good neighbour policy merely for the sake of peace and a better image. The policy had also a material purpose. After 1933 the United States wanted to stimulate the world economy and revive world trade. In the eyes of Roosevelt's advisers, the world economy suffered from three ailments in the 1930s: the collapse of the gold standard, which had led to the disintegration of the world financial system into four regional systems (organized around sterling, the dollar, exchange controls and gold); a stagnation in the flow of capital between creditor and debtor countries; and the pursuit of economic self-sufficiency and protectionism. Under these conditions a sharp fall in the volume of world trade was inevitable, and by the early 1930s it had shrunk to a fraction of what it had been before the crash of 1929.

The headlong flight into protectionism did not even help those countries which hoped it would balance their accounts, for it actually throttled international trade to the detriment of all. Francis B. Sayre, the assistant secretary of state for economic affairs, described the situation as follows:

> Nations entered into feverish competition with each other to sell to foreigners a maximum and to buy from foreigners a minimum of goods. To protect against huge excesses of imports over exports and the consequent outflow of gold, nations sought to cut down their imports by launching intensive drives towards national "autarky" or economic self-sufficiency ... New governmental measures were devised arbitrarily to restrict imports, [such as] quota restrictions, exchange-control restrictions, government trade monopolies, import-licensing requirements ... Nation became pitted against nation in the parry and thrust of bitter trade rivalry.[13]

Free competition, which previously had been carried out by more or less fair means, degenerated into trade war.

Although Germany and Japan pursued the economic objectives outlined above more ruthlessly than most countries, the United States was not entirely blameless in the contraction of international trade after 1929, as indeed a number of American politicians conceded subsequently. In the eccentric to and fro of US trade policy between free trade and protectionism, partly a function of the influence of specific branch interests, the pendulum had swung clearly towards protectionism as early as September 1922, when Congress adopted the Fordney–McCumber Tariff, which raised import duties to the then highest-ever level in US history (on average 33% of the product value). In doing so, however, the legislators failed to take account of the fact that during the First World War the United States had changed, almost overnight, from a major debtor country to a major creditor country. Their action was wholly contrary to the demands of the situation: on the basis of historical experience they should have lowered rather than raised tariff barriers. US congressmen of all people should have recognized that creditor countries — which the United States had been until a decade earlier, borrowing from Europe to build its houses, railroads and factories — needed a significant surplus of exports over imports so as to be able to pay off their accumulated debts. This restrictive trade policy deprived debtor countries, in particular the Latin American republics, of a means of building up a trade surplus, and as a result they suffered from chronic dollar shortages and were unable to meet their financial obligations, or pay for American goods for that matter.

In 1930 Congress raised tariffs to unprecedented heights in order to protect individual economic branches from foreign competition in the wake of the Wall Street crash. In the face of warnings from foreign governments and from more than 1,000 economists at home, the ruling Republicans reached for the protective tariff — the economist Joseph Schumpeter called it their 'household remedy' — at the first hint of trouble in the agricultural sector.[14] The Smoot–Hawley Tariff, signed by President Hoover on 17 June 1930, raised import duties on agricultural raw materials from 38% to 49% and on other commodities from 31% to 34%. Special protection was given to US sugar and textile interests, at the expense of the Caribbean and Central American countries in particular. It brought the Latin Americans to 'a condition of abject destitution', as Welles later admitted.[15]

Smoot–Hawley was important not so much for its impact on the US balance of payments or for debtor–creditor relations as for its sheer irresponsibility in extending protection from the agricultural sector to all kinds of other primary and manufactured goods. This act of folly, taken without the slightest regard for its international implications, had almost immediate consequences. Canada retaliated in kind by raising tariffs on US goods. The British Commonwealth replied in August 1932 with the Ottawa agreements, a system of internal import preferences and external tariffs which would terrify the Americans for years to come because it undoubtedly increased the flow of goods between Britain, its colonies and the dominions at the expense of American exports. British imports from the Commonwealth rose from 30.2% of the total in 1929 to 41.9% by 1938, and exports to the Commonwealth rose from 44.4% to 49.3% in the same period.

A few countries benefited from the protectionism, but overall the mounting trade barriers caused dramatic contraction in the volume and value of world trade, with the latter falling from an estimated $68 billion in 1929 to $24 billion in 1933. This collapse had still not been made good in 1937, when the value of trade was still 3% below the 1929 level in real terms. The US economy was more adversely affected by this contraction than its major European competitors. France, for instance, actually increased its share of world trade from 6.19% to 7.31% between 1929 and 1932, while the US share fell from 13.83% to 10.92%. In absolute figures, the value of US foreign trade dropped from $9.5 billion in 1929 to $2.5 billion in 1933; exports dropped from $5.2 billion in 1929 to $1.6 billion in 1932, the lowest total for 28 years, and rose slightly to $1.7 billion in 1933, the first increase in five years.

American politicians had sleepless nights worrying not only about the 68% decline of US exports in four years. They spent their whole careers taking account of local and sectoral economic interests, and some of these had experienced even greater setbacks on the world market. Exports of cars and spare parts were down from $541.4 million in 1929 to $90.6 million in 1933, iron and steel from $200.1 million to $45.5 million, copper from $183.4 million to $24.9 million, and wheat and flour from $192.3 million to $18.6 million (a decline of 90%, which, ironically, threatened the future of the very agricultural exporters which the Republicans' tariff policy was supposed to protect). 'Trade was being readjusted, and we were losing out at every turn,' Hull noted.[16] The fact that in comparison with agricultural goods exports of manufactured goods overall declined by 'only' 70% provided no consolation whatever, since in this sector too the general figure masked the virtual collapse of various particularly export-sensitive branches.

As they surveyed the world economic situation, the Americans could hardly avoid the conclusion that their protectionist policies had inflicted the greatest economic distress in their own back yard. In 1929 the United States imported raw materials and basic manufactures from Latin America valued at just over $1 billion and exported manufactured goods there valued at slightly less. Four years later the value of imports from the region had fallen to $212 million, with the result that the Latin Americans could buy only $291 million worth of US goods.

The disconcerting trends in trade flows which the Americans could observe at the world level were repeated at the regional level. In the first third of the century trade between the two Americas had increased steadily, but it declined in relative terms after 1929. Between 1927 and 1936 sales by eight of the ten South American republics in the US market fell in relative terms, the exceptions being Ecuador and Paraguay; sales by the United States to Uruguay fell in absolute terms, and particularly to Argentina, Brazil and Chile in relative terms. (Despite this decline the United States remained the largest supplier to five countries and the largest buyer for four of them.)

Around this time the Germans launched their economic offensive. Between 1935 and 1938 Germany increased its share of Latin American imports from 13.1% to 17.3%. And while Latin American exports to the United States stagnated during this period, the Latins delivered 40% more goods to faraway Germany, especially the raw materials which the Reich needed for its burgeoning war machine. The Americans had hardly treated their southern neighbours even handedly by the erecting of their tariff wall, but the German fascists, even less concerned about fair trading practices, outdid them. And unlike the Americans they were initially successful. The state foreign-trade monopoly, which supervised Germany's return to barter trade and bilateral trade, obtained very favourable terms in its dealings with the vulnerable raw-material suppliers of Latin America.

All in all the protectionism of the early 1930s, which the United States promoted like no other, proved an economic boomerang. Rather than serve as economic self-defence, it shook the domestic economy to its core. As foreign trade declined between 1929 and 1932, unemployment soared to 10 millions, national income fell by 43%, farmers' income fell by 58% and industrial workers' wages fell by 53%. In the circumstances it was hardly surprising that the opposition Democrats advocated a less protectionist foreign-trade policy to improve US competitiveness in the world market. During the 1932 presidential election campaign Roosevelt strongly attacked the Smoot–Hawley Tariff as a major cause of the depression.

Hull did not need this particular piece of legislation to be persuaded that protectionism was harmful. He had supported free trade as early as 1916, and fought for his philosophy with almost missionary zeal during his 12 years as Roosevelt's secretary of state. To translate his ideas into practice, he appointed Sayre, a Harvard law professor and President Wilson's son-in-law, as assistant secretary of state. Hull and Sayre formulated the grand lines of the new foreign-trade policy, not without encountering resistance from within the administration, however — for instance from the fanatical protectionist George N. Peek, whom Roosevelt had asked to chair a committee to co-ordinate foreign trade relations. The president himself did not share Hull's optimism in the recovery of lost foreign trade, and he certainly had little time for the philosophical flights of fancy of his secretary of state. But he gave him a free hand. A decade later Welles, who had turned his boss's plans into practice in Latin America, could describe the policy as 'the new deal of US foreign trade'.[17]

Hull's advocacy of free trade was by no means the whim of a starry-eyed ideologue. He recognized that the United States, the country with the largest, most productive and most competitive industrial capacity in the world, could only profit from a liberal trade regime and should therefore promote it vigorously. By the 1920s the United States had overtaken Britain — which, significantly, had supported free trade when it had been the 'workshop of the world' in the nineteenth century — in economic terms. By the 1930s it had little to fear from either Britain or the other European powers. As an economic superpower, especially in its own hemisphere, the United States could now reap the fruits of the international division of labour. And after all, expansionism had always been America's destiny.

In short, the advocates of free trade believed fervently that to prosper and to guarantee its citizens a high standard of living the US economy needed access to foreign markets. The domestic market would never be able to absorb the economy's total production, and certainly not its agricultural surpluses. The closing of foreign markets threatened not only America's prosperity but would eventually also lead to the suffocation of free enterprise under state controls. Moreover, they argued at a more general level, restrictions to markets would lead to conflict, while free trade would ensure peace. For Sayre, 'economic nationalism, and its corollary, imperialistic expansion, alike lead to perpetual conflict' while 'increased trade … is the only sure foundation upon which to build for world peace'; and for Hull, 'unhampered trade dovetailed with peace; high tariffs, trade barriers and unfair economic competition, with war'.[18]

Hull and the others dismissed the claim put forward by the opponents of a free-trade policy that they over-rated the importance of foreign trade for the US economy. Around this time the United States was undoubtedly far less export-dependent than most other leading national economies, exporting only around 8 to 10% of its gross domestic product. But this obscured the fact that certain branches were highly dependent on foreign markets. In 1933, with export opportunities very restricted, the United States still sold 66% of its cotton production abroad, 39% of raw tobacco, 46% of dried fruits, 28% of fruit preserves, 34% of lubricating oil, 37% of aircraft engines, 16% of machinery and 41% of copper, to quote just a few examples. In their efforts to sway the argument, the free traders calculated that 40 million acres of agricultural land would be surplus to requirements if farmers could not export their produce; and that some 10 million jobs would be at risk if manufacturers could not export their goods. In the eyes of the politicians, 10 million jobs meant 10 million votes, reason enough to take an interest in their protection. It should also be remembered in this context that the farm lobby in Washington was highly organized and effective, and exerted far greater influence than could be expected from or justified by the importance of agriculture in the domestic economy, both in terms of its share of the labour force or the gross domestic product.

If certain sectors of the US economy were particularly dependent on exports to sell their surplus products, some industries were almost wholly dependent for their survival on access to the Latin American markets. During the 1930s the southern neighbours bought over 40% of US exports of dairy products, wheat flour, iron and steel, railway cars and parts, and medicinal products; 30–40% of rubber, cotton, synthetic fibres, iron and steel products, and electrical equipment; and 20–30% of leather, timber and paper, agricultural machinery, cars, and industrial chemicals. It was no empty phrase, therefore, to say that American business needed foreign markets to survive.

The reciprocal trade agreements with Latin America

If Hull and his advisers had had their way, the Roosevelt administration would have restored a liberal world-trade regime and its political complement, the open-door policy, at a stroke But the time was not right in 1934, five years after the beginning of the world economic crisis and five years before the outbreak of the Second World War. Reviving multilateral international trade, which had largely disintegrated into bilateral relations, could hardly succeed in the face of increasingly open imperialist rivalries. The free traders' aim 'to restore to international trade its essentially flexible and triangular character' remained for the time being wishful thinking.[19] For the moment they could only reminisce about the colonial period, when American ships carried various colonial products to the West Indies, where they loaded sugar and molasses for Europe, and completed the triangle by returning home with manufactured goods from Europe. Nevertheless, the free-trade philosophy did gain in popularity. Hardline protectionists lost ground as the free traders hammered home the message to American business and the politicians that trade was a two-way, not a one-way street, that those who wanted to sell also had to buy, and that Uncle Sam could not continue to 'play fairy godfather to the rest of the world by making uncollectable loans to finance' their imports.[20]

The Latin Americans were to be the first beneficiaries of the free-trade regime. Initially at least they did not welcome the new concept with any great enthusiasm. Bitter experience had taught them that US goods and dollars were usually followed by the US flag, and that the likely outcome would be an ever greater economic and political dependence on the northern colossus. At the Seventh Pan-American Conference in Montevideo in December 1933 they accepted, at Hull's insistence, a resolution recommending a reduction of existing tariff barriers through the conclusion of bilateral and multilateral trade agreements. But this amounted to little more than an act of diplomatic courtesy. A special economic conference held in Buenos Aires in May–June 1935 produced nothing on trade relations. Although it was generally accepted that this conference should deal primarily with technical issues, the Americans had hinted quite openly that their main interest was in the removal of barriers to trade. The delegates adopted 4 conventions and 60 resolutions, on: the adoption of anti-smuggling measures, the introduction of a regional tourist passport, the construction of a pan-American railway and highway, the standardization of the classification of goods, vaccinations, the position of agricultural attachés in diplomatic missions, the definition of what constituted an immigrant, the creation of national parks and so on. But no sign of a resolution reaffirming the Montevideo recommendations, let alone anything more specific.

The multilateral approach having yielded nothing, the state department switched to negotiating the opening of national markets one by one. This was done on the basis of a series of reciprocal trade agreements, which, the administration later claimed, contributed in large measure to the success of the good neighbour policy in the western hemisphere. In the past the United States had sought from time to time to stimulate foreign trade by making bilateral reciprocal agreements (in which both sides agreed to lower tariffs on a specified range of goods) with various countries, as with Cuba in 1902. This approach was now to be generalized. The Trade Agreements Act was adopted by the House of Representatives on 20 March 1934 and by the Senate on 4 June, against the bitter opposition of the Republicans, and was signed into law by President Roosevelt on 12 June.

The Trade Agreements Act, whose declared intention was to capture and extend foreign markets for American goods, authorized the president for a three-year period to enter into agreements with other countries for the reduction of specific tariffs by up to 50%. These 'executive' agreements did not require congressional ratification, which meant that the administration could act with speed and flexibility. It would use the opportunities offered as often as possible.

On 24 August 1934, less than two months after the Act came into force, the United States and its closest neighbour, Cuba, signed the first reciprocal trade agreement. The two governments reduced import duties on various products: the United States reduced its rates by 20%, and Cuba reduced its rates by 20–40%. Although Hull had argued for the inclusion of a most-favoured-nation clause in the agreement, it was in the end absent. So despite its eloquent complaints of the detrimental effects of preferences and discrimination in world trade, the Roosevelt administration in this case sinned against its own free-trade philosophy by concluding an exclusive treaty. In this regard the Cuban agreement differed from subsequent ones.

Cuba having showed the way, 14 other Latin American countries proved themselves good neighbours and concluded reciprocal trade agreements with the United States over the next eight years. These were Brazil (2 February 1935), Haiti (28 March 1935), Colombia (13 September 1935), Honduras (18 December 1935), Nicaragua (11 March 1936), Guatemala (24 April 1936), Costa Rica (28 November 1936), El Salvador (19 February 1937), Ecuador (6 August 1938), Venezuela (6 November 1939, a provisional agreement having been signed on 12 May 1938), Argentina (14 October 1941), Peru (7 May 1942), Uruguay (21 July 1942) and finally Mexico (23 December 1942). These 15 countries accounted for 90% of all US trade with Latin America. Bolivia, Chile, the Dominican Republic,

Panama and Paraguay did not sign agreements. It is a moot point whether the Americans courted their Latin American trading partners particularly avidly for reasons of their own — above all the looming war — or whether the Latins were already disposed to accept the new initiative. Whatever the case, the trade-agreement policy ensured that it was in Latin America that the Americans first recovered the losses they had incurred during the protectionist aberration.

Worldwide, the United States had signed 16 trade agreements by the end of 1937, covering a third of its foreign trade; 20 by 1939, covering 60% of its trade, and 26 by 1943, covering 65%.

The structure of US–Latin American trade in the 1930s

Although the reciprocal trade agreements between the United States and other countries could never be an adequate substitute for unhampered multilateral international trade, they did prove an effective means of reviving American fortunes. Statistics widely publicized by the state department — they achieved their immediate aim, the renewal of the Trade Agreements Act in 1937 and 1940 — showed that trade with agreement countries developed far more favourably than that with non-agreement countries. While US exports to the latter increased by 32% between 1934–35 and 1938–39, exports to the former increased by 63%; similarly, imports from the latter increased by 12%, but from the former by 22%.

To voters and the business community alike the free traders used the example of Cuba to illustrate the enormous success of reciprocity. Languishing at a mere $7 million between September and December 1933 (at a time when, admittedly, political turmoil hindered economic activity), trade picked up immediately after the signing of the trade agreement and jumped to $17 million for the corresponding months of 1934. US exports to Cuba increased from $35 million in the year preceding the conclusion of the agreement to $55 million in its first year and $64 million in its second. While the state department officials took great heart from this steady upward trend, individual exporters for whom the agreement meant a dramatic increase in business had even greater cause for satisfaction. The car companies, for instance, sold nearly five times more Fords, Buicks and Chevrolets to Cuba in the first six months of the agreement compared with the corresponding period a year earlier.

Export trade with the other agreement countries in Latin America developed equally favourably (see Table 4.1). The value of US exports to these countries increased by 101% overall — it doubled, in other words — between 1931–35 and 1939, while exports to non-agreement countries increased by only 44%. Among agreement countries growth ranged from 251% (Venezuela) to 21% (Haiti), with only one country (Honduras) registering a decline in imports from the United States; the more generally modest expansion among non-agreement countries ranged from 114% (Peru) to 20% (Paraguay), with again only one country (Uruguay) registering a decline.

The situation was rather different with regard to imports from Latin American agreement countries. The flow of goods to the United States did not increase by anything like as much as sales to the south. Some countries even had to cope with significant reductions in their exports to the American market. For instance, between 1931–35 and 1939 exports from Honduras to the United States fell from $8.4 million to $6.5 million, from Colombia from $56.3 million to $43.4 million, and from Costa Rica from $3.3 million to $3.0 million.

Table 4.1
US exports to Latin America, 1931–9
(US$ million)

	1931–35 average	1936	1937	1938	1939*	change 1931–35/1939 (1931–35=100)
agreement countries						
Cuba		64.0			110.8	180
Brazil	34.2	49.0	68.6	62.0	70.0	205
Haiti	3.8	3.9	4.1	3.6	4.6	121
Colombia	17.0	27.7	39.2	41.0	45.3	266
Honduras	5.4	4.9	5.6	6.3	5.3	98
Nicaragua	2.5	2.4	3.4	2.8	3.9	156
Guatemala	3.8	4.6	7.6	6.9	7.5	197
Costa Rica	2.8	3.0	4.5	5.4	8.7	311
El Salvador	2.8	2.8	3.6	3.5	3.6	129
Ecuador	2.3	3.3	5.1	3.3	5.0	217
Venezuela	15.4	24.1	46.4	52.3	54.0	351
non-agreement countries (in 1939)						
Argentina	42.6	56.9	94.2	86.8	60.3	142
Bolivia	2.9	3.6	5.7	5.4	3.9	134
Chile	11.5	15.7	24.0	24.6	22.9	199
Dominican Rep.	5.3	4.6	6.5	5.7	6.2	174
Mexico	48.5	76.0	109.5	62.0	73.3	151
Panama	18.8	22.7	25.0	24.4	27.9	148
Paraguay	0.5	0.3	0.7	0.6	0.6	120
Peru	7.8	13.5	19.0	16.9	16.7	214
Uruguay	5.7	8.5	13.2	5.1	4.3	75

* January–November

Source: Chamber of Commerce of the United States, *Foreign Trade Trends in Items Affected by Trade Agreements*

The development of inter-American trade at this time showed clearly how the new policy brought far greater benefits to the United States than to its trading partners. The Roosevelt administration was extremely fond of the rhetoric of reciprocity, proclaiming that it wanted the United States to be, in Welles' words, 'an equal among equals and, not the notorious big brother armed with the "big stick"'.[21] But the North American economic giant was dealing with Latin American economic dwarves. With sales booming and purchases lagging behind, the overall US trade deficit with Latin American agreement countries was sharply reduced from $141.9 million in 1931–35 to $13.4 million in 1939. During the same period the United States improved an existing trade surplus with non-agreement countries from $27.1 million to $45.5 million. This despite the fact that exports to non-agreement countries increased relatively slowly and that imports from some countries increased significantly, with Peru and Uruguay doubling their sales to the United States, and Paraguay even quadrupling them.

The comparatively slight deterioration in the balance of trade of non-agreement countries suggests that those countries which, for whatever reasons, did not opt for reciprocity or did so only during the Second World War were better able to protect their markets and domestic industries from the powerful northern neighbour. Even so, these countries also eventually lost ground in terms of their trade balance with the north. Latin America as a whole had a favourable balance of trade with the United States between 1910 and 1937, but the situation was reversed for the first time in 1938. It proved a watershed. From then on, with the brief exception of the war years, it would be the Americans who could book a surplus in inter-American trade.

Between 1935 and 1938 the United States increased its share of Latin American imports from 32.2% to 35.1%, and its share of Latin American exports from 32.9% to 33.1%; conversely, Latin America increased its share of US imports from 23.6% to 24.8%, and its share of US exports from 16.5% to 18.2%.

So although Latin American exporters increased their share of the huge American market in both relative and absolute terms in the 1930s, the reciprocal trade agreements ultimately contributed to a further structural deterioration in inter-American trade relations. Economic dependence on the north became greater than ever, particularly because the generous concessions for US manufactures included in the agreements stifled the development of domestic industrial bases in the developing Latin American countries. The local entrepreneurs were simply no match for US big business. Even state department officials openly admitted that the concessions they obtained for US goods put local industries at a disadvantage and 'severely inhibited diversification efforts'.[22] For instance, reciprocity for Costa Rica meant that it could import, duty-free, all its main exports — namely coffee, bananas, cocoa, hides and skins and balsa wood — to the United States. But the Americans exacted a high price for this access to their market. Costa Rica had to reduce its duties on a wide range of US goods, not just essential manufactures but also agricultural products including wheat, flour, fish and milk. Costa Rica's dilemma was shared by all the agreement countries: without granting concessions which favoured US exports above others, they could not obtain reductions in the exorbitant US import duties.

Among the US goods which obtained import concessions from Latin American countries were wheat (granted by El Salvador and Guatemala); flour (Cuba, Costa Rica, Ecuador, Guatemala, Honduras, Nicaragua); potatoes (Cuba, Colombia, Haiti); oranges (Colombia, Guatemala, Costa Rica); pears (Brazil, Costa Rica, Cuba, El Salvador, Guatemala, Haiti, Honduras); preserved fruit (Brazil, Colombia, Costa Rica, Cuba, El Salvador, Guatemala, Haiti, Honduras, Nicaragua); electric motors (Colombia, Cuba, Haiti, Nicaragua); refrigerators (Cuba, Ecuador, Haiti); radios (Brazil, Colombia, Costa Rica, Cuba, Guatemala, Haiti, Nicaragua); construction machinery (Colombia, Cuba, Ecuador, Nicaragua); typewriters (Brazil, Colombia, Costa Rica, Cuba, Ecuador, Guatemala,

Nicaragua); tractors (Brazil, Colombia, Cuba, Nicaragua); and passenger cars (Brazil, Colombia, Cuba, Ecuador, Guatemala, Haiti, Honduras). The list is selective of course, but does indicate the range of goods covered.[23] It also shows that Cuba, only recently freed from the Platt Amendment and hence only recently a sovereign country, was still unable to resist demands by the Americans to grant concessions on almost all their exports. The list also provides an indication of the extent of US dominance of the economies of Central America and the Caribbean in comparison with South America.

For their part the Americans were very sparing with concessions to their trading partners. With the notable exception of sugar and tobacco for Cuba, they preferred to restrict them to items which would not compete with domestic production. Among the Latin American goods granted import concessions were freshwater fish and eels, maize, potatoes, sugar cane, timber and tomatoes (in the case of Cuba), brazil nuts and manganese (Brazil), rum (Haiti), crude oil (Venezuela) and panama hats (Ecuador).[24]

From the perspective of the United States, Latin America and the Caribbean could be divided, both in the 1930s and earlier, into three groups of countries in terms of economic and commercial characteristics:

(a) the mineral-exporting countries: Mexico (silver, lead, copper, oil); Venezuela (oil); and the Andean countries, Colombia (oil, gold), Peru (copper, silver, oil), Bolivia (tin, zinc, silver, gold) and Chile (copper and nitrates);

(b) the agricultural countries of temperate climate: the Southern Cone countries, Argentina (wheat, meat, hides and skins), Uruguay (wool, meat, hides and skins) and Paraguay (meat, hides and skins); and

(c) the agricultural countries of tropical climate: a large part of Brazil (coffee, cotton, cocoa and vegetable oils); the Caribbean countries, Cuba and the Dominican Republic (sugar and tobacco); and the Central American countries and parts of Mexico and Colombia (bananas, coffee, cocoa).

The countries of the first group were in the fortunate position of possessing minerals which were normally in demand in the highly advanced industrial economy of the United States. The countries of the second group, on the other hand, could not find large market shares in the United States because their products, cereals and meat, competed directly with US agriculture. The countries of the third group were in a different situation again, in that they could sell most of their agricultural products to the United States largely without hindrance because they complemented domestic agricultural production. In its promotion of reciprocity, the state department used the argument that in the main the agreements favoured commodities of which there were domestic shortages or which did not compete with domestic products — so farmers did not have to worry about Latin imports leaving them saddled with their own produce.

The economic geography outlined above was mirrored, as a north–south divide, in the US share of the imports and exports of Latin American countries (see Table 4.2). At the top of the list, with the closest links to the northern neighbour, were the countries that had something exotic to offer; at the bottom, the countries which offered something which the Americans produced in great quantities themselves.

Table 4.2
US share in Latin American foreign trade, 1938
(%)

imports from the United States	country/region	exports to the United States
71	Cuba	76
58	Mexico	67
52	Central America	67
51	Colombia	53
56	Venezuela	13*
35	Ecuador	37
24	Brazil	34
34	Peru	26
28	Chile	15
25	Bolivia	5
10	Paraguay	12
18	Argentina	9
12	Uruguay	4

*This figure is somewhat misleading, since most Venezuelan crude oil was first shipped to the Netherlands Antilles for refining.

Source: Behrendt, *Inter-American Economic Relations*

All in all it was not surprising that the traditionally unequal trading partners played out the old roles against the new backdrop of the trade agreements. Whereas the United States swamped the southern markets with its manufactured goods, Latin America had to remain content with supplying raw materials, and could count itself lucky that the markets for its minerals and agricultural commodities were now more secure than they had been in the past.

In 1939 manufactures accounted for 76.9% of US exports to Latin America, and semi-manufactures for 16.1%; in a mirror image, foodstuffs accounted for 43.9% of US imports from Latin America, minerals for 36.2% and semi-manufactures for 14.5%. The main goods which the United States supplied to Latin America were passenger cars, iron and steel products, industrial machinery, textiles and clothing; the main commodities which it bought in the region were coffee, sugar, copper, bananas and oil (see Table 4.3). It is worth noting in this context that Latin America was the United States' primary source for many important raw materials between the wars. In 1938, for instance, it supplied 33% of imports of hides and skins, 99% of bananas, 60% of cocoa, 97% of coffee, 61% of sugar cane, 100% of tobacco, 34% of wool, and 69% of copper.

By imposing an unbalanced trade structure, through the trade agreements but above all through its overwhelming industrial superiority and dominance of regional trade, the United States contributed decisively to the ossification of the Latin American monocultural economies. In 1938 only eight primary commodities (oil, coffee, meat, sugar, copper, wool, cotton, and various ores apart from copper and tin) accounted for 62.1% of the region's total exports. Some countries were dependent on a single export commodity to a disconcerting degree, such as El Salvador on coffee and Venezuela on oil (89% of total exports), Honduras on bananas (82%), Panama on bananas (74%), Cuba on sugar (73%), Bolivia on tin

(71%), Guatemala on coffee (62%), Haiti on coffee (62%), the Dominican Republic on sugar (60%) and Colombia and Costa Rica on coffee (58%).

Table 4.3
Structure of US trade with Latin America
(imports and exports in US$ and as a share of total)

product	value (US$ million)	share of total (%)
exports		
coffee	136.1	27.5
sugar	75.0	15.1
copper	30.0	6.1
bananas	28.8	5.8
oil and oil products	23.3	4.7
hides and skins	19.0	3.8
linseed	18.3	3.7
wool	17.1	3.4
cocoa	13.2	2.7
nitrates	11.4	2.3
imports		
passenger cars (incl. spares)	69.9	12.4
iron and steel products	61.6	11.0
industrial machinery	56.3	10.0
textiles and clothing	41.8	7.4
chemicals and related products	39.2	7.0
rice, flour and other vegetable products	34.5	6.1
electrical equipment	34.1	6.0
oil and oil products	28.5	5.1

Source: Behrendt, *Inter-American Economic Relations*

That most of these countries also relied on a second or third export commodity, so that in many cases two main commodities accounted for between 80 and 90% of exports, usually offered little solace. Every time war was declared, as it was in Europe in 1914 and 1939, or an economic depression broke out, as it did worldwide in 1929, markets collapsed and Latin America's exports plummeted. This set off a chain reaction involving loss of jobs, loss of government revenue, cuts in public spending, inability to fund the government payroll, suspension of debt servicing, and (in extreme cases) virtual national bankruptcy. In some cases this downward slide sparked serious social and political unrest, as in Cuba in 1933.

But not only in times of crisis or war did the skewed trade structure have devastating consequences for the countries under US economic domination. Its effects bordered on the grotesque in normal times as well. Thus, most glaringly perhaps, Latin America, with its abundant land, fertile soils and rich fishing grounds, could not feed its people because the international division of labour condemned it to committing scarce resources to producing crops for the world market rather than for the subsistence. Argentina and Uruguay, with vast farmlands and pastures, had to import potatoes, rice and vegetable oils. Peru and

Bolivia, with fertile highland soils, had to import wheat, cocoa and tea (Bolivia's purchases of foodstuffs accounted for more than a third of total imports). Mexico, with two long coastlines on seas teeming with fish, had to import fish. Panama, with vast tropical forests and fishing resources, had to import timber and fish. Furthermore, Latin American countries found themselves buying, at high prices, goods processed from raw materials which they had previously sold cheaply to the Americans and Europeans. Cuba, for instance, exported around 11,000 tons of tomatoes to the United States annually, most of which returned to the island as tomato paste or ketchup; and Argentina shipped untanned hides and skins, and the quebracho extract for tanning them to Europe and the United States, which returned as shoes.

As the Latin Americans analysed the nature of their predicament and the implications of their unbalanced economies and trade relations, they refused to accept the unfavourable international division of labour as immutable. As a result, from the 1920s onwards the general thrust of national economic policies shifted towards a diversification of foreign trade and a greater degree of economic self-sufficiency.

Apart from the reciprocal trade agreement programme, the Roosevelt administration took several other initiatives to stimulate inter-American trade, of which the creation of the Export–Import Bank in February 1934 was the most important. The bank was originally established to stimulate trade with the recently recognized Soviet Union. But when this failed to materialize it was transformed to assist Latin American countries which lacked the foreign exchange (dollars, in other words) to buy imports from the north. It also came to the aid of governments on the verge of bankruptcy and might therefore be confronted with the kind of social upheaval which threatened the business prospects of American exporters and investors. The Cuban government, for instance, received three silver loans to pay the salaries of its employees. But on the whole the bank operated under such narrow commercial guidelines that it could do little to promote inter-American trade. Washington had yet to recognize the usefulness of foreign credits and aid as instruments of trade policy. Until 1940, Hull and his associates stuck to the view that free trade, not government lending, provided the solution to international problems, both financial and political.

A common front against fascism

As the nationalist, fascist and military regimes of Germany, Italy and Japan gained in strength during the 1930s, and when after 1939 the expansionist wave actually swallowed half of Europe and surged against the US positions in the Pacific, the fear spread in the United States that sooner rather than later the Axis powers would turn their attention to a militarily weak Latin America and pose a threat from there. Washington's strategists and political leaders were deeply troubled by the prospect of the Nazis winning a European war and acquiring French possessions in Africa, including Dakar, which would bring them within reach of the vulnerable north-east coast of Brazil, only 1,500 miles away. This concern over a possible Nazi assault on the hemisphere was shared by most American people. Shortly after the invasion of Poland a Gallup poll showed that four out of five Americans believed that if Hitler were victorious in Europe he would try to penetrate the Americas; and one in two believed that he would attack the United States at the earliest opportunity.

There was, indeed, ample evidence of an advance by the totalitarian regimes. German exporters pursued an aggressive commercial expansionism which enabled them to capture a 14% share of the Latin American market from next to nothing between 1936 and 1939. German and Italian agents were active everywhere, especially in Argentina and Paraguay, where they could rely on the support of large German and Italian immigrant communities (Paraguayan admirers of Hitler founded the first Nazi party in Latin America in 1932, even before he gained power).And there was little doubt that German diplomats played a major role in their country's sophisticated espionage network.

With germanophobia rampant in America, President Roosevelt apparently felt he could resort to a shabby propaganda ploy. On 27 October 1938 he claimed he had in his possession a secret Nazi map for the conquest of certain Latin American countries and their incorporation into a future German world empire. When the next day a reporter asked him to produce the document, he said he could not do so because — a feeble excuse — its notations might divulge the identity of his source. Doubtless he could not produce it because it existed only in his imagination. But even without this overdrawing of the 'German peril', it was deemed serious enough by many leading Americans to invoke the spirit of Monroe and intone the old chant of 'the Americas for the Americans'.

To counter the fascist challenge in the hemisphere effectively, the Americans realized they had to win over the Latin Americans as allies in a possible military conflict with the Axis powers on the one hand and organize the defence of Latin America on the other.

At the instigation of the state department, representatives of the 21 republics gathered in Buenos Aires for a special inter-American conference on the maintenance of peace on 1 December 1936. President Roosevelt had decided to attend the opening in person to underline Washington's desire to be a good neighbour in a time of crisis. It had not been a difficult decision. By its rhetoric and actions his administration had succeeded in improving Uncle Sam's image, and he was confident that he would receive the acclamation of the southern neighbours. And indeed, the Argentines gave him an enthusiastic welcome on his arrival in Buenos Aires. As a symbol of the new spirit of harmony, he greeted President Agustín Justo as 'my friend' and the two leaders embraced.

In his opening address Roosevelt urged the American countries to 'stand shoulder to shoulder' in their determination to resist outside influence and expressed the firm belief that those who 'might seek to commit acts of aggression against us will find a hemisphere wholly prepared to consult together for our mutual safety and mutual good'.[25] During the conference the delegations from north and south affirmed the principle of 'absolute non-intervention' and agreed on voluntary but close consultation in case of one or several countries of the hemisphere being threatened by external aggression.

The American republics again closed ranks two years later, at the Eighth Pan-American Conference held in Lima in December 1938. Haunted by the Munich accord and numerous other indications of fascist expansionism, the conference reaffirmed the Buenos Aires commitments and instituted a machinery for consultation among foreign ministers. The Declaration of Lima, it should be noted, was less outspoken than the Americans would have wanted, largely because of opposition from Argentina, the country which would cause the Americans much aggravation over the next decade owing to its close relations with Germany and Italy and its claims to regional leadership. The Argentine delegate, instructed to avoid any provocation of the Axis powers but faced with a clear anti-fascist consensus, had preferred to absent himself from the signing ceremony and visit the Andean mountains instead.

Ten months after Lima, in September–October 1939, the first consultative meeting of foreign ministers was held in Panama to discuss the international situation in the wake of the German invasion of Poland. In addition to adopting general declarations on economic co-operation, neutrality and the maintenance of peace, the ministers also took one concrete decision (based on a proposal put forward by Welles) to establish a security zone around the Americas. As part of their endeavours to keep the region out of the war, the Americans had one day taken a map and drawn lines roughly 300 miles from the Pacific and Atlantic coasts and proposed to declare the area thus embraced 'sea safety zones'. As if a 'do not enter' sign had been posted on the high seas, the belligerents were prohibited from carrying out military actions within the zone, on pain of punishment by the US and/or other navies. The Latin American foreign ministers accepted the proposal readily enough, since they knew that the burden of ensuring compliance with its strictures would in any case fall on the United States. Two months later the German battleship *Graf Spee* and three British cruisers fought a naval battle, unhindered, only 200 miles off the Uruguayan coast: sufficient reason for satirists to decry Roosevelt and Welles' neutrality zone as more akin to a chastity belt.

The foreign ministers assembled for a second time ten months later, in Havana in July 1940, after German troops had occupied the Benelux countries, Denmark, Norway and three-fifths of France. Alarmed at the possibility that the Reich might demand control of the Danish, Dutch, French, and perhaps eventually the British, possessions in the hemisphere, the conference adopted a convention on 30 July providing for the introduction of provisional administrations in the European colonies should they be in danger 'of becoming the subject of … a change of sovereignty'.[26] An inter-American commission was set up for such an eventuality. The foreign ministers thus in effect endorsed a previous foray on the matter by the Roosevelt administration and Congress. On 17 June Hull had directed the US ambassadors in Berlin and Rome to inform the German and Italian governments that Washington 'would not recognize any transfer, and would not acquiesce in any attempt to transfer, any geographic region of the western hemisphere from one non-American power to another non-American power'.[27] The same day, the Senate passed an almost identically worded resolution. (Incidentally, territories in dispute between European powers and American republics were prudently excluded from the provisions of the agreement. Such territories were not mentioned specifically, but the reference became clear enough when the Argentine delegation signed the document with the reservation that its provisions could not apply to the Malvinas/Falkland Islands on the grounds that these were not a colony of a non-American power but part of Argentine territory.)

While the Convention of Havana — in effect a multilateral affirmation of the no-transfer principle — made the headlines, the adoption of another resolution which linked the two Americas more closely together than at any time since the beginning of the pan-American movement went almost unnoticed. A declaration of 'reciprocal assistance and cooperation' stated:

> Any attempt on the part of a non-American state against the integrity or inviolability of the territory, the sovereignty or the political independence of an American state shall be considered an act of aggression against the states that sign the declaration.[28]

One for all and all for one. Under this motto the American republics sealed their political solidarity against fascism.

The Havana documents provided a useful enough ideological indication of increased inter-American co-operation in the face of external pressures, but no regional government ever enforced them to prevent or punish European aggression in the hemisphere.The main problem for the Americans was that between December 1938 and July 1940 nothing more could have been achieved even against the background of imminent war. For despite the dangers looming from the other side of the Atlantic, the Latin Americans were far too concerned for their sovereignty to countenance the kind of formal defensive alliance of American states proposed by Roosevelt in Lima. They saw clearly that US military superiority would allow the United States to use a multilateral pact, once it had served its immediate purpose of common defence in the current war, to meddle in the internal affairs of its neighbours or even to intervene directly as it had done unilaterally in the past.

The results of the consultative meetings of foreign ministers in Panama and Havana nevertheless would have serious implications for the balance of inter-American relations. The various agreements of this time, above all the Havana declaration on reciprocal assistance, certainly created an embryonic pan-americanized Monroe Doctrine; but they also portended the so-called Rio Pact of 1947, which on a broad interpretation allowed the United States to claim a right to intervention, as it did, for instance, with regard to Grenada in October 1983.

The Latin Americans had more success in protecting their territorial integrity from US encroachment. In the light of the balance of military power between north and south — Brazil's navy, for instance, was so small that 14 of its 15 admirals had to stay at home at any one time and use their imagination to execute brilliant manoeuvres and win famous victories — the Americans thought it reasonable to request temporary, if not permanent, leases for military bases from their neighbours. But no Latin American country was prepared to surrender even an inch of territory. After protracted negotiations the Americans obtained several bilateral agreements with Latin American governments which allowed them only to construct such army and navy installations on these countries' territories that could be staffed with unarmed technicians.

In the wake of the Havana meeting the United States did manage to 'borrow' naval bases from another ally, however. On behalf of his government, the British ambassador in Washington, the Marquess of Lothian, on 2 September 1940 offered the use of British islands and territories in the hemisphere as naval and air bases. These included the eastern side of the Bahamas, the south coast of Jamaica, the west coast of Saint Lucia, the west coast of Trinidad, the island of Antigua and an area around Georgetown, the capital of British Guiana. Since President Roosevelt and the British prime minister, Winston Churchill, had already discussed the matter the previous August, Hull could accept the offer and inform Lothian of the administration's return present, 50 over-age destroyers, the same day.

After the Japanese sneak air and naval attack on Pearl Harbor on 7 December 1941, which destroyed a large part of the US navy, the Latin American countries promptly gave proof of their solidarity with their ally. Nine Central American and Caribbean countries declared war on Japan on 12 December. Three days earlier the Chilean government had cabled the Pan-American Union in Washington calling for an immediate consultative meeting of foreign ministers to discuss the unjustified aggression against the United States by a non-American power. Such a meeting was convened in the Tiradentes palace in Rio de Janeiro on 15 January 1942. After a long wrangle over the final resolution, with Chile (fearing Japanese retaliation) and Argentina arguing for a mild response to Pearl Harbor, the foreign ministers eventually agreed to recommend breaking off diplomatic relations with Japan, Italy and Germany. Colombia, Mexico and Venezuela had in fact already done so; Bolivia, Paraguay, Peru and Uruguay did so even before the conference adjourned; Brazil announced its decision at the closing plenary session, and Ecuador the following day.

The Roosevelt administration scored another diplomatic success in Rio, even though once again it was more modest than hoped for, with the creation of a joint defence council, the Inter-American Defense Board (IADB). It held its first meeting on 30 March 1942, met regularly during the war, and in fact survived to become a permanent inter-American institution. Although the Americans would have preferred a true defence pact, the IADB, which functioned as a kind of regional war college, nevertheless gave them an opportunity to impress on their Latin guests the benefits of receiving US training and equipment and to influence the outlook a Latin American military class which had hitherto relied much more on Europe.

Apart from pushing for the multilateral agreements, the US government sponsored a wide range of other measures to consolidate the Pax Americana and protect the New World from attacks by the old. From 1938 onwards it expanded its military missions to counter the growing influence of the Axis rivals. It set up the Inter-American Financial and Economic Advisory Committee (FEAC), which met first on 15 November 1939 to discuss financial problems as well as urgent economic and commercial issues. On the basis of a joint resolution of

Congress, known as the Pitman Resolution, approved on 15 June 1940, the FEAC furnished the Latin American countries with military equipment (although the arms, mostly coastal artillery and anti-aircraft guns, were outdated and sold on restrictive terms). On 16 August 1940 it established by executive order the Office for Coordination of Commercial and Cultural Relations between the American Republics, later renamed the Office of the Coordinator of Inter-American Affairs (OIAA), and appointed Nelson Rockefeller as co-ordinator. On 24 March 1942 it founded, under the auspices of the OIAA, the Institute of Inter-American Affairs (IIAA), which offered the Latin American countries technical aid and support for the development of their health services.

With regard to economic co-operation, the administration proposed the formation of an inter-American trade cartel under the leadership of the United States, which would have provided central planning and a bargaining agency for all regional trade, and revived an earlier proposal for an inter-American bank. Both plans foundered, however, the first primarily on the resistance of the Latin Americans and the second on the resistance of US banks and Congress.

The administration's less ambitious economic initiatives had more success. It granted credits to Latin American countries to help them stabilize their currencies against the dollar; it signed a convention with the region's 14 coffee-exporting countries to prevent price declines (due to the loss of European markets); it greatly increased the lending funds of the Export–Import Bank; and it sent development experts to the Latin American countries within the framework of a co-operation programme co-ordinated by Welles himself.

For their part, the Latin Americans made considerable contributions to the US war effort and the defence of the hemisphere. For instance, thousands of Mexican volunteers enlisted in the US army, the two countries signed a defence pact, and a Mexican air squadron fought on the Pacific front; Brazil declared war on Germany and Italy in August 1942, and an expeditionary force left for Italy in July 1944, the only Latin American force to fight on the European front (the close co-operation with the United States enabled Brazil to become Latin America's strongest military power); and Cuba signed an agreement of military co-operation with the United States in June 1940.

In economic terms the region's contribution was also important. The US Board of Economic Warfare persuaded the Latin Americans to change their agricultural production to help the war effort. But above all, the southern neighbours supplied the United States with crucial, perhaps even decisive, strategic minerals. Once the Pacific area had been closed off, Latin America became the United States' only source of manganese, copper, tin, antimony, vanadium, tungsten and zinc.

Inter-American co-operation during the war also meant considerable sacrifices. For one thing, any profits to be made tended to be pocketed by US firms. By agreeing to the defence-oriented programmes Latin Americans accepted the postponement of their own development and diversification programmes or a further distortion of their economies, either in the direction of monocultural agriculture or unbalanced industrialization. In most countries food production and other key areas of economic activity were seriously hampered during the war, whether in Mexico because of the forced cultivation of oil-bearing seeds, in Bolivia because of increased tin and tungsten mining, or in Brazil because of accelerated arms production. More often than not, farmers and miners had to accept even worse working conditions.

In short, the price the Latin Americans paid for their contribution to the US war effort was a high one. Economically, they ended up with a new inflationary spiral (due to the influx of American money) and even greater interdependence with the United States (as indicated by the growth of the US share of the region's trade from one third in 1939 to half by 1945). Politically, they ended up with much closer institutional links to the northern neighbour, many of which survived the war and were consolidated in the Rio Pact and the charter of the Organization of American States adopted in 1948.

Notes

1. Inaugural address, 4 March 1933, quoted in Gantenbein (ed.) 1950 p. 159ff.

2. Address to the Pan-American Union, 12 April 1933, quoted in Gantenbein (ed.), op. cit., p. 160.

3. Hull 1949 p. 324.

4. Address to the Seventh Pan-American Conference, 26 December 1933, quoted in Gantenbein (ed.), op. cit., p. 763.

5. Article 8, Convention on Rights and Duties of States, signed 26 December 1933, quoted in Gantenbein (ed.), op. cit., p. 761.

6. Welles 1935ap. 14.

7. Quoted in Merle, *Moncada*, p. 37

8. Official statement by President Roosevelt, 24 November 1933, quoted in Welles 1935cp. 11.

9. Welles, op. cit., p. 12.

10. Agreement [on Haitian Finances] to Replace the Agreement of August 7, 1933, signed 13 September 1941, quoted in Gantenbein (ed.), op, cit., p. 938ff.

11. Joint statement by President Roosevelt and President Arias, 16 October 1933, quoted in Hoyt 1966 p. 296.

12. Quoted in Galeano 1973 p. 126.

13. Sayre 1936 p. 2ff.

14 . Quoted in Kindleberger 1973 p. 294.

15. Welles 1944 p. 191.

16. Hull, op. cit., p. 354.

17. Welles 1941 p. 5.

18. Sayre 1937 p. 13ff; Hull, op. cit., p. 81.

19. Sayre, op. cit., p. 12.

20. Welles 1934 p. 5.

21. Welles 1935c p. 17.

22. Welles 1934 p. 11.

23. A full list is provided in Chamber of Commerce of the United States 1940 pp. 9–19.

24. A full list is provided in Chamber of Commerce of the United States, op. cit., pp. 20–30.

25. Address to the Pan-American Conference on the Maintenance of Peace, 1 December 1936, quoted in Gantenbein (ed.), op. cit., p. 176.

26. Act of Havana on the Provisional Administration of European Colonies and Possessions in the Americas, signed 30 July 1940, quoted in Gantenbein (ed.), op. cit., p. 800.

27. Statement by the US Department of State, 19 June 1940, quoted in Gantenbein (ed.), op. cit., p. 417.

28. Declaration of Reciprocal Assistance for the Defense of the Nations of America, adopted 30 July 1940, quoted in Gantenbein (ed.), op. cit., p. 799.

5. The East–West conflict and anti-communism

Latin America overshadowed by the cold war

Despite great losses in men and materials, the United States emerged on the whole relatively unscathed from the Second World War. Because of its geographical position and the course of the war, it suffered far less damage than the other major powers. In fact, it had profited from the war. US industrial output, for instance, rose sharply between 1941 and 1945, as did people's standards of living. The value of the gross domestic product grew from $116.8 billion to $201.0 billion during this period, and national income increased from $104.7 billion to $181.2 billion. Apart from the government, whose share of national income increased by $26.3 billion, it was above all the agricultural, manufacturing, commercial and transport sectors (up by $6.4 billion, $19.0 billion, $10.7 billion and $4.2 billion respectively) which profited from the wartime economic boom. The fact that at this time three-quarters of the world's invested capital and two-thirds of industrial capacity was concentrated in the United States provides an indication of its overwhelming economic dominance.

In 1945 American economists and politicians lost sleep not over how to stimulate a depressed economy, but over quite the opposite, how to deal with the huge surpluses created by the dramatic expansion of productive capacity during the war. Between 1939 and 1945 the federal government alone had built new factories valued at $16 billion, a sum equivalent to a quarter of all US factories before the war. Moreover, rationalization and modernization had increased labour productivity (output per person-hour) by nearly 20%.

So industrialists and politicians looked towards VE Day and VJ Day, which marked the victories over Germany and Japan, not only with satisfaction, but also with a certain degree of anxiety. Once the war was over, it would become apparent whether the transition from a war to a peace economy could proceed smoothly, and, above all, whether the change could be achieved without mass unemployment and social conflict.

According to the widely held, even commonplace, hypothesis, the US economy would have to curb its production, leading to a dangerous rise in unemployment, unless markets for surplus production and investment opportunities for surplus capital could be found. Just as their predecessors had done during the crisis of the 1890s, the politicians of the Roosevelt era dramatized the consequences of such a depression. They were as certain of their prediction that mass unemployment would lead to social conflict as they were of their apocalyptic vision that this would spell the end of free enterprise and the collapse of America's free-market society. Francis B. Sayre, an assistant secretary of state, put these widespread fears in a nutshell: 'When our soldiers return from the battlefields we will have to find a way to give them work and security. Otherwise our system of free enterprise is damned, and we will reap the storm'.[1]

The politicians found a way out of the looming calamity by the trusted means of expanding export markets. They recalled with some gratitude the 'open-door' policy first proposed in 1899 by John Hay, the secretary of state, by which the imperialist powers accepted each other's rights to trade freely in China. In 1944 all senior American foreign-policy experts of the day (among them Dean Acheson, W. Averell Harriman, Donald Nelson, Edward Stettinius, Adolph A. Berle Jr, John Foster Dulles, Eric Johnston, William C. Foster and James Forrestal) and perhaps even President Roosevelt himself were convinced that only a worldwide open-door policy would secure America's prosperity and its democratic structure. This view continued to dominate US foreign-policy thinking after 1945.

One obstacle to the global open door was of the Americans' own making, however. When the United States, the Soviet Union and Britain divided the world, and above all Europe, into spheres of influence at the Yalta Conference in February 1945, the Americans did not foresee that this would bolt the open door in some parts of the world. They saw Yalta purely as a political agreement with the Soviet Union on how to share the role of world policeman; they did not expect one of the essentials of US foreign policy, free trade, to be affected in any way. When it emerged that the Soviet Union was aiming to prevent, on the grounds of national security, its encirclement by antagonistic neighbours (as had happened in the past), and that it was also encouraging changes in the socio-economic structures within its sphere of influence, the US government had to recognize that the notions of spheres of influence and open door were incompatible.

At this point the critics of the western powers' alleged appeasement at Yalta, in particular Senator Arthur H. Vandenberg, chair of the Senate foreign affairs committee, pressed their case. It was left to Harry S. Truman, who succeeded Roosevelt on the latter's death on 12 April 1945, to spell out, with the help of the foreign-policy hawks in Washington, his predecessor's vague and self-critical doubts about the policy of spheres of influence and to adjust it accordingly. 'Reverse the decisions of Yalta and the realities created in Eastern Europe' became the political, diplomatic and strategic slogan of the day. US foreign policy was under this revisionist spell until 12 March 1947, when Truman proclaimed the anti-communist doctrine named after him that promised ideological and material support for countries of the 'free world' threatened by communism.

Whatever Stalin's policies in Central and Eastern Europe may have contributed to the origins and escalation of the cold war, there can be no doubt that the United States was primarily responsible for this confrontational phase in super-power relations. For one thing, even people like Vandenberg held the view that the United States, the leading world power, was vastly superior to the Soviet Union in its ability to determine the course of international relations. Dominance in the military sphere was evident enough: the US possessed a large strategic airforce; it had access to some 400 military bases surrounding the Soviet Union; its troops were deployed (in 1946) in 56 countries and on every continent; and above all, during the height of the cold war (until 1949) it was the world's sole nuclear power, holding, in the telling words of the secretary of war, Henry L. Stimson, the 'master card', a kind of strategic joker which it could play at any time without fear of a nuclear counterstrike.[2]

In truth, then, the United States had already effectively succeeded in containing the Soviet Union when George F. Kennan outlined the new policy of 'containment', first in a lengthy telegram from Moscow dated 22 February 1946 and then in a famous anonymous article 'The Sources of Soviet Conduct' published in the July 1947 issue of *Foreign Affairs*. In this ideological contribution to the anti-communist strategy (which ensured his promotion to the top of the US foreign-policy establishment), Kennan used the term containment in a very broad sense. He did not stop at declaring the containment of communism within the territorial boundaries it had achieved as a result of the war as an imperative of US foreign policy. He also enjoined the American people to accept

> The responsibility of moral and political leadership that history plainly intended them to bear [and] to increase enormously the strains under which Soviet policy must operate ... and in this way to promote tendencies which must eventually find their outlet in either the breakup or the gradual mellowing of Soviet power.[3]

When five years later the new secretary of state, John Foster Dulles, advocated 'rolling back' communism, he was not diverging from current thinking but merely putting forward a more militant version of what had gone before, and making more explicit what had been until then the United States' goal in the confrontation between East and West — namely to keep markets open for American capital or, more stridently, to reopen those markets which had been lost to communism.

US foreign policy during the cold war subordinated everything, including relations with Latin America, to the global confrontation between East and West. Whenever a Latin American government or liberation movement initiated moves in these years to overcome glaring injustices through social reforms or revolution, politicians in Washington inveighed against the 'red peril'. And by labelling all social change, no matter how moderate and cautious, as 'communist-inspired', they also gave themselves the perfect excuse for their countermeasures. Depending on the situation and relative importance of a particular country, these could include information and disinformation campaigns, counter-insurgency programmes, covert actions by the secret service, political destabilization, economic blackmail through the International Monetary Fund (IMF), 'subliminal warfare' with the help of research and social organizations, military aid of all kinds, intimidatory naval manoeuvres, and, as last resorts, support for armed insurgency and direct military intervention.

The new policy of containment went much further than that of President Monroe had done with regard to the European powers. The two policies were comparable in that they were supposed to keep non-American powers or systems and their interests out of the hemisphere — in the 1820s the autocratic monarchies of Europe which lacked any democratic legitimacy, in the 1950s Marxism or communism with its opposition to the capitalist system, in particular the American way of life. But while Monroe's aim had been to contain the power-political ambitions of the European states, the Truman administration's Latin American policy sought to block or reverse any undesirable *social* changes. That is why the new policy had a more direct effect on the internal structures of the Latin American countries than the interventions during the period 1898–1933. Because the economic interests at play at that time were still disparate and limited, the earlier interventions had often consisted of little more than providing US investors with a bodyguard of marines or allowing them to collect debts by gunboat. But American export, raw-materials and investment interests became so intertwined with strategic prerogatives in the decades after 1945 that any social change in countries to the south, no matter how harmless, very quickly ran the risk of being depicted as a danger to US national security.

When in doubt, back the economic and social status quo. That was — and is — the maxim of Washington's Latin American policy. Any attempts by Latin American governments or social movements to address the underdevelopment that condemned the mass of the people to abject poverty was put within the context of East–West conflict, the struggle between good and evil, in which every social change that threatened to go beyond the free-enterprise model became a communist machination. The logic was simple enough: whoever was not for America was against America, and therefore a communist. Bearing the stamp of that paranoid style of US foreign policy, the stereotyped reactions followed in quick succession: conjuring up the spectre of communism, attempting to kill off the reform movement by economic pressure or, in the last resort, initiating a covert action by the secret service or an overt military intervention in favour of the opposition, whoever they might be — compliant conservatives or ruthless dictators — as long as they supported the star-spangled banner and the dollar.

In a kind of self-fulfilling prophecy, Washington brought to pass in Latin America precisely what it deplored so strongly. The foolish attempt to put revolutions or reforms under quarantine like infected cattle, to prevent the communist 'bacillus' from spreading from one region to another, left belea-guered reformers no option but to look for economic aid and political support to the Soviet Union and Cuba, countries which initially they would probably not have seen as natural allies. It was only at that point that the anti-communist premise that Moscow and Havana fomented all liberation and reform movements in Latin America came somewhat nearer the truth.

As far as US foreign policy was concerned, in particular Latin American policy, revolutions were a thing of the past. Both the revolution in the British colonies in the 1770s and the liberation struggles of the South America of the 1810s and 20s were glorious events, of course — but they were history. In the present, home-grown revolutions arising wholly or primarily out of social contradictions could not be, and therefore should not be.

The preceding paragraphs were written in the past tense, referring to the climate of the late 1940s and 1950s, but they could just as easily be written in the present tense. Because the distorted standpoint of US foreign policy in Latin America is only the ideological reverse of economic interests intent on preserving existing economic and social structures (such as low wages or restricted trade-union rights), it would be futile to pin one's hopes on the American political system's ability to learn from the past and develop a different relationship with Latin America. A fiasco like the Washington-sponsored Bay of Pigs invasion (by opponents of Castro) in 1961 makes US governments reconsider the costs and benefits of such adventures, but no more; it never seems to provide an impetus to learn from mistakes. For learning from mistakes would mean nothing less than holding world public opinion and the legitimate interests of the Latin Americans in higher regard than national economic and strategic preferences. National egotism and the country's status as military superpower almost predestines the United States to lapses into arrogance and the politics of the big stick. At any rate it is always the Latin Americans who foot the bills, both for the victories of US foreign policy and for its defeats.

Dumbarton Oaks, Chapultepec and Rio: stages towards disillusionment

By 1945 the United States had become the leading world power, a mantle it had been preparing to take on — with Britain as a junior partner, as outlined in the Anglo–US Atlantic Charter of August 1941 — even during the war. Many Americans, including political leaders, at this time hoped that their country would become an example for all to follow in the post-war 'one world' (the title of an influential book by Wendell L. Wilkie, the Republican candidate in the 1940 presidential elections) and would be able to impress its economic preferences and political principles on a future world state. But the dreams of some kind of worldwide American commonwealth were shattered in the frost of the cold war. What remained, however, was the globalism in US foreign policy: the claim to be leading the 'free world' in a crusade against totalitarianism. The shift from anti-fascism to anti-communism was accomplished even before the allied victories in Europe and the Pacific. During the debates on the foundation of the United Nations in early 1945, the Roosevelt administration tried uncompromisingly, and in the face of strong Soviet opposition, to impose its globalist preconceptions (admittedly in watered-down form) on the future world order.

Those Latin Americans who thought that their willing co-operation with the United States during the Second World War would be repaid politically and economically would be bitterly disappointed in the early post-war years. Quite independent of whether the United States was a reluctant superpower or whether it strove actively for world hegemony, its new role meant that in future Washington would subordinate inter-American relations to the demands of global strategy. In other words, the era of the 'special relationship' between north and south had gone, as had the 'western hemisphere idea' as a bond, at least in American eyes, between the two halves of the hemisphere. Such ideas were considered anachronistic now that the United States had outgrown its role as the dominant regional power and had advanced to world power. No wonder, then, that Washington's interest in inter-American conference diplomacy waned noticeably, even before victory over the anti-fascist coalition had become inevitable.

Not that the Americans could have done without Latin America, nor did they think they could. It should be remembered that many Americans, particularly those who wanted to follow the victory over fascism with a war on communism, regarded the post-war period potentially as a pre-war period. The cold war thus counted as a half-war, and the administration attached great importance to strategic considerations and the safeguarding of supplies of raw materials. As had been the case during and before the war, Latin America still supplied the United States with agricultural products and minerals without which it would be hard-pressed to survive. Brazil still supplied more than half of the US imports of coffee, Cuba of sugar, Venezuela of oil, Chile of copper and nitrates, Argentina of tinned meat, Mexico of tomatoes. Almost all supplies of strategic minerals like antimony, cadmium and mica came from Latin America, as did the lion's share of imports of bismuth, iodine, tin zinc and sisal. Washington's Latin American policy in effect pursued the dual goals of securing strategic political interests by economic means (what might be called 'economic defence') and protecting economic interests by power-political means.

Overall, US imports from Latin America had tripled during the war in comparison to the 1930s, and total trade had doubled. The prospect of the flow of goods returning to pre-war levels made the Latin America experts fear for the prosperity of the US economy, particularly the size of the gross domestic product, which it did not seem possible to maintain without the Latin American market. Moreover, by 1943 American businesses had invested around $3.5 billion in Latin America, mostly in infrastructure, which benefited US foreign trade, and in oil, which benefited the US economy as a whole. For despite its own oil wealth, the United States now partly relied on imported oil to fuel continued growth. If this relative dependency did not make the Americans eye the south with some concern, the fear that the black gold and other strategic minerals might fall into communist hands certainly did.

To consolidate their economic prosperity and leadership role in the world the Americans needed their southern neighbours now as much as they had at the outbreak of the Second World War. But politically they needed them only as bit-part players on the international stage. With the notion of globalism in the ascendant, neither President Roosevelt nor his secretary of state, Cordell Hull — who considered his foreign-trade philosophy a panacea for all international conflicts — had much time for the regionalist approach of the Latin Americans.

The administration now held that regional institutions should be subordinated to world institutions and that initiatives on the maintenance of peace and security, for instance, should become the prerogative of the new worldwide organization. The dismissive attitude towards the Latin Americans was evidenced by the fact that they were not even invited to the conference in Dumbarton Oaks (outside Washington) in August–October 1944 at which the structure and authority of the United Nations were being discussed by American, British, Chinese and Soviet representatives. Bland briefings by US diplomats were the Latin Americans' only source of information on the discussions by the great powers regarding the new world order. Of course, once the UN charter was finally signed in San Francisco after lengthy negotiations on 26 June 1945, the Americans were very keen to welcome their Latin neighbours as members of the western 'family of nations'.

Because relations with the Soviet Union had turned sour, even Argentina, previously criticized for having assisted the Axis powers during the war, was soon allowed to join to swell the Latin and pro-US bloc. Hull, a member of the US delegation at the San Francisco conference but too ill to attend, described Argentina as a 'refuge and headquarters in the hemisphere of the fascist movement' and a 'bag neighbour', and from his hospital bed urged his successor as secretary of state, Edward Stettinius, to keep Roosevelt's promise to the Soviets that Argentina would not be admitted to the United Nations for the time being.[4] But to no avail: over the objection of the Soviets, Argentina was admitted by 31 votes to 4. (The state department cobbled together a thoroughly disingenuous justification for the sudden gentle treatment of Argentina. It argued that the Argentine government, not its people, had offered the country to the Axis powers as a base for their operations; it would therefore be wrong to punish a people which in the past had proven itself a friend of the United States for the deplorable actions of its government.)

As a concession to the co-operative Latin Americans, the UN charter did in the end contain a compromise between globalism and regionalism. In return for the Latin American countries' support for the formation of the United Nations, article 51 of the charter recognized Latin America's inherent right of individual and collective self-defence against armed attack; and article 33(i) urged states to settle disputes through regional bodies before bringing them to the UN Security Council. As a result of this compromise, the OAS, founded in 1948, retained a high degree of autonomy in the handling of peace and security matters in the hemisphere, and the United Nations — the world organization to which the OAS was supposed to be subordinate — had no effective control over its activities. This remained the case from the 1950s until the US-led invasion of Grenada in October 1983.

Further mollifying their southern neighbours with generous military aid, the Americans could now count on their unwavering support. Since the Latin American republics accounted for 20 of the UN's 49 founding members, the Americans had 'built a steamroller in the United Nations', as the New York *Herald Tribune* observed even before the organization had been formally set up, and could always muster an anti-Soviet majority.[5] In fact, in its first decade the

United Nations was little more than an instrument of US foreign policy. Between 1946 and 1953 the General Assembly adopted over 800 resolutions, and the United States was defeated on no more than 20, none of which involved important security interests. In these eight years only two resolutions supported by the United States failed to get adopted.

As far as regional relations were concerned, the Latin Americans had served notice of their desire to put them on a new footing at an early stage, with an initiative launched in June 1944 by the Mexican government in conjunction with its Brazilian, Cuban and Uruguayan counterparts. But the Americans, fully occupied with formulating the post-war open-door policy and preparing for the role of world power, ignored the call for an inter-American conference on the issue. Only when the initiative gained momentum and the danger loomed that the Latin Americans might proceed without the northern neighbour did Washington change tack, pretending that nothing would be more welcome than a meeting of foreign ministers to discuss the future of the inter-American system.

Representatives of all the American republics (with the exception of Argentina, which was yet to be rehabilitated) met in the Chapultepec palace in Mexico City on 21 February 1945 for the Inter-American Conference on Problems of War and Peace. The conference agenda was as wide-ranging as its title, including the issue of the regional organization, its relationship to the fledgling world organization, arms control, the co-ordination of the various inter-American institutions, and the Argentine question. But above all the conference dealt with economic issues.

The Latin Americans intended to consolidate the modest industrial development they had achieved during the war as a result of protectionist policies, the temporary withdrawal of the European powers from their traditional markets, and better trade relations. They brought a long list of demands to the Chapultepec palace reflecting this. They called for: massive foreign investment in their countries, so that they could diversify their economies and one day perhaps substitute expensive imports with domestic products; recognition of their need, as weaker links in the world division of labour, to use tariffs to protect their vulnerable industrial sectors; the abandonment of protectionism by the Americans (in particular, the policy of imposing high tariffs on imported manufactured goods, which in effect perpetuated the existing division of labour between north and south as suppliers of manufactures and raw materials respectively); greater control over foreign capital; measures to stabilize their export revenues (which they feared would collapse with the expected deterioration of the terms of trade); and an end to the stranglehold by US firms on the transport of Latin American goods, which artificially inflated transport costs and hence the prices of imports and exports. All in all, the Latins' objective at Chapultepec was nothing less than a more equitable distribution of the profits of the inter-American division of labour.

But, just as in the 1970s the call by the developing countries as a whole for a new international economic order would encounter stiff resistance from the industrialized countries, the Latin Americans found no enthusiasm for their proposals within the Truman administration. It had no intention of acceding to their wishes and instead proposed something quite different. At Chapultepec the US delegation tried to push through its thesis of the unrestricted freedom of trade — the conventional wisdom in Washington since the 1930s — in the grandiosely entitled 'economic charter for the Americas', which became known as the Clayton Plan, after Will Clayton, the assistant secretary of state for economic affairs.

Under the Clayton Plan the United States specifically proposed to enshrine equality of access to raw materials and manufactures, reduction of trade barriers, the elimination of economic materialism in all its forms, equal and just treatment for foreign capital and enterprises, encouragement of private enterprise and rejection of state enterprise, agreements on the marketing of primary commodities, and respect for the rights of workers. No doubt laudable principles as far as many contemporaries were concerned. But the Latin Americans, representing un- or under-developed economies, knew all too well that by opting for free trade rather than moderate protectionism and for private enterprise rather than moderate planning they would in effect give *carte blanche* to unrestrained exploitation by the north.

The Clayton Plan found no takers in Latin America. Most unusually, it was opposed in equal measure by capital and labour. In Mexico, for instance, the National Chamber of Mexican Industrial Development, the Confederation of Chambers of Commerce, the Confederation of Mexican Workers and Vicente Lombardo Toledano, president of the Confederation of Latin American Workers, issued a joint statement warning against acceptance of 'the North American free trade' which would 'never be convenient to us, because of our backward conditions'.[6] The formal report presented to the first congress for industrial development in Mexico, held in April 1947, contained a critique of the free-trade proposal which could have been written by the later theorists of dependence (*dependencia*). It argued that the Clayton Plan

> means nothing but a plan to world dominion and for the abolition of competition and freedom. The role which the United States plays in it is that of a metropolitan country, while the other countries are on the level of satellite states. Only the United States is defending this neo-liberalism. The other countries, all over the world, are opposed to the total loss of their independence on the altar of something which pretends to be democracy and liberty but which is nothing more than egotistic and cunning libertinism.[7]

In the face of implacable Latin American opposition the Americans were forced to accept a systematic dilution of the Clayton Plan, with, for instance, the objective of 'the elimination of economic nationalism in all its forms' becoming that of 'the elimination of excesses of economic nationalism'. At the same time, however, the Latin Americans were unable to secure Washington's endorsement of any of their major economic proposals for regional development.

Early in the proceedings it had in fact become clear that the US approach at Chapultepec was to offer advice and make recommendations rather than pledge direct assistance or enter into specific commitments. The main thrust of the Truman administration's foreign-aid policy was not the development of Latin America but the reconstruction of Europe and its consolidation as a bulwark against communism. Since the dollars were pledged to Europe, Latin America had to make do with vague promises. Thus Clayton sought to assure the delegates that the economic recovery of Europe would also benefit their countries in that it would 'restore former markets and perhaps open new and greater ones'.[8]

Owing to Washington's globalist preoccupations, most of the Latin Americans' regionalist proposals advanced at Chapultepec made no headway. An inter-American investment bank, for instance, was rejected for the simple reason that the United States had already created the instruments for its world economic policy, the World Bank and the IMF, at the Bretton Woods conference in July 1944. The Truman administration also saw regional financial institutions as potential obstacles to the realization of the free-trade idyll or open-world policy. For similar reasons, and also because of the vexed Argentine question, the plan for a collective regional security system was out of favour in Washington, for the time being at least. Attention focused instead on turning the planned UN Security Council into the instrument of US global security policy and the signing of bilateral agreements with individual Latin American countries to secure US influence (rather than peace) in the hemisphere.

The conference concluded on 23 March with the adoption of a bland document, the Act of Chapultepec, which contained little of substance. The Latin Americans left Mexico City with at most some satisfaction that the act reaffirmed the Declaration of Havana, which by its reciprocal assistance formula had pan-americanized the Monroe Doctrine and politicized the pan-American movement.

Although the Havana and Chapultepec commitments on regional defence co-operation existed only on paper, this did not mean that the Americans remained inactive in this field. The military aid granted to Latin American countries during the war under the lend-lease programme, in which the United States had donated $262 million to its economically weak allies ($150 million to Brazil alone), was considered such a success in US military circles that plans were soon afoot to expand it after the war. The reasons for this were diverse: it would mean good business for the booming arms industry, contain anti-US nationalist sentiment in the region, and prevent the emergence of so-called communist-inspired subversive movements.

To achieve these objectives, a bill on inter-American military co-operation was introduced in Congress and recommended for adoption by President Truman in May 1946. Not least because it wanted to clear the arsenals of old weapons (to replace them with new ones to counter the communist threat), the administration wanted to offer the Latin Americans a programme for the standardization of training, organization and equipment of their armed forces. But both leading Republicans and Democrats objected to the proposal on the grounds that the transfer of weapons to the south, even outdated ones, might spark civil wars and regional conflicts. The bill languished for months in the Senate foreign affairs committee and in fact never came to a vote.

This means of organizing military co-operation being denied to it, the administration once again warmed to the notion of a regional defence treaty. One obstacle to this had been removed when Argentina finally declared war on

Germany and Japan in March 1945 and thus cleared the way for its return to the community of American republics. But above all it was the escalation of the cold war which brought about a change of outlook in the White House, the state department and the Pentagon. Washington's policy makers recognized the importance of securing their more aggressive policy of a systematic encirclement of the Soviet Union at the regional level. Specifically this meant gaining the support of Latin American governments in the fight against allegedly or actually Soviet-backed social and political movements in the hemisphere.

Representatives of the United States and 19 Latin American republics (Nicaragua was absent) gathered on 15 August 1947 in Quintandinha, near Rio de Janeiro, for an inter-American conference on the theme of 'the maintenance of continental peace and security'. Highlighting the overriding need to counter the communist threat, the United States managed to gain acceptance for its conception of a regional security system. Vandenberg, the rabid anti-communist senator from Michigan, proved a key figure in the US delegation, for it was he who fought down Argentine counterproposals in a dramatic session on 30 August.

The Inter-American Treaty of Reciprocal Assistance, signed in Rio on 2 September and commonly known as the Rio Pact, formalized a recommendation in the Act of Chapultepec by declaring that 'an armed attack by any state against an American state shall be considered as an attack against all the American states'.[9] The treaty was a setback for Latin American emancipation, however, because it was not restricted to deterring external aggression, but once again opened the back door to US intervention in the region. For article 6 stated that

> If the inviolability or the integrity of the territory or the sovereignty or political independence of any American state should be affected by an aggression which is not an armed attack or by an extra-continental or intra-continental conflict, or by any other fact or situation that might endanger the peace of the Americas, the organ of consultation [of foreign ministers] shall meet immediately in order to agree on the measures which must be taken.[10]

This clause provided the Americans with the maximum leverage to intervene, if they so chose, in any dispute or crisis in the hemisphere. Some US politicians reputedly claimed that the Rio Pact fulfilled the dream of Bolívar: in fact it made a mockery of the sovereignty of Latin American countries which it was supposed to protect. The treaty was ratified by the US Senate on 8 December, with only one senator voting against.

The Rio Pact has been invoked by US presidents and secretaries of state on more than 20 occasions since it entered into force with the deposit of the fourteenth ratification in December 1948. Ironically this treaty, essentially designed for defence of the hemisphere from outside attack, became invariably, in its application, a legal front for aggression within the hemisphere. The first time the Americans hid behind article 6 to justify an intervention was in Guatemala in June 1954, the last, at the time of writing, was in Grenada in October 1983. (In the latter case the Reagan administration did not even bother to convene the consultative conference as required under the treaty.) Far from eliminating arbitrary use of power by the stronger, the Rio Pact actually gave it a semblance of legitimacy. The *claim* to intervention, which the Roosevelt administration had solemnly relinquished in the 1930s, returned in US foreign policy as a *right* to intervention. Over the years many Latin American governments had to pay a high price for their predecessors' willingness to give up a slice of national sovereignty in the (false) hope that their political solidarity with the United States in the anti-communist crusade would bring them economic dividends.

The *bogotazo*, the red peril and the foundation of the OAS

To put the emerging inter-American system on a permanent footing, as envisaged in the Act of Chapultepec, representatives of the 21 American republics gathered in Bogotá, the Colombian capital, on 30 March 1948 for the Ninth Pan-American Conference, the founding conference of the OAS (although Chapultepec could be regarded as such with some justification).

Both the timing of the conference and the choice of venue proved to be extremely unfortunate. It started inauspiciously when the Americans insensitively insisted on the diplomatic custom, to which exception had often been made in the past, of offering the foreign minister of the host country the presidency of the conference. This meant handing the gavel to Laureano Gómez, a man who could only be described as a fascist in the strict sense of the term (he was a close friend of Franco, in whose arms he was to flee soon afterwards). On the opening day the conference thus lost the confidence of Colombian public opinion by giving its highest honour to the country's most notorious reactionary.

During the conference's first week the situation in the city grew increasingly tense as supporters of the governing Conservatives and the opposition Liberals confronted each other in the streets. Then, on 9 April, the assassination in the centre of Bogotá of Jorge Elicier Gaitán, the Liberal presidential candidate in the 1946 elections and a charismatic reformer and populist leader, provided the spark for a spontaneous and undirected uprising. Once it had overcome its shock the crowd pursued the assassin and lynched him in the street. Anger quickly turned against the Conservative government, which was held responsible for the murder. A general strike was called, paralysing the city. In the growing chaos the poor of Bogotá vented their anger by rioting and looting. Several government buildings were put to the torch. With both the conference venue and their hotels being attacked by the mob, the foreign ministers had to postpone their sessions and find refuge wherever they could. (Not so the senior members of the US delegation, however, who had left the conference for a leisurely weekend in a mansion outside the capital an hour before the outbreak of violence on the fateful Friday.) It took the military ten days to restore order. Around 1,200 people lost their lives in the conflagration, which became known as the *bogotazo*.

Although they had been in no position to observe and analyse it, the American diplomats readily offered official explanations for the rebellion. As usual, the economic and social roots of the anger of the masses were ignored or discounted. Instead, the reported identification of some Colombian communists in the crowd was 'proof' that the entire affair had been 'communist-inspired'. Almost as if stage-managed by Washington's policy makers, the uprising could, thus interpreted, be used to prove that a pan-American defensive alliance against the communist threat was more necessary than ever.

The US delegation found eager supporters among those regimes, like the Dominican and Paraguayan, which on the agenda item 'defence and preservation of democracy' had nothing to offer but cant. Their support ensured the adoption a resolution (proposed by Brazil, Chile, Peru and the United States) declaring that 'the political activity of international communism or any totalitarian doctrine is incompatible with the concept of American freedom'.[11] The pan-American anti-fascist front had been decisively transformed into an anti-communist front.

Not all Latin American governments committed themselves to anti-communist solidarity out of political conviction, however. As at the Rio conference the previous year, they made it clear that they expected economic aid from the United States in return for their political support. They had good reason to attempt to shift the focus of the conference away from political stability towards economic development. They saw how the the Americans were pumping huge amounts of money into Europe as part of the European Recovery Programme (Marshall Plan), and they felt that their support of the allies during the war entitled them to a similar level of aid to deal with problems of dislocation and readjustment.

The hope for a massive injection of dollars had already faded at Rio, when the Americans had tried to gain understanding for their decision to allocate the lion's share of US foreign aid to the reconstruction of the European economies, and that therefore Latin America would have to wait. And that is what happened. For example, while West Germany alone received $613 million in a single year (1948/9), Latin America as a whole received only $16 million in economic aid and $235 million in military aid in the first four post-war years. The discrepancy was even more glaring over a longer time frame: between 1945 and 1960 Latin America received $625 million in US aid, while the rest of the world received $31,000 million. During the same period the Philippine government could collect more in US grants than its 20 Latin American counterparts put together. Of the total US foreign aid disbursed between 1945 and 1956 — some $57 billion — Latin America received a consistently low share: 1.6% of military aid and 2.7% of economic aid.

Despite overwhelming evidence to the contrary, the Latin Americans still hoped that George C. Marshall, the US secretary of state, would unveil a Marshall plan for the region at Bogotá. But he arrived empty-handed. All he had to offer was ideological fare: 'encouragement for private enterprise', 'fair treatment of foreign capital' and, in a nostalgic reference to US history, a positive assessment of the role of foreign capital in economic development.[12] Addressing the conference's economic committee, Averell Harriman, the influential secretary of commerce, hammered home, somewhat less diplomatically, the conviction of US politicians and economists that private investment provided the key to a solution of Latin America's economic problems:

The most decisive factor in our success has been freedom of business. The United States and its people are accustomed to this system ... and they desire for the same conditions in Latin American countries that desire to be served by our experience. We are called to collaborate with Latin American economies, but I have the feeling that although we are invited, you tie our hands at the same time. We make no progress this way.[13]

Not surprisingly, the Latins gave the economic lectures a decidedly cold reception. To recover the situation, Marshall asked the conference secretary to read to the conference an address from President Truman to the US Congress in which he requested authorization for the Export-Import Bank to increase its loans to Latin America from $166 million to $500 million. But this gesture was received in total silence, all the more so because, embarrassingly, it seemed to suggest that the administration thought that the friendship and political solidarity of Latin America could be bought.

Despite the general acrimony the Latin Americans — most of whom once again feared the colossus of the north now that it was returning to its old ways, poignantly at this time by harassing the Perón regime in Argentina — agreed to set up the OAS/OEA as the successor to the pre-war International Union of American Republics. Signed on 30 April and in force from 13 December 1951, the charter of the OAS included in its first eight chapters virtually every basic principle of inter-American relations evolved and accepted since the early nineteenth century, such as:

- states are juridically equal;
- every state has the duty to respect the rights enjoyed by every other state in accordance with international law;
- the political existence of a state is independent of recognition by other states;
- the jurisdiction of states within the limits of their national territory is exercised equally over all the inhabitants, whether nationals or aliens;
- the territory of a state is inviolable.

Article 15 in particular could be used by the Latin Americans to keep their intervention-happy northern neighbour in place. It declared that 'No state or group of states has the right to intervene, directly or indirectly, for any reason whatever, in the internal or external affairs of any other state'.[14]

The institutions created to guard these principles and to implement OAS policies were the following:

- the inter-American conference, the organization's supreme organ, in which each member country had one vote; it would meet every five years, or in emergency session with the approval of two-thirds of members;
- the meeting of consultation of foreign ministers, which had only an advisory function; it would meet at the request of one member, by majority decision of the council or in case of an armed attack on a state or within the security zone;
- the permanent council, the organization's standing committee, based in Washington and comprising representatives (with the rank of ambassador) of each member state; it would deal with all matters referred to it by the conference or

the foreign ministers and would be the provisional consultative body in case of an external attack; and

- the general secretariat, the successor to the Pan-American Union, based in Washington and led by a secretary-general elected by the council for a ten-year term; it would promote economic, social, juridical and cultural relations, as well as provide technical and information services.

The already existing Inter-American Defense Board (IADB), the Inter-American Juridical Committee, the Inter-American Cultural Council and the Inter-American Economic and Social Council (IA–ECOSOC/CIES) were incorporated into the new OAS structure.

It is interesting to note that the Economic and Social Council, originally set up at Chapultepec, would for years be overshadowed by a regional organization of the United Nations system, namely the Economic Commission for Latin America (CEPAL/ECLA). At Chapultepec and Rio the Latin Americans had realized that inter-American co-operation aimed primarily at strategic and political objectives would not serve their countries' economic interests. So they insisted, against the opposition of the US government (which warned of unnecessary duplication of work), on the formation of CEPAL in February 1948 as one of the UN's regional commissions. Its headquarters was established in Santiago de Chile, as far away from Washington as possible, almost as if the Latin Americans wanted to document their desire for independence and the divergence of views on economic issues. The UN commission soon outshone IA–ECOSOC, not least because it employed competent and committed experts rather than untrained career diplomats, but also because it was endowed with a far larger budget. CEPAL produced a number of outstanding reports and special studies, and took the lead in promoting two of the most important initiatives in recent Latin American history, namely the plans for economic integration in Central America and for the larger Latin American Free Trade Association (ALALC/LAFTA).

By the early 1960s the permanent council had become the major political institution of the OAS. This had seemed unlikely at the beginning. With their traditional hostility to supranationalism and their renewed fear of US dominance, the Latin Americans had initially rejected a council with broader powers than those invested in its predecessor, the governing board of the Pan-American Union, which had been allowed to do little more than keep its own offices in order. Under US pressure they eventually accepted a compromise under which the council was empowered to deal with any matter referred to it by other OAS organs. Despite its tightly circumscribed authority the council did carry some weight in inter-American politics, because both the Rio Pact and the OAS charter granted it the power to act as a provisional consultative organ in times of crisis until a meeting of foreign ministers could be called. Such meetings were expensive, inconvenient and time-consuming, however, and so it often happened that once the council had become involved in disputes and conflicts it remained involved.

The permanent council developed into a useful forum for conciliation because it could meet in permanent session and because it could carry out its work away from the public eye, something rarely possible for the foreign ministers. The council's ability to smooth a course for mediation certainly contributed to the early resolution of many regional conflicts without loss of face for the adversaries and, most importantly, before they had moved to armed confrontation. A similar function was fulfilled by the Inter-American Peace Committee, in practice the second most important institution of the OAS after the council. Set up at the 1940 Havana conference but not actually in operation until 1948, it acted as a watchdog and assisted the council in identifying disputes at an early stage.

The OAS undoubtedly had some merit, but because of its relative weakness compared to corresponding UN institutions and above all its undeniable political servitude to Washington it incurred the ridicule and criticism of many. In what it called 'the Second Declaration of Havana', the Cuban government, recently suspended from the activities of the OAS for its communist leanings, on 4 February 1962 pilloried the regional organization as the 'US colonial department' and the 'repressive apparatus against the liberation of the Latin American people'.[15] Others called it the organization of the 'majority of one', or recasting its Spanish acronym OEA, 'another American deception' (*otro engaño americano*). A Latin American delegate to an inter-American conference reportedly confided to a journalist that 'If the United States wanted to badly enough, it could have a resolution passed declaring that two and two are five'.[16] And while the politicians showered the OAS with praise, every major study of the organization referred to its structural crisis and political feebleness.

The crisis of the OAS had its roots primarily in the tendency of US Latin American policy to exclude economic problems as much as possible from the purview of the organization. But it was precisely these that most concerned the Latin Americans. Not surprisingly, after neither the Economic Agreement adopted in Bogotá, nor the Tenth Pan-American Conference in Caracas in March 1954, nor the OAS economic conference in Buenos Aires in November 1957 brought any concrete results, they moved increasingly from inter-American co-operation to intra-Latin American co-operation.

To recover lost prestige and stature, the OAS embarked on a reorganization. The Protocol of Buenos Aires, effective from 1970, established the annual general assembly as the highest body of the organization in place of the cumbersome inter-American conference, which according to the statutes should have met every five years but in fact had not done so since 1954 because of political disagreements. In addition, several tasks previously carried out by the council were transferred to the general assembly. The Latin Americans had tried to shift the balance of power within the organization in this direction, to extricate it from Washington's clutches, ever since the 1950s and especially after the US intervention in the Dominican Republic in April 1965.

The Dominican crisis, the suspension of Cuba and the intervention in Guatemala provided salient examples of the way in which the Americans manipulated the OAS to gain moral cover for their unilateral imperialist actions, to multilateralize them and justify them in international law. In these and other cases they provided an object lesson on how to use an international organization as an instrument of national political and economic policy. So the denunciation of the

OAS as a vehicle for US hegemony and as the US colonial department rang true. But although the critics' anger was understandable enough, this kind of polemic overshot the mark. The other members of the alliance did not unquestioningly support the US line. On a number of occasions the Americans had to work hard to obtain the required majorities for their interventionist policies and in some cases they had to bring out the chequebook to secure much-needed votes. The voting pattern of Latin American countries within the OAS illustrates the extent to which their foreign policies gradually emancipated themselves from Washington. Already between 1948 and 1974 the United States lost no less than 25% of the 297 roll-call votes: only 2% of votes on cold-war-type resolutions, but 29% on other political, juridical and security questions, and 45% on economic and social questions. Ironically, the OAS would make a decisive move towards greater autonomy and independence over its attitude to Cuba, a matter on which it had initially served most willingly as Washington's colonial department.

Notes

1. Hearings of the House of Representatives committee on ways and means, 21 February 1943, quoted in US Congress 1943 p. 4.

2. Diary, 16 May 1945, quoted in Alperovitz 1967 p. 11.

3. Kennan, George F. ('X') 1947 p. 582.

4. Hull 1949 p. 1419.

5. Editorial in *The Herald Tribune*, 2 May 1945, quoted in Horowitz 1965 p. 39.

6. Report in *El Tiempo*, 9 March 1945, quoted in Behrendt 1948 p. 54.

7. Report to the Congress for Industrial Development, 9 April 1947, quoted in Behrendt, op. cit., p. 54 (translation by Behrendt.)

8. Address to the Inter-American Conference on Problems of War and Peace, 4 March 1945, quoted in Green 1971 p. 174.

9. Article 3, Inter-American Treaty of Reciprocal Assistance, signed 2 September 1947, quoted in Gantenbein (ed.) 1950 p. 823f.

10. Ibid. (article 6), p. 825.

11. Declaration and Resolution 23 [regarding preservation and defence of democracy in America], Ninth Pan-American Conference, adopted 2 May 1948, quoted in Gantenbein (ed.), op. cit., p. 838.

12. Address to the Ninth Pan-American Conference, 1 April 1948, quoted in Gantenbein (ed.), op. cit., p. 279.

13. Report in *El Tiempo*, 18 April 1948, quoted in Inman 1965 p. 247.

14. Charter of the Organization of American States, signed 30 April 1948, quoted in Gantenbein (ed.), op. cit., pp. 855–71.

15. The Second Declaration of Havana, 4 February 1962, quoted in Aguilar 1968 p. 122f.

16. Report in *New York Times*, 8 March 1954, quoted in Meek 1975 p. 311.

6. The era of 'anti-communist' interventions

Guatemala 1954

The first country to experience at first hand the implications of Washington's determination to see everything that happened south of the Rio Grande through an east-west prism was Guatemala. This Central American country had been ruled since 1930 by a *caudillo* of the old school, perhaps the last of his type, General Jorge Ubico y Castañeda. Even during Roosevelt's 'good neighbour' years the Americans did not object to the ways in which this brutal tyrant tormented his people — by imposing forced labour for instance. He served their purpose because he guaranteed law and order and held back on the kind of industrialization programmes that might damage the interests of foreign capital. Ubico ruled for 14 years. He was finally ousted in a bloody revolution in October 1944 by a coalition of students, middle-class professionals, workers, peasants and progressive elements in the armed forces. A three-member junta took power and called elections for December, which were won by Juan José Arévalo, a reformist university professor, who received 86% of the votes cast.

The government of Arévalo, who described himself as a nationalist and a democratic socialist, rang in a nine-year era of reform which brought the country a range of economic, social and political benefits. The new democratically elected administration concentrated its efforts above all on transforming the two-crop economy of coffee and bananas so as to reduce the country's vulnerability to the wild fluctuations in the prices of these commodities. It took steps, in short, to diversify agriculture and accelerate previously neglected industrial development. The reform programme brought immediate improvements in the economic situation in general and in living conditions in particular. The government also allowed the formation of new political parties, legalized trade unions and peasant organizations and lifted censorship, thus stimulating a revival of political activity. In a climate of social and political renewal and innovation, a constitutional transfer of power took place in March 1951 after Jácobo Arbenz Guzmán, a member of the 1944 junta, had won the election four months earlier.

Being a rich landowner and an army officer, Arbenz was widely expected to steer a more conservative course than his predecessor. But he continued the reform programme, and his first move was to raise the daily minimum wage to $1.08. Foreign business interests accepted this attempt to help the poor farm-workers and the few industrial workers just as they had grudgingly put up with all the reforms introduced in the previous six years. But in the eyes of the Americans in Guatemala and the politicians in Washington the Arbenz government passed a point of no return on 17 June 1952 when it launched an ambitious land-reform programme with the promulgation of the famous Decree 900, which called for the expropriation and redistribution of uncultivated or fallow land. In March 1953 the government expropriated 234,000 of the 295,000 acres of such lands owned by the United Fruit Company in the Tiquiaste district on the Pacific coast. This precipitated the first serious friction in relations between Guatemala and the United States.

Now United Fruit, the huge banana conglomerate with interests in many countries, had over the years secured economic and political control over Guatemala. Through bribing political leaders, pressuring governments and intimidating opponents and detractors, it had obtained extremely favourable concessions and could act almost as a state within a state. It could do so all the more effectively for two reasons. For one, it owned and operated much of the country's infrastructure, including, for instance, the whole railway system and Puerto Barrios, the main port on the Atlantic coast. And for another, its senior management was extraordinarily closely intertwined with the government bureaucracy in Washington. Thus the secretary of state, John Foster Dulles, was a shareholder in United Fruit and a long-time legal adviser of the company; the director of the CIA, his brother, Allan Dulles, had been a president; and the assistant secretary of state for inter-American affairs, John Moors Cabot, was a major shareholder.

Not surprisingly, then, under these circumstances Washington showed impressive concern for the fate of United Fruit. It responded to the modest attempt by the Guatemalan government to exercise its sovereign right to constrain a foreign economic giant and help its peasants and farmworkers as if the gravest sin known to western civilization had been committed. No matter how cautious the land reform, when it affected American property big business and its allies in the state department saw red — also in the political sense. The Eisenhower administration rejected the proposed level of compensation and demanded that it be 'prompt, adequate and effective'.[1] And United Fruit let it be known that the issue was no longer the opposition between the people of Guatemala and itself, but the threat which communism posed for the right of property, life and security in the western hemisphere.

Much has been written about the role of the communists in the Arbenz government, and opinions differ about the extent of their influence. However, it would be grotesque to claim — although many did at the time and have subsequently — that the country was being run by the communists and not by the deeply anti-communist army, whose representatives retained many of the levers of power throughout the Arévalo–Arbenz era. Whatever the truth, the spectre of communism, much inflated by pressure groups and a section of the American press, haunted the western hemisphere after the launch of the Guatemalan land reform.

Ideologically the US government had long been prepared for the strangling of the reforms in Guatemala. The anti-communist declarations adopted at the Rio conference in 1947 and at the OAS founding conference in Bogotá in 1948 had already provided a suitable means for intervening against economic reforms in the region under the pretence that they were acts of communist subversion. At the fourth consultative meeting of OAS foreign ministers in Washington in March–April 1951 — at the height of the Korean War — this line was pushed even further. Instead of discussing economic development, as the Latin Americans wanted, President Truman called for economic mobilization against 'communist imperialist attacks' and the 'aggressive expansion of Soviet power':

> In these uneasy times [he went on more specifically] production for defence depends on our economic strength. We need to increase production of strategic raw materials ... We must establish the principle of the equitable sharing of this responsibility.[2]

To counter the red peril, then, the southern neighbours had to step up production of strategic minerals, so that the United States would be fully prepared in case of a full-blown world war. The assembled Latin American foreign ministers duly adopted a resolution to this effect, accepting four specific measures which entrapped them even more inextricably in the web of US interests. They agreed to assign responsibility for military planning of common defence to the Inter-American Defense Board (IADB), to actively support the work of the board, to strengthen their armed forces, and to enact the necessary legislation to prevent the subversive activities of international communism.

What happened in Rio, Bogotá and Washington was more or less repeated at the Tenth Pan-American Conference in Caracas in March 1954. The Latin Americans hoped for a programme of international economic co-operation, but yet again the Americans put their own self-interest above that of the hemisphere and turned the meeting into another battleground against the alleged penetration of international communism.

Although the agenda was kept general, all those gathering in the Venezuelan capital knew that the main purpose of the meeting was to try, and then convict, the reforming Arbenz government. The 'democrats' who would sit in judgement over the 'communists' included such unsavoury characters as the host, Marcos Pérez Jiménez, one of the most repugnant dictators in Latin American history, Fulgencio Batista of Cuba, Anastasio Somoza of Nicaragua, Héctor Trujillo (brother of the even more notorious Rafael) of the Dominican Republic, Oscar Osorio of El Salvador, Manuel Odría of Peru and Gustavo Rojas Pinilla of Colombia. Leaders and representatives of all American republics came, with the exception of the Costa Ricans, who had no stomach for debating inter-American problems as guests of a notorious murderer.

Dulles warned darkly that 'There is not a single country in this hemisphere which has not been penetrated by the apparatus of international communism, acting under orders from Moscow'.[3] He received warm applause from the dictators present when he argued eloquently in favour of the draft resolution which declared communism a threat to the Americas. But the Guatemalan foreign minister, Guillermo Toriello, received twice the ovation that Dulles did when he rejected both any resolution which, 'on the pretext of communism, may contravene the fundamental principle of democracy ... or infringe the principle of non-intervention' and the 'internationalization of McCarthyism'.[4]

But although the delegates offered applause, most offered precious little in terms of solidarity with the hard-pressed Guatemalans. By 17 votes to 1 (Guatemala), with two abstentions (Argentina and Mexico), the conference adopted Dulles' resolution, which stated that:

> the domination or control of the political institutions of any American state by the international communist movement, extending to this hemisphere the political system of an extra-continental power, would constitute a threat to sovereignty and political independence ... endangering the peace of America.[5]

Immediately after bulldozing through his resolution, which in effect gave the administration a free hand to carry out its unilateral actions against the Guatemalans under the guise of joint OAS measures, Dulles flew back to Washington and left his colleagues to discuss for another two weeks the main topic for which they had come to Caracas, economic development.

The preparations for Arbenz's overthrow had in fact been in hand for some time. The plans centred around Colonel Carlos Castillo Armas, an exile who had staged an abortive coup five days before the 1950 elections and then escaped to the United States shortly afterwards. Making no attempt to hide his intentions, he was training, with CIA experts at his side, an invasion force composed of other exiles and mercenaries. The final decision to invade was taken some time in mid-May at a White House meeting attended by President Dwight D. Eisenhower, the Dulles brothers, representatives of the joint chiefs of staff and Thruston Morton, the assistant secretary of state for congressional relations (who had previously briefed a few key senators about the true nature of the CIA-sponsored operation). Morton later recalled that Eisenhower had asked the men around the table whether they were sure that the invasion plan would succeed. Told that it would, he reportedly said: I'm prepared to take any steps that are necessary to see that it succeeds. For if it succeeds, it is the people of Guatemala throwing off the yoke of communism. If it fails, the flag of the United States has failed'.[6] The plot against the democratically elected government of Arbenz had been well prepared and it did not fail.

Towards the end of May 1954 the Americans found the excuse they needed to justify moving against Arbenz. For years the Guatemalan government had been vainly seeking to buy arms, first in the United States and then in other western countries. Finally it opened negotiations with the Czechoslovak government in January 1954. When the Swedish ship *Alfhem* arrived at Puerto Barrios on 15 May carrying $10 million worth of Czech arms, the Americans claimed to have proof of their widely broadcast suspicion that the communists now also exercised military control over the country. At a press conference on 25 May, Dulles even suggested that Guatemala might intend to use the arms 'to develop a communist strongpoint dominating the Panama Canal'.[7] Perhaps he thought it a super-power's prerogative to insult the intelligence of his audience in this way, by claiming that a country of 3 million people, more than 1,000 miles and four countries away, and at this time without either a navy or an airforce, could pose a threat to the canal.

Events moved swiftly. In response to the arms purchase the United States airlifted arms and equipment to Nicaragua and Honduras, countries with which the administration had signed treaties (on the basis of the Mutual Security Act of 1951) on 23 April and 20 May respectively. On 27 May three B-36 bombers paid a 'courtesy visit' on Managua. On 8 June the Guatemalan government declared itself in a state of siege. On 18 June, Castillo Armas launched his invasion from his base in Honduras with 2,000 men and six US planes and US pilots to fly them. In the next few days the Americans followed a delicate strategy. The aim was to give Armas sufficient time to overthrow Arbenz while preventing the latter from obtaining help from the United Nations or the OAS. To this end it was necessary for the OAS to take just enough action to justify the exclusion of the United Nations, but not so much as to endanger the success of the coup. And so it happened. Deserted by the military on 27 June, Arbenz resigned his office to prevent further bloodshed. As a result of ensuing negotiations with the new anti-communist junta, facilitated by the US ambassador, John E. Peurifoy (who had been sent to Guatemala specifically to 'get rid of the reds'), Castillo Armas became president on 1 September.

The new president did as requested. Among his first acts in office he granted potentially lucrative concessions to international oil cartels, reversed the land reform and labour programmes, and disenfranchised the illiterate masses. All that remained for the Americans was to create the fiction that the people of Guatemala had rid themselves of a gang of communists who had usurped the levers of power and acted on the orders of Moscow. But no one really believed this version, least of all the American politicians themselves. John C. Dreier, for instance, for many years the US representative on the OAS council, described the change of power in Guatemala bluntly as a 'successful counterrevolution, led by Colonel Castillo Armas with US backing'.[8]

Cuba under quarantine

On New Year's Day 1959 Fulgencio Batista, the Cuban tyrant who during his 25-year rule had shown greater concern for the creases in his trousers than for the hunger and poverty of his people, fled the island for the Dominican Republic. A few days later Fidel Castro Ruz, his brother Raúl, Ernesto 'Ché' Guevara, Camilo Cienfuegos and the other 'bearded ones' (*barbudos*) entered Havana in triumph. The first stage of the Cuban revolution, launched on 26 July 1953 with the uprising against Batista in Santiago de Cuba led by Castro and his associates, had been completed.

The second stage centred on the internal Cuban debate over the aims of the revolution and on the conflict with the northern neighbour. The Americans had unreservedly supported Batista for nearly 25 years, until even President Eisenhower — a man not known for his political vision — ruled out continuing support for a 'self-enriching and corrupt dictator'.[9] In March 1958 the state department suspended a shipment of arms to Cuba, and the following month it effectively declared an arms embargo. The Americans undermined the dictator in this way no doubt in the expectation that he could be replaced by a new, more reform-minded and less autocratic leader, but still a *caudillo* in the Latin American mould whom they could control. Very soon after Batista's departure and Castro's arrival they had to recognize that the Cuban revolution was not one of the usual coups but a determined attempt to transform Cuban society. They began to condemn the radicalization of the revolution — as if they had approved of it in the first place — and spoke shamelessly about the 'betrayal' of the revolution (the word that would also be used 20 years later in the case of the Sandinista revolution in Nicaragua). A showdown became inevitable when the Castro government began to implement its reform programme.

The spark for the 'economic war' which the powerful United States unleashed against its small underdeveloped neighbour was the first agrarian reform law proclaimed on 17 May 1959. Although still a cautious measure in that it declared the expropriation of large estates of over 400 hectares, the US government reacted — echoes of Guatemala — as if the law constituted an onslaught on the fundamental values of western civilization. Not surprisingly, perhaps, since most of the properties seized were owned by US citizens. On 11 June the Eisenhower administration protested against what it considered inadequate compensation — yet again echoes of Guatemala. But after decades of exploitation of the island's resources by American sugar barons and so soon after the conclusion of an economically damaging liberation war the Cuban government was in no position to meet US demands.

The nationalization of the economy was swiftly achieved. On 29 June 1960 the government took over the foreign-owned oil refineries after the Esso, Shell and Texaco corporations had refused to refine Soviet crude oil. On 6 August it seized another 26 US-owned companies, on 17 September it nationalized the banks, and on 24 October it expropriated and nationalized the remaining 166 US-owned companies on the island.

The Americans knew very well how to punish their recalcitrant neighbour for the radicalization of its revolution. Cuba was economically highly dependent on the United States, and therefore vulnerable, with, for instance, 62% of the country's exports sold to the United States. The key was of course sugar. Exports of this commodity accounted for a quarter of the island's gross domestic product in 1958, and for over four-fifths of Cuban exports to the United States between 1949 and 1958. In retaliation for the alleged economic aggression perpetrated by the revolutionaries, the Eisenhower administration stepped up the pressure in January 1960 by asking for congressional approval to reduce the Cuban sugar quota. Armed with that authority, the president on 6 July announced a cut in the permitted sugar imports by 700,000 tons, and on 16 December he fixed the quota at zero for the first quarter of 1961, thus establishing the policy of cutting the

Cuban quota entirely.

Even before the completion of the nationalization programme, the Americans also retaliated with an economic, political and diplomatic blockade of Cuba, a measure strongly advocated by Richard Nixon, the vice-president and Republican presidential candidate. On 19 October 1960 the administration prohibited the export to Cuba of all American goods with the exception of non-subsidized foodstuffs, medicines and medical supplies for humanitarian uses. On 3 January 1961 it broke off diplomatic relations in protest against 'a long series of harassments, baseless accusations and vilifications'.[10]

The Americans simply tried to starve out the Cuban revolutionaries. The general idea was to put Cuba under quarantine, as it were, to isolate the revolutionary anti-capitalist and anti-American contagion at the centre of the United States' Caribbean sphere of influence and thus prevent it from infecting other Latin American countries. That is why the blockade introduced in stages over the next two years covered potentially catastrophic sanctions like the ban on sugar imports as well as ridiculous 'punishments' like the ban on the importation of Cuban ideas. (Even in May 1981 the Reagan administration, invoking the Trading With the Enemy Act of 1917, confiscated 30,000 Cuban newspapers and periodicals and informed subscribers that if they wanted to continue to receive these vehicles for Cuban propaganda they would have to register with the treasury. A huge outcry and threats of legal action followed, and the ban on Cuban publications was lifted in January 1982.)

Economic and political decisions in Cuba, US reprisals and more radical actions by Havana followed in quick succession, escalating to a total economic war between the two countries. On the basis of this sequence some analysts developed a kind of revenge theory, arguing that it was not class antagonism or the social contradictions prevailing in pre-revolutionary Cuba which caused and accelerated the shift from a nationalist to a socialist revolution but mere irrational anti-Americanism. Some observers even concluded from this exchange of blows, with all its fateful economic consequences for the island, that to achieve their goals the revolutionaries needed a bogey, and they would have had to invent the United States if it had not already existed. The complement to this argument was that if the United States had been less extreme and more flexible in its attitude to Castro's Cuba it might have spared itself the socialist experiment on its doorstep. But these interpretations fail to acknowledge the Cuban revolution as an autonomous development and ignore its roots in the 1940 constitution, whose democratic and reformist elements were invoked by Castro when he came to power, or the Manifesto from the Sierra Maestra of 12 July 1957, in which the revolutionaries had declared their intention to carry out extensive expropriations and a comprehensive redistribution of land.

Be that as it may, President John F. Kennedy's Proclamation 3447 issued on 3 February 1962 formalized a virtually comprehensive embargo on exports to and imports from the island. The embargo was further perfected in subsequent months. On 23 March it was extended to include all goods containing raw materials from Cuba, such as metal products containing Cuban nickel. (In November 1983, during the new cold war with the Soviet Union, the Reagan administration renewed this chicanery by banning the import of goods from the Soviet Union which contained Cuban nickel.) From 4 October onwards all ships which had carried cargo to and from Cuba were banned from carrying American goods and foreign-based subsidiaries of American corporations were not allowed to trade with Cuba. To make absolutely sure that Cuba could not trade normally, an article was inserted in the 1961 Foreign Assistance Act which provided for the suspension of aid to any country which refused to ban its ships from plying Cuba.

The Americans did not stop at economic war. They harassed the Cuban socialists with all the means at their disposal short of direct military intervention. Covert plans for an invasion of the island were being drawn up by the CIA, and with the approval of the executive it began to train Cuban exiles and mercenaries for such an operation. At the May Day rally in 1960 Castro predicted that the Americans would attempt an invasion, that it would be sponsored by the CIA and that it would be launched from US military bases in Guatemala. (At this mass meeting he first uttered the rallying cry of '*¡Cuba sí, Yanquí no!*', which would echo around the world for years to come.) Considering the invasion to be imminent, he called a mobilization on 31 December 1960. Much ridiculed by his opponents, his fears proved correct. President Kennedy, who had inherited what was euphemistically known as the 'Cuban project' from his predecessor, gave his blessing to the operation in a meeting with his closest security advisers on 3 April 1961. (Publicly he maintained even nine days after this meeting that 'the government of the United States will not permit the organization of an invasion of Cuba from US territory'.)[11]

On 15 April, at 6 o'clock in the morning, American B-26 bombers — piloted, it emerged later, by Cuban exiles — attacked the cities of San Antonio de los Baños, Havana and Santiago de Cuba. The Cubans rightly interpreted this as the prelude to invasion. But the planning had gone seriously awry and the invasion force of 1,500 Cuban exiles and others, which was already on its way, would not get the sea and air support it was relying on. The landing on 17 April at the Bahía de Cochinos (Bay of Pigs), 90 miles south of Havana, ended in disaster. The invasion did not get much further than the Playa Girón and the marshes of the Zapata peninsula, and it was crushed by the Cuban army and militia within 72 hours. President Kennedy had little choice but to take responsibility for the fiasco. He did so on 20 April, but not without warning defiantly that the inter-American doctrine of non-intervention should never 'conceal or excuse a policy of non-action'.[12]

Soon afterwards negotiations began for the release from Cuban prisons of the men who thought that they could smash the Cuban revolution with the help of the masses who would enthusiastically flock to their cause. The efforts to free the victims of the CIA and Pentagon bungling, known as Project X, bore fruit in November 1962. Twenty months after their capture 1,113 prisoners were returned to Miami, where they could continue to dream of the victorious counter-revolution. In compensation for the damage caused by the invaders Cuba received 500 tractors, medicines, food and surgical instruments.

Despite this, above all moral, defeat, Washington's political and military sabre rattling against Cuba continued unabated. On 7 September 1962 President Kennedy asked Congress for the authority to call up 150,000 reservists, a measure justified officially by the situation in Berlin but really taken with reference to Cuba. On 3 October, Congress adopted a joint resolution which in effect gave him the authority to order an intervention in Cuba should he consider that country a threat to the national interest of the United States, specifically if Cuba became an 'offensive military base ... for the Soviet Union'.[13] The notion that the presence of an offensive and threatening foreign military power in Cuba would constitute a direct threat to the security of the United States and the western hemisphere as a whole became known as the Kennedy Doctrine, a modern, anti-communist update of the Monroe Doctrine.

Three weeks later Washington considered that threat to have materialized. US reconnaissance aircraft — which until today monitor everything going on in Cuba — had alarmed the Pentagon with evidence that the Soviet Union was building, rapidly and secretly, missile bases on the island equipped with nuclear-capable missiles with a range of 1,100 miles and with launching pads for missiles of double that range. The Soviets had signed a defence treaty with Cuba in September and had repeatedly warned the Americans against attacks on Cuba, using the plausible enough argument that they need not install *offensive* missiles on Cuba since the United States could already be targeted from bases in the Soviet Union. The general view among disinterested military analysts was that Cuban-based Soviet missiles did not alter the global nuclear balance of power, nor, apart from the destabilizing effect of shorter warning times, did they create a greater danger to the United States than had existed previously. It should also be borne in mind that the Kennedy administration never actually accused the Soviet Union of harbouring direct or concrete plans to use its Cuban bases to launch a nuclear attack on the United States or Latin American countries.

Even so, President Kennedy knew he had the support of public opinion in the 'free world' when he reacted to the Soviet moves with measures which brought the superpowers to the brink of nuclear war during what became known as the Cuban missile crisis of October 1962. For regardless of the motivations, the deployment of Soviet missiles not just anywhere in the back yard but actually at the back door must have elicited a psychological reaction from the American people and their allies similar to that which the earlier deployment of US medium-range missiles in Turkey had had (or the deployment of cruise and Pershing missiles in the 1980s would have) on the Soviet people.

On 22 October, President Kennedy announced that 'to halt this offensive buildup' he had imposed 'a strict quarantine on all offensive military equipment under shipment to Cuba'; he also demanded the immediate withdrawal of existing Soviet facilities.[14] After four days on the nuclear abyss the Soviet Union, on 26 October, proposed the removal of the missiles in exchange for a US guarantee against an invasion of Cuba by its own forces or exiles. Although Washington did not clearly signal its acceptance, the Soviet Union began dismantling the bases two days later. On 20 November, Kennedy confirmed the removal of the bases, while at the same time reiterating his administration's commitment to an anti-Cuban policy.

The Americans certainly continued their attempts to destabilize Cuba, by means of a shabby covert war. Once the predominantly middle-class exiles in Florida and the politicians in Washington realized they could not challenge the Castro government directly because of its widespread support among the people, it was decided to remove one of the source's of the people's loyalty to the revolution, Fidel Castro himself. Had the critics of Washington's Cuba policy been imaginative enough to suspect CIA involvement in most of the attacks on Cuba, and had they made their suspicions public, they would surely have been decried as victims of communist conspiracy theories. But a Senate special committee on the intelligence services, chaired by Senator Frank Church, reported in November 1975 that the CIA had conceived at least eight separate plots to assassinate Castro between 1960 and 1965. Among the schemes considered by the agency's dirty-tricks department were: spraying the walls of Castro's office with a drug similar to LSD; impregnating his cigars with a chemical that would cause temporary mental dislocation, in the hope that he would smoke one before one of his major speeches and then make a fool of himself; poisoning his cigars and his food; and even hiring Mafia bosses and other underworld figures to make attempts on his life.

A number of epidemics afflicted Cuba in 1979 and 1980, and the Americans were soon suspected of having 'introduced' them to the island. There were certainly many indications that a covert chemical and bacteriological war was being waged. Early in 1980 — the 'year of troubles' or the 'year of plagues' — swine fever broke out in the eastern province of Guantánamo, resulting in the loss of hundreds of thousands of animals; tobacco mould destroyed 27% of all tobacco plants, with the result that the processing plants, which annually generated around $100 million in export revenues, had to close for six months; and part of the sugar crop was lost to sugar-cane rust. In 1981 an epidemic of haemorrhagic dengue fever killed 113 people and affected 273,000 others. Until then the Cubans had shown remarkable restraint regarding the suspicion that these diseases might be traced to the laboratories of the US intelligence services. But on 26 July 1981 Castro openly accused the United States of waging 'biological warfare' against Cuba and demanded to know whether 'the CIA has been authorized ... to use epidemics against our vegetation, animals and population'.[15] To exhaust the full range of destabilization measures, the US government in January 1982 decided to finance a radio station, Radio Martí, to broadcast Spanish-language propaganda to Cuba.

Of course the Americans did not stop at unilateral actions against Cuba. From the beginning they tried to rope in the southern neighbours for their policy to eradicate socialism, that un-American foreign body, from the hemisphere. During the wave of nationalizations, in August 1960, they pushed through without too much resistance a resolution at the seventh consultative meeting of OAS foreign ministers in San José, Costa Rica, which grandly rejected:

> the attempt of the Sino-Soviet powers to make use of the political, economic and social situation of any American state, inasmuch as that attempt is capable of destroying hemispheric unity and jeopardizing the peace and security of the hemisphere.[16]

By the time of the next foreign ministers' meeting, in Punta del Este, Uruguay, in January 1962, attitudes had changed somewhat, however. No matter how strongly the US representatives reviled Castro as an agent of Moscow or decried Cuba as a bridgehead of international communism, by no means all Latin Americans responded with similar anti-communist slogans or eagerly joined the US-led anti-Cuban bloc. The administration actually had to resort to considerable arm twisting to get the 14 votes (a two-thirds majority) needed for proposed sanctions against Cuba. Although US diplomats brought enormous pressure to bear on wavering Latin American governments, at one point only 12 other OAS members supported the US proposals, while six (Argentina, Brazil, Bolivia, Chile, Ecuador and Mexico, which became known in the press as the 'soft six') preferred to defer a decision. Only Haiti's vote was still uncertain. Some days before the opening of the conference the Haitian president, François Duvalier, had complained of the lack of US aid his country had received in recent years. Cleverly seizing the opportunity offered by the balance of forces, Haiti's foreign minister, René Chalmers, suddenly waxed lyrical about the principle of non-intervention and his country's long-standing neutrality in Caribbean affairs. The soft six seemed about to become the soft seven. A story did the rounds at the conference that the Americans were informally advised what the crucial fourteenth vote would cost them: a 1,500-bed hospital, a new jet airport, a road from there to the capital and $15 million in cash. True or not, the Haitian delegation subsequently abandoned its moral and legal scruples over imposing sanctions against Cuba and voted with the United States, and the following month Pan American Airways announced that it would construct a new airport at Port-au-Prince.

The final resolution adopted by the conference on 31 January 1962 declared that 'the principles of communism are incompatible with the principles of the inter-American system' and that therefore any country which espoused Marxist-Leninist ideology placed itself outside that system.[17] Cuba was thus suspended from the OAS. Cuba voted against the resolution, and the soft six abstained. In view of the fact that the latter included the three most important Latin American countries (Argentina, Brazil and Mexico), the numerical two-thirds majority which the United States marshalled against Cuba could hardly be considered an overwhelming victory.

At the ninth consultative meeting of OAS foreign ministers in Washington in July 1964 the Americans called for specific sanctions against Cuba. Most governments agreed to 'suspend all their trade, direct or indirect, with Cuba' and to 'suspend all the sea transport between their countries and Cuba', in both cases with the exception of 'foodstuffs, medicines and medical equipment that might be sent to Cuba for humanitarian reasons'.[18] Once again Washington had considerable problems in forming a decent anti-Cuban majority within the OAS. The most prominent of the four countries which refused to carry out the terms of the resolution was Mexico, which continued to maintain political and economic links with Cuba throughout the US and OAS blockades.

For years there existed a state of permanent cold war between Cuba and its neighbours. The eventual improvement in relations did not take place at OAS level but at bilateral level. The first crack in the anti-Cuban bloc occurred in November 1970, when the newly elected left-wing Allende government of Chile announced the resumption of diplomatic ties. A four-week official visit by Castro to Chile in November–December 1971 marked the new friendship between the two countries. The Chilean people gave him a rapturous welcome and the time seemed ripe to launch the second stage of Latin American liberation, namely emancipating the continent from the overwhelming economic and political dominance of the colossus of the north. Although the US-backed coup in Chile of September 1973 dashed that hope, the door to regional detente had at least been opened, and remained open. In the course of 1972 Barbados, Guyana, Jamaica, Peru and Trinidad and Tobago normalized their relations with Cuba, and most Latin American countries followed their example over the next few years.

Several factors accounted for the change of attitude towards Cuba in the early 1970s. Above all, the relative weakness of the United States because of its involvement in Vietnam and other foreign-policy disasters meant that the Latin Americans gained some room for manoeuvre and were able to resist Washington's dictates within the OAS. It was precisely such an assertion of national sovereignty that the Cuban government demanded of its future partners as a precondition for a rapprochement. Furthermore, Havana took a more pragmatic line than in earlier years and accepted the validity of all attempts to reduce dependence on the north, whether nationalist, socialist or anti-imperialist. The Cubans were also able to convince their neighbours that the official reason for the OAS blockade (namely that Cuba interfered in the internal affairs of other countries) no longer applied; for while they still declared their solidarity with revolutionary movements elsewhere in the region, they stressed that each of them had to find its own path to national independence and development.

But in the final analysis economic factors motivated the Latin American countries to end their blockade of Cuba. The island was becoming an increasingly attractive trading partner. Symptomatic of the importance of economic interests in the political normalization process was the Argentine government's decision, despite all the ideological differences, to grant a $1.2 billion loan to Cuba only a few months after the resumption of diplomatic relations between the two countries in May 1973. Under a trade agreement signed at this time Cuba undertook to supply nickel, tobacco and sugar to Argentina, while Argentina would supply Cuba with tractors, lorries, farm machinery and railway equipment, and also with $150 million worth of cars built by Argentine subsidiaries of General Motors, Ford and Chrysler. This agreement thus made the largest breach hitherto in the economic blockade of Cuba.

Rapprochement between Cuba and the OAS took much longer than the bilateral normalization of relations. The lifting of the blockade appeared on the agenda at successive meetings of the organization, but the Americans, relying in particular on the support of the Central American countries, still exercised sufficient control to thwart any serious discussion of the issue. A proposal to leave the nature of relations with Cuba at the discretion of individual members was defeated at a council meeting in Washington in June 1972 by 13 votes to 7.

Once again the OAS showed itself a willing instrument of US foreign policy, and once it again held together as the embodiment of the updated Monroe Doctrine. But not for much longer.

At the meeting of foreign ministers in Mexico City in February 1974 the Americans still succeeded in excluding Cuba from the much vaunted 'new dialogue' between the United States and Latin America. But some governments also openly expressed the view that an inter-American system without Cuba was no longer viable. At a meeting in Quito, Ecuador, in November, 12 Latin American countries inflicted a serious defeat on US foreign policy by issuing a joint declaration rejecting the blockade as an anachronism, deploring OAS loss of authority, and demanding a fundamental reform of the inter-American system. One of Washington's worst fears, that with Cuba the OAS might develop into an anti-US organization and could be transformed into a Latin American raw-materials cartel, appeared a step nearer reality. The Quito conference showed that the policy of opposing the reintegration of Cuba into the inter-American system had actually increased rather than diminished the likelihood of a Latin secession.

At the annual OAS general assembly in Washington in May 1975 the Americans, although they were the hosts, had to put up with strong criticism of the one-sidedness of the 'new dialogue', demands for equality within the inter-American system, and even a call for a compromise on the Cuba question. As an outward sign of the shift on this issue, the conference adopted a resolution which allowed governments freedom of action to resume diplomatic and commercial relations with Cuba. And at a special consultative meeting in San José, Costa Rica, on 29 July, the foreign ministers in effect decided to lift the blockade altogether.

Despite this decision the US government took no significant steps to improve its bilateral relations with Cuba. Even gestures of good will from Havana could not persuade it to end the now unilateral trade embargo. The few signs of a rapprochement included a memorandum of understanding signed on 15 February 1973 to curb the hijacking of aircraft and ships between the two countries and the partial lifting of the trade embargo on 21 August 1975 by permitting foreign subsidiaries of US firms to trade with Cuba. But when other western countries began to re-establish diplomatic links with Cuba in the mid-1970s, the Ford administration refused to do the same ostensibly because of Cuba's military involvement in Angola (which happened to be under attack by South African troops and CIA-backed mercenaries). What relations there were deteriorated markedly in the course of 1976 as a result of the increasing terrorist activities of Cuban exiles based in the United States.

The inauguration of President Jimmy Carter as president in January 1977 brought a temporary improvement. In June that year both governments agreed to exchange diplomats and to establish interest sections in the Swiss and Czechoslovak embassies in Havana and Washington respectively. But the new administration's 'soft policy' did not last long. In November 1978 Carter ordered the resumption of reconnaissance flights over Cuba, and large-scale manoeuvres were held in the Caribbean. In October 1979 he announced increased surveillance of Cuba and the formation of the Caribbean Joint Task Force, and 1,500 marines made a simulated assault landing at Guantánamo, the US naval base on the island. Relations worsened in the following year. When in April 1980 thousands of Cubans disillusioned with the revolution and wishing to leave the country gathered in the grounds of the Peruvian embassy, Carter warned the Latin American countries to be wary of Cuban intentions and even spoke of a threat to the Caribbean and Central America. On 11 April the Pentagon announced that the Solid Shield manoeuvres, an annual event hitherto largely held on American soil, would that year be held in the Caribbean. The unprecedented show of force involved the deployment of 20,000 soldiers, 42 warships and 350 aircraft off the coast of Cuba, a simulated landing of 3,000 marines at Guantánamo and the use of B-52 bombers. For the first time since the missile crisis of October 1962 American civilian personnel were evacuated from Guantánamo.

The flight of 125,000 Cubans to the United States in the spring of 1980, the sending of Cuban troops to Ethiopia to assist that country in its defensive war against neighbouring Somalia, and above all Cuban aid for the Sandinistas in Nicaragua contributed to a hardening of US policy in the final months of the Carter administration. President Castro in turn declared his government's resolve to resist US aggression, but also stated that 'if an olive branch is extended we will not reject it'.[19]

The election of Ronald Reagan in November 1980 led to a further serious deterioration in bilateral relations. Hardly in office, the new administration in February 1981 published a special report accusing Cuba of covert activities in Central America, and notably of abetting communist aggression against El Salvador by providing military support to guerilla forces there. Although the evidence for this involvement was so sketchy that the serious American media even began to question the authenticity of the documents contained in the report, the state department sent out its emissaries to rope the allies into the new hardline anti-communist policy. In April, 20 years after the Bay of Pigs fiasco, the secretary of state, Alexander Haig, revealed that the possibility of an invasion of Cuba was again being considered. As a result, Cuba had to divert scarce resources to improve its military preparedness and create a new territorial militia, both of which of course had a detrimental effect on economic performance. It should be noted that despite the massive threats at this time, the Cubans declared their willingness to enter into a dialogue with Washington to ease the tension and to do so even before the embargo had been lifted.

The US trade embargo inflicted tremendous damage on Cuba, of that there can be no doubt. But in its ultimate goal, squeezing the Cuban economy to the point where the revolutionary government would have to give in and abandon socialism, it failed utterly.

The Dominican tragedy

At the time of the inauguration of President Kennedy in January 1961, Rafael Leónidas Trujillo, one of Latin America's longest-surviving and most notorious dictators, had ruled the Dominican Republic as his private estate for 31 years. After usurping power in a coup in February 1930 he used the eight years of his first official presidency to put members of his family in key government positions and to launch an unprecedented personality cult. This actually allowed him to relinquish the office of president on two occasions (one of his successors was his brother, Héctor Bienvenido) while retaining a total hold of the government and increasing his hold over the country's wealth. Squeezing the people mercilessly, he was thought to control and own 65–85% of the national economy by 1961. Too much, as far as the local agrarian oligarchy and the American investors were concerned.

Crucially, the Americans had to content themselves with a small share of the key sugar industry, a situation they were particularly keen to remedy after 'losing' their highly profitable sugar mills in Cuba. But only, quite literally, over Trujillo's dead body would they be able to change the balance of ownership in the Dominican Republic in their favour. It was the dictator's attempt to restrict American economic interests, not his brutally repressive rule, which led to his assassination on 30 May 1961. The deep involvement of the CIA in the plot, widely suspected at the time, was later confirmed by the Church committee.

Juan Bosch, a radical democrat, was elected president with the support of 62% of the Dominican electorate in December 1962. The new president, the first to be popularly elected since 1924, had a unique opportunity to reform and develop the country's economy because Trujillo's inestimable wealth had come under state control after his death. But two factors thwarted Bosch's reformist ambitions, the factional fighting of the numerous political groups, also on the left, and the opposition of the generals (who had enjoyed power, property and privilege under Trujillo) to his anti-corruption campaign.

After only seven months in office, Bosch, a firm anti-communist, was deposed in October 1963 for allegedly being too lenient towards the communists. The coup was led by General Elias Wessin y Wessin, the commander of the country's largest military base, and had the approval of Washington. Donald Reid Cabral, nicknamed 'the little American' (*el americanito*), was put in charge of the government. The new administration imposed an austerity programme which restricted not only luxury imports, which hurt the rich, but also food imports, which hurt the poor and unemployed masses particularly during the persistent drought that afflicted the country at this time.

From exile Bosch had in the meantime been able to forge an alliance, backed by anti-Trujillo sections of the army, to restore the 1963 constitution. This constitutionalist alliance, having also gained strong support from the urban working class and sections of the middle classes, removed Cabral the day after rioting broke out in Santo Domingo on 24 April 1965. An interim junta headed by Colonel Francisco Caamaño was installed pending the return of the elected president. General Wessin y Wessin retreated to the San Isidro airbase 20 miles outside the capital. The reactionary forces found themselves in a hopeless position, particularly after the junta began distributing arms to the people, but they still tried to march on Santo Domingo and bombed the city on the orders of the US ambassador, William Tapley Bennett.

The revolution was not even a revolution when the American politicians already saw a danger to national security. Ostensibly to protect the 2,300 US citizens on the island, President Lyndon B. Johnson decided on 28 April to send in the marines, initially 400 men from Task Force 124, who arrived on the aircraft carrier *Boxer* and were supported by the 82nd airborne division. In a press release Johnson claimed that the Dominican 'authorities are no longer able to guarantee the safety [of American citizens], and they have reported that the assistance of military personnel is now needed for that purpose'.[20] He did not mention that the 'authorities' referred to was the junta of Colonel Pedro Bartolomé Benoit, whom the CIA had picked as an alternative to the constitutionalist junta of Caamaño. Benoit had initially requested Bennett for troops because he feared a communist takeover. But since US intelligence reports had stated the same day that only two leaders of the rebel forces had communist leanings, this argument lacked all credibility, and Bennett had informed Benoit that US troops could only be used to protect US lives. Thereupon Benoit had sent a second cable with the alarming message: 'Regarding my earlier request, I wish to add that American lives are in danger'.[21] Now the marines could be brought in, and after the first 400 another 30,000 were landed in Santo Domingo over the following week.

With all Americans evacuated and the fighting over by 30 April, Washington had to resort to the international-conspiracy argument after all to justify the continued presence of the marines: 'Meanwhile there are signs that people trained outside the Dominican Republic are setting to gain control', according to President Johnson.[22] The same day the CIA duly published a list of 58 communists among Bosch's supporters whom it claimed had played a major role in the revolution. The list drew much criticism from many quarters, and it hardly seemed reliable enough to base a policy on, certainly not a policy of the big stick. Many observers questioned the administration's argument that the neutralization of 58 communists within a mass insurgent movement led by be avowed non- and anti-communists required the deployment of 30,000 heavily armed US troops. But Johnson stuck to his theory that international communism had been able to establish a bridgehead in the Dominican Republic and so posed a threat to the Caribbean — the region which the Americans are wont to call their southern flank — and by implication the United States itself. In a television address on 2 May he declared categorically that 'the American nations cannot, must not and will not allow the establishment of another communist government in the western hemisphere'.[23]

Yet another foreign-policy doctrine had seen the light — the Johnson Doctrine, according to which a domestic revolution in the western hemisphere ceased to be an internal matter when its object was the establishment of a communist government. In essence the new doctrine held that: the existing order must be preserved at all costs because it guaranteed continued US influence; any violation of this order, whether of an ideological nature or otherwise, became an attack on it and an attack on US hegemony; and under the prevailing cold-war mentality and after years of tendentious political propaganda, it was of course 'international communism' which presented the concrete 'threat' to the existing order. The Johnson Doctrine, ostensibly intended to shield Latin America from outside threat, quite blatantly attempted nothing less than impose the will of the powerful onto the weak. Its enunciation met with immediate widespread criticism in the media, mainly because the doctrine harked back to the imperialist language of the turn of the century to express the illusion of American omnipotence and the self-designated role of world policeman.

The deployment of the marines clearly violated article 15 (later 18) of the OAS charter, which explicitly prohibits intervention in the internal or external affairs of another state. So as not to appear wholly on the wrong side of international law in the eyes of world public opinion, the administration tried to argue in the UN Security Council that the OAS had played a decisive role in the Dominican affair. At the tenth consultative meeting of OAS foreign ministers, convened in Washington three days later, the representatives of Chile, Mexico, Uruguay and Venezuela in particular deplored the violation of the OAS charter by the United States. But they were the only countries to vote against a resolution adopted on 6 May which in effect legitimized the unilateral action by authorizing the creation of an inter-American force to restore order in the Dominican Republic.

By 28 May, Nicaragua, Honduras, Costa Rica and Brazil had sent small contingents to Santo Domingo to join US troops in the international force. The participation of Brazilian troops seemed particularly poignant in view of the fact that a year earlier the right-wing army had deposed, with US support, President João Goulart, who had initiated a reform programme including restrictions on land ownership and foreign investments and the legalization of the Communist Party. The participation of Brazil in the peace-keeping mission or the participation of Haiti and Paraguay in the OAS effort to 'protect' democracy in the Dominican Republic could hardly be considered great moral victories for US foreign policy.

The intervention in the Dominican Republic proved very costly: it left around 3,000 Dominicans and 44 Americans dead, damaged the Alliance for Progress (the inter-American development programme launched with great fanfare in 1962), torpedoed the project for a standing inter-American task force, undermined morale at the OAS secretariat, and threw the inter-American system into a crisis of credibility. OEA, the Spanish acronym for the OAS, once again meant 'another American deception'. Anti-Americanism, which Washington had been at such pains to neutralize since the late 1950s, made a comeback with a vengeance.

But the intervention also brought the Americans considerable gains. It ensured the victory of their favoured candidate for president, Joaquín Balaguer, one of Trujillo's trusted advisers, in elections held in March 1966. An invasion of American capital could now follow the invasion of the marines. The new government created the right climate for big business by introducing a range of incentives for foreign investment, including generous tax concessions and the creation of 'free zones' in which foreign firms were tempted to set up assembly plants exempt from taxes for 10 to 20 years. The Dominican Republic thus lost all control over its natural resources to the United States.

Chile 1973: the crushing of socialism

For the Americans, Chile has traditionally been a strategic and economic cornerstone of their back yard. US direct private investment in Chile in 1970 stood at $1.1 billion, concentrated in the mining of a range of strategic minerals, primarily copper, the country's only important foreign-exchange earner and four-fifths under the control of US corporations. To protect this valuable investment, successive US administrations tried to promote anti-socialist candidates and keep socialists well away from the Moneda, the Chilean presidential palace. As the secretary of state, William Rogers, put it at a meeting with executives of six US corporations with holdings in Chile in October 1971: 'The Nixon administration is a business administration in favour of business and its mission is to protect business'.[24] To prevent a 'second Cuba' the Americans also pumped around $1.3 billion in foreign aid into Chile between 1960 and 1970, which made it the largest recipient on a per-head basis of loans under the Alliance for Progress programme.

The Church committee, which also investigated the activities of the United States in Chile, uncovered US intervention in Chile's internal affairs from 1963 onwards. Its report concluded laconically that during the Kennedy, Johnson and Nixon administrations covert intervention of the United States in Chile was 'extensive and continuous'.[25] Direct US intervention began with massive support for Eduardo Frei, the Christian Democratic candidate in the 1964 presidential elections. Around $20 million flowed from various American sources into Frei's campaign coffers, and at least 100 so-called 'special personnel' were sent to Santiago to bolster his campaign against his socialist opponent, whose name was Salvador Allende. Intervention in Chile in 1964 was 'blatant and almost obscene', as a key US intelligence officer at the time later remarked.[26]

The worst-case scenario occurred in September 1970, when Allende, the candidate of the Popular Unity (UP) alliance of left-wing parties, gained a plurality of votes in a three-cornered race. He had campaigned on a platform which included what to the US political establishment and big business were the most horrendous abominations: extensive land reform; nationalization of the US mining companies, the banks, the textile, chemical and cement industries, and the energy and transport sectors; the establishment of diplomatic relations with China, North Korea, North Vietnam and East Germany and the resumption of ties with Cuba. The alarm bells must indeed have rung loudly in Washington. Not surprisingly, the administration tried its utmost to prevent the confirmation of Allende as president by the Chilean parliament (which had the final say since no candidate had gained an absolute majority in the popular vote).

The prospect of an extensive nationalization programme prompted one major US transnational corporation with interests in Chile, the International Telephone and Telegraph Corporation (ITT), to act. Behaving more like a government than a business enterprise, ITT became the pivot of the conspiracy against Allende. Its directors offered the administration seven-figure sums to thwart Allende's accession to office and consulted a former director of the CIA and a dirty-tricks expert, John McClone, on how to destabilize his government should he gain power. They had quite precise ideas: it would be necessary to force several banks into defaulting, which in turn would lead to a run on the financial institutions, the bankrupting of some key businesses and a rise in unemployment; as social tension heightened and chaos ensued, the army would offer itself as the saviour of the nation and bring the socialist nightmare to an end.

The state department, influenced by the domino theory, attached high priority to Chile in its Latin American policy, and it was not difficult for ITT and the CIA to co-ordinate their joint strategy with the executive. Closely following the original ITT scheme, the Nixon administration's policy for the removal of Allende consisted of two 'tracks', one involving political, economic and propaganda activities, and the other involving direct contact with plotting elements of the Chilean armed forces. Although the dual-track strategy could not prevent Allende's election by parliament on 24 October and the formation of the UP coalition, its implementation had immediate effect. As a first indication of the US administration's intentions, President Nixon refused Allende the courtesy of congratulating him on his election. Much stronger stuff was to follow.

On the economic front, the Americans imposed a credit squeeze on Chile. The Export-Import Bank, which had made $234 million available to Chile in 1967, reduced its credit lines to nil during the Allende years. The World Bank — an international organization, but invariably bowing to US wishes — followed suit. The administration also refused to begin negotiations on Chile's huge foreign debt, a legacy of the Frei era, which in turn further complicated the contracting of essential new loans. On the military front, the administration increased its aid to the Chilean army to $14.5 million of military aid in 1972–73 (up from $5 million in the previous year) and quietly urged it to use the funds for the preparation of a coup attempt. While the armed forces found themselves awash with resources, the civilian population suffered from the shortages caused by the financial blockade, which made purchases abroad of wheat, fertilizers and spare parts increasingly difficult (because of the government's lack of foreign exchange and reduced credit rating).

Enraged by the resumption of diplomatic relations between Chile and Cuba in November 1970 — described by President Nixon as a 'challenge to the inter-American system' — and the nationalization of the copper industry in December 1971, US big government and big business in concerted action tried to build an international anti-Allende front.[27] To coerce the Chileans to instant payment of compensation, the Kennecott mining company, still describing itself as the rightful owner of its Chilean operations, in October 1972 took action in the courts of consumer countries, particularly in Western Europe, to secure an embargo on copper exports from the El Teniente mine. Kennecott's strategy was to use legal means to seize El Teniente copper wherever it could be traced so as to block payments being made to the Chilean Copper Corporation (CODELCO). In another ploy to inflict economic damage on Chile, the Americans engineered an artificial collapse of world copper prices. They fell from 85 to 51 cents per kilo in the three Allende years, equivalent to a loss for the Chilean state of several hundred million dollars of foreign exchange.

In addition to the external pressures, the UP government also had to withstand domestic pressure in the form of terrorist attacks, acts of sabotage, and above all the lorry owners' strike of October 1972, which had a devastating effect on the national economy. It could not survive these assaults in the long term. The bosses' strikes of late 1972 — the dress rehearsal for a right-wing coup — were followed by the bloody drama of 11 September 1973, when General Augusto Pinochet ousted the elected government and Allende was killed.

The bodies of the thousands of Chilean patriots had not even been buried, or perhaps just dumped in mass graves, when Washington let it be known, un-prompted, that it had not been in any way involved in the coup. It was a case of deciding that attack was the best form of defence: those who had pulled the strings behind the massacre in Chile now tried to proclaim their innocence. (Pinochet, incidentally, had been little more than a US puppet until the coup, but was apparently allowed to be his own man once in power.) Henry Kissinger, national security adviser and from September 1973 secretary of state in the Nixon administration, one of the politicians most deeply implicated in the destabiliza-tion strategy and the coup itself, was frivolous enough to maintain this line even after the actual background to the affair had been uncovered. In 1982 he wrote the following about the end of Allende:

> contrary to anti-American propaganda around the world and revisionist history in the United States, our government had nothing to do with planning his overthrow and no involvement with the plotters. Allende was brought down by his own incompetence and inflexibility. What happened, happened for Chilean reasons, and not as a result of acts of the United States.[28]

All evidence points to the contrary of course. Allende's socialist experiment foundered not on economic mismanagement but on external and externally sponsored pressure. Tellingly, in January 1974 the leading right-wing daily, *La Tercera de la Hora* elected Pinochet *and* Kissinger men of the year.

Notes

1. Memorandum to Guatemalan government, 28 August 1953, quoted in Krakau 1968 p. 28.
2. Address to the fourth consultative meeting of OAS foreign ministers, 26 March 1951, quoted in Schlesinger (ed.) 1973 p. 141.
3. Address to the Tenth Pan-American Conference, 4 March 1954, quoted in Schlesinger (ed.), op. cit., p. 238.
4. Quoted in Aguilar 1968 p. 102.
5. Declaration of Solidarity for the Preservation of Political Integrity of the American States against the Intervention of International Communism, adopted 28 March 1954, quoted in Schlesinger (ed.), op. cit., p. 261.
6. Quoted in Wise and Ross 1964 p. 176.
7. Press conference, 25 May 1954, quoted in Horowitz 1965 p. 172.
8. Dreier 1962 p. 4.
9. Eisenhower 1963 p. 520.
10. Quoted in Morris (ed.) 1976 p. 490.
11. Press conference, 21 April 1961, quoted in Schlesinger (ed.), op. cit., p. 543.

12. Address to the American Society of Newspaper Editors, 20 April 1962, quoted in Schlesinger (ed.), op. cit., p. 551.

13. Congressional joint resolution 230, 3 October 1962, quoted in Schlesinger (ed.), op. cit., p. 590.

14. Radio and television broadcast, 22 October 1962, quoted in Schlesinger (ed.), op. cit., p. 593.

15. Speech on the anniversary of the Cuban revolution, 26 July 1981, quoted in *Keesing's Contemporary Archives*, 16 April 1982, p. 31438.

16. Declaration of San José, adopted 28 August 1960, quoted in Schlesinger (ed.), op. cit., p. 451.

17. Final Act of Punta del Este, adopted 31 January 1962, quoted in Schlesinger (ed.), op. cit., p. 507.

18. Final Act of Washington, 25 July 1964, quoted in Schlesinger (ed.), op. cit., p. 638ff.

19. Report to second congress of the Cuban Communist Party, 17 December 1980, quoted in *Keesing's Contemporary Archives*, p. 30817.

20. Press release, 28 April 1965, quoted in Schlesinger (ed.), op. cit., p. 644.

21. Cable to Bennett, 28 April 1965, quoted in Pearce, *Under the Eagle*, p. 63.

22. Radio and television broadcast, 30 April 1965, quoted in Schlesinger (ed.), op. cit., p. 648.

23. Radio and television broadcast, 2 May 1965, quoted in Schlesinger (ed.), op. cit., p. 654.

24. Quoted in Petras and Morley 1975 p. 70.

25. US Congress, *Report of the Select Committee to Study Governmental Operations with Respect to Intelligence Activity ('Church Report)*, Covert Action in Chile, p. 1.

26. Laurence Stern in the *Washington Post*, 6 April 1973, quoted in Petras and Morley, op. cit., p. 20.

27. Report to Congress, 25 February 1971, quoted in Petras and Morley, op. cit., p. 53.

28. Kissinger 1982 p. 374.

7. More of the same: US–Latin American economic relations 1950–80

The 1950s: the years of 'benign neglect'

After the Second World War, European interests in Latin America retreated in the face of US dominance. Commerce and investment became American domains — Wall Street took the place of Lombard Street. As a result, the Americans could reap even richer rewards in their back yard from what others had sowed for them. In 1940, US exports to Latin America and the Caribbean totalled $1 billion, imports $900 million. Twenty years later, on the eve of the creation of the Alliance for Progress, US exports to the south totalled $5.2 billion and imports from there $4.7 billion; between a fifth and a quarter of total US exports went south, and around a third of total imports came from there (primarily Venezuela, Mexico, Cuba, Brazil, Argentina and Colombia). Latin America and the Caribbean in turn conducted almost half of its collective foreign trade with its unloved northern neighbour. The structural balance of trade during this period was much the same as in the 1930s: the Latin Americans supplied raw materials to the north (coffee, oil, meat, sugar, copper, wool, bananas, tin, timber, cocoa, natural fibres), while the Americans supplied manufactures to the south (textiles, chemicals, oil products, iron and steel, machinery, cars, paper, ceramics). Still lacking an industrial base, the Latin Americans continued to find themselves in a position of buying back at high prices manufactured goods made from raw materials which they had produced and sold cheaply in the first place. Not only did particular American companies, particular branches and the American economy as a whole make lucrative profits from trading with Latin America; as a result of the imbalance an ever increasing share of Latin American wealth was actually being transferred to the north.

This 'creaming off' occurred also in another way — through the huge profits generated by American investments. The repatriation of profits to the United States led to a constant drain of capital from a not exactly overcapitalized continent. Latin America had always been a desirable prospect for American investors, because there more than in any other region of the world were they guaranteed a quick and high return. It has been calculated that every invested dollar yielded a return of three within a few years. If one ignored the farmworkers on the estates and the mineworkers in the mines, one could have thought that the dollars 'worked' by themselves. It was always likely, then, that once the United States had become the world's major creditor country after the First World War and had accumulated huge amounts of surplus capital after the Second World War, the Americans would invest billions of dollars in Latin America and the Caribbean. Direct investment in the region grew from $2.8 billion in 1940 to a peak of $9.1 billion in 1959 and stood at $8.4 billion in 1960, higher than in any other world region.

In the light of these close economic relations, it was only natural that Milton S. Eisenhower, the brother of the president and a special ambassador who kept an eye on the back yard, prepared reports in November 1953 and December 1958 which stressed that 'no area in the world is of more importance to us than Latin America'.[1] Although he was by no means alone in this view, official US Latin American policy in the 1950s did not reflect it at all. In the 1930s and 40s questions concerning Latin America had received top priority, usually figuring prominently in the meetings of the Standing Liaison Committee, the predecessor of the National Security Council, for instance (not least because of the Roosevelt administration's concern about German activities in the region). But this changed completely during the cold war. If ever Washington lacked a clearly defined Latin American policy, then it was in the 1950s; and if ever a policy of 'benign neglect' applied to Latin America, it was in the 1950s. What policy there was was an anti-policy — a policy against communism. Thus while inter-American commercial relations flourished as never before, the US political establishment seemed quite simply to have forgotten Latin America.

Throughout the 1950s the Latin Americans' complained bitterly about US attitudes and policies. Although their criticisms focused also on political issues — such as Washington's insistence on supporting brutal dictators, like Batista in Cuba, as part of the effort keep communism out of the hemisphere — it was above all the unwillingness to tackle economic problems that riled the Latin Americans. A major source of aggravation was the Americans' determination to close their markets to imports whenever market conditions or special interest groups demanded it, while at the same time preaching free trade, private enterprise and similar notions. In 1959, for example, the Eisenhower administration bowed to domestic pressure from both the mine owners and the mineworkers' union to limit imports of oil, zinc, lead and copper because owing to a slight recession consumption of these minerals was falling while domestic production was rising. This affected above all Chile, Mexico, Peru and Venezuela, which depended on sales of these commodities to obtain hard currency but lost out both because access to their main market was restricted and world prices were falling. Trade barriers existed not only for Latin America's minerals but also for many agricultural products (such as cotton and peanuts) which American farmers produced in large quantities themselves and therefore did not want to allow into the United States. Latin American governments consistently urged their US counterpart to devise means of stabilizing world commodity prices. But all appeals were ignored.

Had Washington been more willing to provide foreign aid to the southern neighbours to compensate them for what were in effect losses of earnings, then the Latin Americans might have viewed matters differently. But there was precious little aid on offer between between 1945 and 1960 — in fact less than $2.5 billion for the whole continent. And four-fifths of this amount consisted of loans whose servicing subsequently burdened government budgets. The thorny problem of aid arose at nearly every inter-American conference during the cold war: ar Chapultepec in 1945, Rio in 1947, Bogotá in 1948, Washington in 1951, Caracas and Rio in 1954 and Buenos Aires in 1957. On each occasion the Latin Americans pressed home the point that to modernize their semi-colonial and monocultural economic structures they needed money — money for industrialization and diversification of agriculture and money for raising people's living standards. But here, too, Washington turned a deaf ear. It usually argued that the loans supplied through the Export-Import Bank and private investment were sufficient to stimulate the Latin American economies.

Vice-president Richard Nixon experienced directly the Latins' ire during a goodwill tour to six South American countries in May 1958. At every stopover in Uruguay, Argentina, Bolivia, Peru, Colombia and Venezuela he was greeted by thousands of demonstrators protesting against the presence of this representative of dollar diplomacy who brought with him only empty words and empty hands. He found himself even in some physical danger. On 14 May in Caracas, the Venezuelan capital, he had to flee into the US embassy to protect himself from stone-throwing demonstrators, and some reports even spoke of a 'near lynching' of the vice-president. The administration reacted by mobilizing paratroopers and marines to free him from his predicament, but in the end they were not deployed. Nixon's experience provided a potent indication of the extent of Latin American anger with the United States, and it certainly shook the White House and the state department.

Eisenhower, Operation Pan America and Castro

The outbursts of popular resentment during the Nixon tour brought home to the Eisenhower administration that burgeoning nationalism and anti-Americanism posed a danger to the American economic empire in Latin America and the Caribbean. This realization led to a hurried review of US Latin America policy, and for the first time since the Second World War Washington's politicians began to treat the region as a high priority.

To improve knowledge of the neglected neighbours, President Dwight D. Eisenhower set up a national advisory committee of private citizens chaired by the secretary of state. Its brief was to examine the cause for the turbulence in inter-American relations and to devise a strategy for putting them in order. He also dusted off the good neighbour policy of his predecessor Franklin D. Roosevelt, who had understood like no other president before or since how to negotiate with the Latin Americans and how not to alienate them with arrogant political gestures.

The change of heart paid off for the Latin Americans, first in institutional terms and later also in cash terms. In August 1958, soon after the disastrous Nixon visit to the region, the secretary of state, John Foster Dulles, rushed to Brazil to try to smooth down the wave of anti-Americanism by publicly affirming that 'Latin American has an important role to play among the nations of the world' and by signalling the administration's interest in 'Operation Pan America', the development programme for Latin America proposed by President Juscelino Kubitschek the previous May.[2] President Eisenhower himself visited Brazil, Argentina, Chile and Uruguay in February–March 1960 to spread the new message. Trying hard to dispel the impression that the United States was less generous to the southern neighbours than to its partners elsewhere in the world, he called for a 'crusade for economic development' and enthusiastically endorsed the Kubitschek plan. (He also spoke of 'misunderstandings which needed to be corrected', however, thereby implicitly denigrating Latin American criticisms as arising merely from an inadequate understanding of US intentions.)[3]

The first concrete step in the new direction was taken at the OAS economic conference in Buenos Aires in April 1959 with the creation of the Inter-American Development Bank (IDB), a project suggested as long ago as 1890 but since then always rejected by the Americans. All American states bar Cuba became members and the United States agreed to subscribe $450 million of the total capital stock of $1 billion. At an OAS economic conference in Bogotá in September 1960 the American republics (once again bar Cuba) agreed unanimously to adopt a social and economic development programme for Latin America and the Caribbean. At the same time the US government pledged $500 million to get Operation Pan America off the ground.

That would probably have been the end of American generosity had it not been for the Cuban revolution. The agrarian reform law of May 1959 provided the first indication that the Castro government was different from the usual. The trade agreements with the Soviet Union and other communist countries and the nationalization first of the American-owned oil companies and then of all American interests in the course of 1960 left big business and big government in no doubt that they were dealing with a real revolution. What the Latin American policy was to prevent at all costs, namely the supplanting of the hallowed free-enterprise system by a socialist system, was unmistakably taking shape.

This very painful realization unleashed an almost hysterical anti-communism. Anti-communism had of course been latent in US Latin American policy from the beginning of the cold war, but from now on it dominated every aspect of relations with Latin America. Since the conventional wisdom in Washington held that it was inconceivable for a small Latin American country to break out of the capitalist system and the American empire of its own volition and under its own steam, the Americans imagined a huge communist conspiracy at work in the region. Four senators who visited South America in November–December 1961 to look into the economic plight of the region reported 'communist activity', 'communists exploiting situations' and 'elements of cold-war machinations' at every turn.[4] Apparently an alleged 250,000 card-carrying party members south of the Rio Grande devoted all their energies to making propaganda for the Russian, Chinese and Cuban revolutions.

Because communist activities were orchestrated at international level, they had to be confronted at international level, that is, politically within the framework of the OAS and economically within the framework of Operation Pan America and its successor, the Alliance for Progress. US political leaders argued quite openly that these development programmes were intended not so much to secure the prosperity of Latin America but more to counter what they called 'subversion', or to be more exact, to prevent any social and economic change contrary to US interests. In other words, without Castro these development programmes would never have seen the light of day.

The Alliance for Progress: instrument of US foreign policy

The inauguration of John F. Kennedy as president of the United States on 20 January 1961 appeared to mark the dawning of a new age in international relations, in particular in inter-American relations. In his inaugural address the new president offered the southern neighbours 'a special pledge — to convert our good words into good deeds, in a new alliance of progress, to assist [them] in casting off the chains of poverty'.[5] At a reception for Latin American ambassadors on 13 March he invited Latin America to join with the United States in 'a vast cooperative effort, unparalleled in magnitude and nobility of purpose, to satisfy the basic needs of the American people', to be known as the Alliance for Progress.[6] (Kennedy showed he had taken to heart the lesson of his predecessor Theodore Roosevelt to 'speak softly and carry a big stick' in dealings with Latin America. As he made the apparently generous offer of massive new foreign aid, he had full knowledge of the preparations for the invasion of Cuba, and he gave the go-ahead to the Bay of Pigs operation three weeks later.)

In the same way that the Marshall Plan had allowed Western Europe to rise from the ashes of the Second World War, the Alliance for Progress was to overcome underdevelopment in the western hemisphere. In June 1961 President Kennedy sent one of his closest associates, Adlai E. Stevenson, the US representative at the United Nations, southwards to test the waters. On his return Stevenson reported — rather optimistically — widespread support for the alliance plan among government leaders, and, underlining the explosive differences between rich and poor which left little time for social reforms, he recommended moving ahead as quickly as possible. The four senators who visited South America later that year described the alliance plan as 'the most exciting new idea in Latin America, perhaps in this century'.[7] The usual hyperbole, one might have thought, but this time deeds did follow words, at least in the short term. On 27 May 1961 Kennedy signed into law an aid programme for Latin America totalling $600 million in the first instance, just over half of which would be disbursed by the IDB. Having formally put the alliance plan on the inter-American agenda the previous month, the administration in effect unilaterally called the Alliance for Progress into existence by this increase in foreign aid.

The Latin American countries gave their blessing to the venture at a meeting the following August of the IA–ECOSOC/CIES in Punta del Este, Uruguay. The choice of venue was perhaps not wholly coincidental. For Punta del Este, a seaside resort and playground of the rich and super-rich from Argentina, Brazil and Uruguay, this was the off-season. The economics ministers of the 21 OAS members could meet in isolation from mistrustful compatriots who might choose to demonstrate against the plan had they gathered in a big city like nearby Montevideo. For there was a widely expressed view in the region, also articulated at the meeting, that the alliance amounted to little more than a continuation of US hegemony under a different guise. Many Latin American representatives, who on other matters could happily co-operate with the northern neighbour, feared that they would be expected to relinquish part of their national sovereignty and autonomy in exchange for economic aid. Nevertheless, after ten days of debates the assembled delegations adopted the Declaration to the Peoples of America and the Charter of Punta del Este on 17 August. The formal planning for the alliance could now begin.

The charter talked not only of the noble values of freedom, democracy, civilization and human dignity, but also of the urgent need for reforms and the money which was to make it all possible. The aim was to inject the enormous sum of $100 billion into Latin America over a ten-year period. The Latin American countries committed themselves to put up a fifth of the total. The Americans, who had disbursed an average of $335 million of foreign aid to the southern neighbours between 1946 and 1961, committed themselves to more than quadrupling the annual economic aid to the region. The Alliance for Progress thus became the largest single foreign-aid programme of the US government. And in the beginning the money flowed so generously that one could have been tempted to think that altruism had finally become an element of US Latin American policy.

But of course it was not altruism which prompted President Kennedy and his advisers to take up the challenge of alleviating the misery in the south. Despite the lofty rhetoric employed by a young, charming and charismatic president, the alliance was anything but a work of charity. The plan arose from the renewed realization — it surfaces time and again in US history — that the prosperity of the American economy and the stability of American society depended very largely on developments in Latin America. When the Kennedy administration spoke of the inter-American common interest it thought first and foremost of the United States' particular interest. It thought specifically of the importance of Latin America's raw materials to the United States, the strategic minerals and key commodities without which a highly industrial economy would grind to a halt and lose its pivotal position in international relations: bauxite, manganese, copper, iron ore, lead, zinc and oil.

Oil, the most important commodity on the above list, held an unusual position in that the United States strictly speaking could have satisfied demand from domestic sources, for the black gold flowed richly in Texas and other states. The fact that from 1950–58 the value of oil imports from Latin America increased by some $80 million every year — so that by the end of the period it constituted about a quarter of all US imports from the region — had more to do with the relative cheapness of third-world oil than with any shortages. In the 1950s producing a ton of oil cost $20 in the United States, but only $7 in Venezuela. Small wonder, then, that for many years the Americans had invested heavily in oil extraction — in 1964, 36% of US direct investment in Latin America went on this lubricant of industrial society.

The situation was different for some metals, including iron ore, copper, lead, zinc, nickel and bauxite. Although itself well endowed with these mineral resources, the United States had become a net importer during and after the Second World War. That is to say, the American economy relied on raw-material imports to sustain high-technology sectors like the arms industry and space exploration. The production of jet engines, for instance, required nickel. This was in short supply in the early 1960s, and while in the past America's industrialists would have turned to Cuban supplies, since they owned all nickel mines on the island, they could no longer do so after the nationalizations. This experience would have concentrated their minds on the implications of other Caribbean islands or smaller Latin American countries going the way of Cuba. Guyana, Jamaica and Surinam, for instance, were among the world's largest bauxite producers, and in the 1960s the United States became heavily dependent on bauxite imports: by 1966 imports exceeded domestic production by a factor of six, and by 1969 as much as 99% of imports came from Latin America and the Caribbean. All good reason to remain on good terms with the southern neighbours who sat on these riches.

The goals of the Alliance for Progress were ambitious indeed. As set out in the Charter of Punta del Este, they were:

- to achieve … a substantial and sustained growth of per-capita income [of at least 2.5% per year];
- to make the benefits of economic progress available to all citizens … through a more equitable distribution of national income;
- to achieve balanced diversification in national economic structures;
- to accelerate the process of rational industrialization;
- to raise greatly the level of agricultural production [and] to encourage a programme of comprehensive agrarian reform;
- to eliminate adult illiteracy;
- to increase life expectancy by a minimum of five years;
- to increase construction of low-cost housing for low-income families;
- to maintain stable price levels;
- to strengthen economic integration [in Latin America and the Caribbean]; and
- to develop programmes to prevent the harmful effects of excessive fluctuations in foreign-exchange earnings.[8]

Within the space of decade, the foreign-aid programme was to substantially raise living standards and improve living conditions and health and educational facilities for millions of impoverished Latin Americans. To turn these ambitious plans into reality, the United States pledged $1.1 billion every year in the form of loans and subsidies and $300 million as direct private investment, Japan and Europe $300 million and the international financial institutions (primarily the World Bank and the IMF) another $300 million.

In President Kennedy's vision the Alliance of Progress would have created by the end of the decade 'an American civilization where spiritual and cultural values are strengthened by an ever-broadening base of material advance, where, within the rich diversity of its own traditions, each nation is free to follow its own path toward progress'.[9] Needless to say, however, the aims of the alliance were actually rather more prosaic. As President Rómulo Betancourt of Venezuela noted more perceptively at the time: 'We must help the poor ... in order to save the rich'.[10] In other words, the Americans and the Latin élites, faced with social contradictions which threatened to explode into popular uprisings, tried to channel and control social change; they tried to engineer a revolution from above to prevent a revolution from below. Even at the time it did not require great prescience to see that where the Americans envisaged their brave new prosperous world there would still be poverty, unemployment and slums for years and decades to come. And indeed, in the end the alliance proved to be a misalliance; it achieved none of its goals and fulfilled none of its promises.

The alliance shaped up well enough in its first year. The funds flowed almost as planned, with the 18 participating Latin American countries investing $8 billion, the United States contributing $1 billion, and the European countries and the international financial institutions contributing another $700 million, so that the target of $10 billion was nearly reached. But after this good start the dollar transfer declined considerably. Four years into the alliance the United States had transferred a total of $4.2 billion to Latin America in loans, grants, technical aid, Peace Corps projects and donations within the framework of the Food for Peace programme. Over the same period the Latin American countries themselves had invested $23.1 billion in development projects and borrowed a further $1 billion from the international institutions. This made a total of $28.3 billion, or just over $7 billion a year, well short of the target. On average every Latin American received the meagre sum of $2.73 in foreign aid per year. During the Johnson administration, from 1963 until 1969, Congress became increasingly unwilling to authorize even the curtailed foreign-aid programmes largely because the war in Vietnam was already swallowing up huge resources and probably also because no second Castro seemed to be in sight in Latin America. In the early Nixon years US contributions to the alliance fell dramatically, to $976 million in 1969 and $625 million in 1970, down from $1.7 billion in 1968. The stock-taking after ten years showed that not even half of the initial target had been achieved. Instead of the projected overall $20 billion transfer of resources, only $9.4 billion had found their way southwards.

In itself this sum was certainly substantial. However, American 'aid' had several catches. Already by 1964 the dollar injections failed to compensate the Latin American countries for the loss of income as a result of deteriorating terms of trade. Nor could the funds fulfil their intended purpose as catalysts for progress, since a large proportion was often used to meet growing budget deficits rather than finance key development projects. While the US government allo-

cated public funds for development in Latin America, the US corporations active
there made excess profits. The Latin American countries' chronically weak
balances of payments showed all too clearly that there could hardly be talk of a
net capital inflow.

What the foreign 'aid' did do was benefit the US economy. Whenever President Kennedy or President Johnson had problems in getting congressional
approval for the ostensibly large budget allocations for the Alliance of Progress
they stressed the benefits which the aid programme brought the US economy.
For one thing, they argued, even if the communist threat abated and the cold war
came to an end the United States would still have to find markets to absorb its
products, and Latin Americans could only buy these if they had some money in
their pockets. They would also point out that, to promote exports, the overwhelming part of US foreign aid had for some years now been dispensed in the
form of so-called 'tied' loans. This meant that the dollar loans or grants donated
to the developing countries had to be spent on purchasing American goods and
services. In January 1968 Johnson could assure Congress that more than 90% of
US foreign aid in 1969 would be applied to finance purchases in the United
States. These purchases often had to be made at prices 30–50% above world
market levels, so that in real terms the value of the aid was little more than half
of the nominal amount. Moreover, the goods which the developing countries
bought within the framework of not-quite-aid were rarely state of the art. More
often than not American freighters transported to Latin America goods which
could no longer be sold on the US market. And then there was a major political
disadvantage which further diminished the value of US aid for the south, the
Hickenlooper Amendment to the 1962 Foreign Assistance Act, which called for
the automatic suspension of US aid to any country which expropriated or
nationalized the property of US citizens.

Under the Alliance for Progress foreign aid for Latin America was as much an
instrument of US foreign policy as it had been in the past. The United States
would reward with dollar credits and grants those countries which created a
favourable investment climate, and would withdraw from those countries which
pursued a more independent economic policy less accommodating to US interests. Despite the alliance's multilateral character, the Americans had sufficient
means at their disposal to ensure they had their way, whether through their veto
in the IDB or through the Agency for International Development (AID), the
main vehicle for distributing alliance funds, which restricted the sovereignty of
recipient countries by linking, on the model of the IMF, the disbursement of aid
to the fulfilment of economic and social targets.

No wonder, then, that already after two years of the Alliance for Progress the
Latin Americans were disillusioned. At the meeting of IA–ECOSOC in São
Paulo in November 1963 they sharply criticized the failure of dialogue between
the two Americas and the continued US control over decision making on
development priorities. All too aware that the meeting revealed far more than
a momentary political disagreement — in fact a fundamental structural crisis of
the alliance — the Americans tried to salvage what they could. After the debacle
of São Paulo a co-ordinating committee was set up to breathe new life into the

alliance, the Inter-American Committee for the Alliance for Progress (CIAP), whose main purpose was to carry out special studies on the social and economic development of the Latin American countries. In May 1964 President Johnson reaffirmed his administration's support for the goals of the alliance and ordered several institutional changes to the management of the programme to improve its performance. And in October 1969 President Nixon proposed to strengthen the role of the CIAP and removed the 'buy American' clause of the tied loans, so that henceforth loan dollars could be used to make purchases anywhere. But it was already too late. The alliance had been quietly buried long before Nixon implicitly acknowledged as much in February 1970, when he referred not to an 'alliance' but to an 'action programme for progress'.[11] The abolition of the CIAP in June 1974 marked the formal end of the Alliance for Progress.

The failure of the alliance was admitted in US government circles, albeit in coded form. Nelson Rockefeller, who had been asked by President Nixon to head a special mission to Latin America in May–June 1969, noted rather coyly: 'To be sure, actual progress under the Alliance has not come up to the grand hopes entertained in 1961 at Punta del Este'.[12] Quite. While regional trade between the two Americas flourished under the auspices of the alliance, with Latin American exports to the north increasing by 40% in the 1960s, the hoped-for changes in the structure of commercial relations did not happen. The meagre economic growth was swallowed up by a population growth of 2.8% per year, so that income per head could not be raised. A redistribution of wealth did occur, but in exactly the opposite direction to that intended — from the poor to the rich. Hardly any more Latin Americans were literate at the end of the decade than at the beginning, with almost one-third of the continent's people still unable to read or write. Life expectancy increased by a mere two years. Housing shortages were not overcome, with an estimated demand for some 20 million units in 1970. Inflation spiralled unabated. And, above all, no significant land and tax reforms were carried through.

The reasons for the failure must be sought primarily in the inherent contradictions of the whole alliance project. In the final analysis the planned reforms were neither in the interest of the Latin American élites, because they undermined their very basis of existence, nor of the Americans, because they undermined their economic and political interests. The business community wanted political stability to make profits and the government wanted social peace to keep out communism. Both of these could be provided in Latin America by the armed forces. In most countries the generals received large quantities of dollars within the framework of the alliance, a favour for which they showed appropriate gratitude. Just as the alliance of equals had proved illusory, so too did the alliance of the free.

Most reformist presidents of the early 1960s shared a similar fate: in Argentina, Arturo Frondizi was ousted by the military in March 1962; in Peru, Víctor Raúl Haya de la Torre won the elections in June 1962 but was prevented from taking office by a military coup the following month; in the Dominican Republic, Juan Bosch was ousted by the military in October 1963 after less than a year in office; in Brazil, João Goulart was ousted by the military in April 1964. In the meantime the military had taken power also in Guatemala, Ecuador and Honduras, so that, in 1964, 6 Latin American countries were ruled by provisional military governments (11 were ruled by elected governments and 3 by dictators). The Americans were not too concerned. They had trained most of the officers now in power, and knew them to be a strong anti-communist core willing to defend the social status quo. Many influential leaders in Washington actually considered the Latin American military a stabilizing, progressive force. More often than not they preferred to ally themselves with the dictators because of their anti-communist credentials rather than with the true democrats; in a fateful travesty they often saw the dictators as the democrats and the democrats as the communists.

US foreign trade policy after 1970: the ill-fated 'new dialogue'

One of the main goals which had eluded the Latin American countries during the Alliance for Progress years was the substitution of expensive imports — which presented such a drain on their international reserves — by domestic production. But thanks to relatively favourable price trends, especially for tin and copper, they were able to increase their export earnings at a faster rate than in previous years, by 5.2% per year from 1961–69 compared to 1.8% per year in the corresponding period of the 1950s. They were also able to loosen slightly the commercial chain that tied them to the colossus of the north by seeking out and finding markets for their products in other parts of the world. Whereas 53% of the continent's exports went to the United States and Britain in 1960, only 44% went to these traditional markets in 1968, with the European Community countries accounting for 20%, and Canada, Japan and non-EC European countries for 14%. And they were able to change, at least moderately, the structure of their exports away from raw materials towards manufactured goods. Foodstuffs, beverages, tobacco, agricultural raw materials, minerals and fuels accounted for around 90% of exports in 1960, but for only 82% in 1968.

The Latin Americans did not have to thank their northern neighbour for these modest successes. On the contrary, they progressed because of their own efforts and despite US economic policies. The creation of ALALC/LAFTA in February 1960 played a key role in this regard by opening markets and thus extending intra-Latin American trade. Inter-American trade between north and south declined in importance. The Latin American share of US imports fell from 31% in 1957 to 17% ten years later, and to 15% in 1970; it rose to 18% in 1974 but then settled at a fairly constant 14% in the following years. But the trade gap between the unequal partners grew ever larger. In the early 1960s the deficit reached around $260 million a year, but by 1970 it had increased to $1.3 billion. Moreover, contrary to the alliance rhetoric, the Americans continued to put barriers in the way of Latin American imports, which not only thwarted access to the US market but also consolidated the existing unequal structure of commerce. Economic relations between the two Americas remained unchanged in other areas as well. For instance, US companies continued to make far greater profits on their investments in Latin America than on their operations in the industrialized countries.

All in all the Latin Americans had little reason to lament the passing of the Alliance for Progress. While airing their grievances at every available opportunity, especially over the import restrictions, they also began to take unilateral action. At Punta del Este in April 1967 the heads of government of the Latin OAS members agreed to form a Latin American common market from 1970 onwards. Two years later, at a conference of the Special Commission for Latin American Coordination (CECLA) in Viña del Mar, Chile, in May 1969, the assembled ministers adopted the Latin American Consensus of Viña del Mar, a document which did not couch criticisms of the US policy in the usual diplomatic jargon. In effect it declared that the Latin American countries were tired of being treated as second class and as the work-horses for the industrial countries, and demanded a radical reorientation of relations with the industrial countries and a more just international division of labour. Specifically from the United States it demanded — as had been done before and would be done again in future — the liberalization of trade policies, opening of markets to products from the south, including manufactures, and a commitment to set the interests of Latin America above those of other world regions in economic policy making. The document stressed the conflicts of interest between the two Americas, referred to a crisis in inter-American relations, and deplored the disappointing results of co-operation. In a nutshell, the Latin Americans wanted an overhaul of a relationship in which they gave up more of their continent's wealth than they received in return, a relationship quite simply in which they, not the Americans, provided the foreign aid.

Rockefeller's report on his mission to Latin America, published in August 1969, admitted that many of the Latin Americans' grievances were justified. Particularly regarding trade he observed that there was 'an imperative need for export trade' and that 'It comes down to the elemental fact that trade expansion is essential to support accelerated economic development in the hemisphere'. He also added that 'Increasing imports by the United States from the hemisphere nations will help expand US exports to them'.[13] Responding to the report, President Nixon in October 1969 promised change and announced steps to reduce non-tariff trade barriers, which marginally improved access for Latin American goods to the US market.

But these views could not prevail against the short-term and short-sighted protectionism which the United States, like all other industrial countries, always resorted to in order to keep foreign goods at bay during times of economic recession. In August 1971, not that long after he had invoked a new partnership with Latin America and promised to remove non-tariff barriers, President Nixon used his powers under the 1930 Tariff Act and the 1962 Trade Expansion Act to increase tariff barriers by 10%. Understandably enough the move provoked a tremendous outcry in Latin America, which was hit hardest by it.

A similar snub followed. On the one hand the American politicians moved verbal mountains to improve Latin American access to the US market. Proposals to this effect were put forward in May 1973 by the secretary of state, William Rogers, during a tour of the region and in February 1974 by his successor, Henry

Kissinger, at the OAS foreign ministers' conference in Mexico City. But then in January 1975 a new Trade Act came into force which enabled President Gerald Ford to exclude from its tariff concessions developing countries which belonged to producer cartels, particularly the Organization of Petroleum Exporting Countries (OPEC), of which Ecuador and Venezuela are members.

Not only did the protectionist US trade policy deal a mortal blow to the 'new dialogue' with Latin America which the Americans had launched with much fanfare in February 1974. Along with other factors, the realization that the United States would invariably subordinate its 'partnership' with Latin America to its own commercial interests even if it caused economic and social hardship in the region brought about a lasting change in relations between the United States and Latin America. On 22 March 1975 the presidents of Mexico and Venezuela, Luis Echevarría Alvarez and Carlos Andrés Pérez, issued an influential joint statement declaring that the US Trade Act offended against the principle of equality in international relations and violated the principles of the inter-American system. They also called for much more consultation and greater co-operation among Latin American governments on economic issues. One outcome of this was the creation on 17 October of the Latin American Economic System (SELA), which was to enable the region to speak with one voice (independently of and perhaps also against Washington) in the current international debate on a new international economic order.

During the 1970s the American politicians, preoccupied with Vietnam, Watergate and other problems, on the whole once again neglected the southern continent — as in the 1950s — which was left to deal on its own with the intractable problem of development in the shadow of the northern economic giant. The Americans rediscovered their interest in the region, particularly in the Caribbean, once the 'red peril' re-emerged in the form of popular revolutions in Grenada and Nicaragua in March and July 1979 respectively. The response was predictable. In February 1982 President Ronald Reagan proposed a $350 million aid programme for the region, the Caribbean Basin Initiative (CBI), which, like earlier similar plans, was more concerned with stemming the communist advance in the back yard than with economic development. It did not take much foresight to predict that the CBI would go the way of the Alliance for Progress.

Notes

1. Report on United States–Latin American relations, 27 December 1958, quoted in Schlesinger (ed.) 1973 p. 417.

2. Joint US-Brazilian communiqué, 5 August 1958, quoted in *Keesing's Contemporary Archives*, p. 16423.

3. Radio and television broadcast, 8 March 1960, quoted in Schlesinger (ed.), op. cit., p. 444.

4. Report by Senator Gale McGee *et al.* to the Senate committee of appropriations, 13 February 1962, quoted in US Congress 1962cp. 6ff.

5. Inaugural address, 20 January 1961, quoted in US Congress 1969 p. 268.

6. Address at reception for Latin American diplomats, 13 March 1961, quoted in Schlesinger

(ed.), op. cit., p. 503.

7. Report by Senator Gale McGee *et al.* to the Senate committee of appropriations, 13 February 1962, quoted in US Congress 1962c p. 2.

8. Charter of Punta del Este, adopted 17 August 1961, quoted in Schlesinger (ed.), op. cit., p. 563ff.

9. Address at reception for Latin American ambassadors, 13 March 1961, quoted in Schlesinger (ed.), op. cit., p. 502.

10. Quoted in Aguilar 1968 p. 119.

11. Message to Congress, 21 February 1970, quoted in US Congress 1970 p. 41.

12. Report of the US presidential mission for the western hemisphere ('The Rockefeller Report on the Americas'), 30 August 1969, quoted in Schlesinger (ed.), op. cit., p. 763.

13. Ibid., p. 766.

8. The 1980s: focus on Central America

Capital expansion and liberation movements

The immediate post-1945 period, in particular during the years of the Korean war, saw a boom of unprecedented proportions and a huge expansion of productive capacity in the American economy. This was the time of the 'economic miracle', of optimism and blind faith in the ability of capitalism 'to multiply benefits to humanity just like the five loaves and two fishes were multiplied to feed the five thousand', as the president of the Pennsalt corporation, Richard L. Davies, enthused in 1956.[1] But the miracle lost some of its mystique in 1957, when overproduction caused a short recession and a decline of the gross domestic product by 1.2% in 1957–58. A brief upturn ended abruptly with a strike in the steel industry in June 1959, and the renewed recessionary phase, accompanied by a sharp fall in demand for steel and cars, caused unemployment to exceed 5 million.

During the 1950s the American politicians devoted themselves mostly to the flashpoints of the cold war rather than the back yard. Similarly, the big corporations turned away from Latin America because of the uncertain business climate and instead concentrated more on other regions of the world. This changed from the Kennedy years onwards, no doubt also as a result of the recession. Latin America was rediscovered as an important new market for American goods.

The business community as well as the trade union movement provided institutional support for the new economic advance southwards. Major investors in Latin America set up the Council of the Americas (the successor to the Council for Latin America) as their mouthpiece in April 1965. Based in New York and chaired by no less a person than the financier David Rockefeller, this business circle could boast over 200 corporate members two years later, which between them accounted for more than 85% of US investments in Latin America and the Caribbean. Its main function was public relations and the promotion of a favourable investment climate in the region, which as far the investors were concerned meant, among other things, special privileges for foreign capital (such as tax concessions), orthodox financial policies to control inflation, balanced government budgets, security of ownership and the existence of basic infrastructure. At an international level, the capitalist élite created the Atlantic Community Development Group for Latin America (ADELA) in April 1963 to promote exports and investment in the region. The trade unions acted in concert with big government and big business with regard to the promotion of investment abroad. Big labour ran the American Institute for Free Labor Development (AIFLD), a body created in 1962 by the Alliance for Progress and the US labour movement and chaired by a businessman, J. Peter Grace, whose ideological training programmes produced compliant Latin American union leaders who could be counted on to argue against strikes and for hollow compromises.

New in this expansion southwards was the determination of big business to penetrate local industrial production, in addition to carrying off raw materials and agricultural goods. The main field of US investment shifted from the traditional areas of agriculture and mining to manufacturing. The move into industrial activities was most marked in the five Central American countries, Costa Rica, El Salvador, Guatemala, Honduras and Nicaragua (see Table 8.1). The investors encountered few obstacles as they turned their acquisitive urge from coffee and bananas to the region's fledgling manufacturing sector. For one thing, potential US rivals carved up the region into spheres of influence (for instance, tyre production and sales were controlled by Goodyear in Guatemala, and by Firestone in Costa Rica); second, the national bourgeoisie in each country could not compete with US transnational corporations; and third, European competitors posed only a marginal threat. In short, American investors fared well in Central America in the 1960s and 70s. In 1969 their share of total foreign direct investment stood at 75% in Costa Rica, 60% in El Salvador, 86% in Guatemala, 95% in Honduras and 80% in Nicaragua. By 1980 total US private direct investment in Central America amounted to $1,025 million ($210 million in Costa Rica, $145 million in El Salvador, $260 million in Guatemala, $250 million in Honduras, and $160 million in Nicaragua).

Table 8.1
Direct US investment in Central American industries,* 1970 and 1979
(US$ million)

	1970	share (%)	1979	share (%)
mining and steel	10	2	24	3
oil	160	26	72	8
manufacturing	74	12	304	34
transport			75	8
commerce			102	11
finance and insurance	380	61	56	6
other industries			262	29
total	624	100	895	100

*Costa Rica, El Salvador, Guatemala, Honduras, Nicaragua

Source: US Department of Commerce

Big business skilfully adapted the form of its investments to the changed political conditions in Central America, in particular to the much discussed and also much maligned 'nationalism' of the Latin Americans. It certainly bought up local companies wherever it could, by the trusted means of concluding agreements on loans, technical aid, licenses and production quotas, thereby making them dependent, and then acquiring full control. But the new investment in the industrial sectors of the Central American countries more often than not occurred in the form of joint ventures with local companies. This had the inestimable advantage for the Americans of bringing sectors of the local economy under their direct or indirect control while reducing the risk of expropriation or nationalization, because joint ventures linked, if only superficially, the interests of the local bourgeoisie to those of the neo-colonialists.

With part of these investments the US corporations tried to penetrate, capture and monopolize the consumer markets of Central America. However, in the late 1950s and early 1960s it was not clear who would consume the goods made in the USA, Honduras or wherever. The peasants and urban workers could hardly fulfil this role, since they could only just feed themselves on what they earned and often enough not even that. The middle class was the only group to come into consideration, but it was far too small to buy in sufficient quantities the goods produced by the American subsidiaries. The first step, then, the Americans decided, was to convert the rising expectations of the masses into purchasing power and demand. This in turn required certain reforms, not least a redistribution — on a moderate scale, of course — of social wealth. It suited the American market strategists that among its goals the Alliance for Progress espoused precisely that.

Another matter that caused the US corporations some concern was the size, or rather the lack of it, of the closed national markets of the Central American countries. They were therefore well pleased when the Central Americans themselves began to open their markets towards the end of the 1950s. On 24 February 1958 the five governments approved in principle two economic treaties designed to create a regional free-trade zone for a limited number of products, a development which aroused great interest in the United States.

So as not to lose control of developments, the US government decided to take a leading role in the regional integration movement. One reason behind this close interest was Washington's obsessive determination to use whatever means available, including economic ones, to prevent other countries going the way of Cuba. Another was the desire to reduce the influence of CEPAL/ECLA, which argued persuasively for gradual integration and co-ordinated industrial planning. CEPAL argued specifically that investment decisions should be based on agreed planning priorities and that limited protectionism was justified as part of a policy of import substitution. Both these tenets were of course anathema to the Americans, the prophets of free enterprise and free trade as the absolute principles of economic relations, and some circles in Washington decried them as overly interventionist and even tending towards socialism.

In March 1959 the Eisenhower administration sent a fact-finding mission to Central America (composed of two state department officials, Isaiah Frank and Harry Turkel) to gather information but also to promote US policies. To make the Central American partners more amenable to the US strategy of unrestricted free trade, the mission offered an aid package worth $100 million. The governments of El Salvador, Guatemala and Honduras could not resist the temptation and began negotiations for a trilateral agreement on free trade for nearly all goods and on free movement of capital and labour. Concluded in February 1960, the agreement which handed part of Central America over to market forces had one blemish — it was drafted in English, and had still to be translated into Spanish.

The Americans continued to dominate, if not control, the integration process as it developed along the desired free-market lines, culminating in December 1960 in the formation of the Central American Common Market (MCC, Mercomún or CACM). Having thus seen off the CEPAL model of integration and imposed its own, Washington ensured, not least thanks to the sheer weight of its financial resources, that all the new organizations' strategic decisions were taken on the basis of the principles of absolute free trade, unrestricted operation of the 'free market' and absolute freedom of movement for foreign capital in Central America.

But in the end the Americans never fully enjoyed the fruits of the free-market strategy they had imposed on Central America. After a few years of trade liberalization and market expansion the integration movement lost impetus. It soon emerged that the MCC did not relieve Central America of its dependence on external factors, especially overseas demand for its raw materials. Furthermore, as the integration process stalled, inequalities within the common market increasingly came to the fore. Honduras, Costa Rica and to some extent Nicaragua began to complain that free trade only benefited El Salvador and Guatemala, the more industrialized members, and created serious balance-of-payments problems for themselves. The military conflict between El Salvador and Honduras in July 1969, which had its roots in this tension but became widely known as the 'football war', led to the withdrawal of Honduras from the MCC and the collapse of the integration efforts.

Washington had to admit defeat on one of its foreign-policy aims. Although individual US corporations made healthy profits, the Central American market as a whole, and the US share of it, did not expand as envisaged. In the second half of the 1960s the US share of foreign investment in the region fell from 92 to 86%, as did the US share of regional trade, in particular with Guatemala. These setbacks were related both to faltering integration and to increasing competition from Western European and Japanese companies. But the relative failure of the market expansion in Central America was primarily attributable to the internal contradictions of US strategy. Crucially, the potential buyers of American goods remained desperately poor because the ambitious reform plans of the Kennedy era for the redistribution of wealth and the raising of living standards remained unfulfilled. It was of course impossible to square mass production with low levels of consumption. And so in the 1970s the Americans prescribed a dose of austerity for the satellites on the isthmus — a one-sided strategy oriented towards world markets and exports, carried out on the backs of the region's peasants and workers. The unholy alliance of the traditional ruling families, transnational corporations and military regimes guaranteed — and still guarantees ruthlessly — capitalist investment and growth in the region.

The creation of 'free-trade zones' formed one particularly offensive element of this strategy. Conceived as high-tech production centres, they exploited the reservoirs of cheap labour in the backward economies, benefited from generous financial incentives and fiscal concessions, and, moreover, suspended basic democratic rights such as freedom of association. Workers' attempts to improve the starvation wages being paid in the zones — the minimum wage in El Salvador stood at the equivalent of 30 cents per hour or $2.50 per day, among the lowest levels in the world and around a tenth of corresponding wages in the United States — met with brutal repression. Hundreds of trade unionists in the region were abducted (often even before they had articulated any demands), tortured, killed and dumped on street corners to deter their fellow workers. On the rare occasions that big business did not receive sufficient backing from the local oligarchies in its extraction of super-profits from these production centres, it simply dismantled them and relocated them in a country where political repression guaranteed undisturbed operations. El Salvador in particular thus became converted into what one analyst aptly called a 'service station of international capitalism'.[2]

This example also illustrates the inherent contradictions of US policy which in the long term meant that it could not prevail over the basic interests of the peasants and urban workers. Washington's economic strategy for the region, which first stressed dependent industrialization and then austerity and cheap labour, contributed to growing turmoil in the back yard by accelerating the trend towards proletarianization and class polarization. In turn, the social processes of commercialization, urbanization and capital inflow, partly induced by the United States, contributed to a revival of revolutionary social movements similar to those which comparable economic pressures had spawned in the 1930s and 40s.

Where wages were too low to achieve the production and reproduction of labour, where in other words the workers had nothing to lose but the chains which shackled them to US capital, the rise of home-grown liberation movements against both local ruling oligarchies and the colossus of the north could not be long in coming. This social and political inevitability was unaffected by the Americans' blinkered view that external powers and alien ideologies, and not the voracity of transnational corporations, gave rise to these movements. The argument that the peoples of Central America were passive victims of communist infiltration from which they needed to be protected rather than active agents in rebellion against glaring social injustices, used as much today as it was 30 years ago, lacked all credibility even then.

The US government tried its utmost to prevent the impending political upheaval in Central America — for instance, by pumping huge sums of economic and military aid into the region (see Table 8.2). The international financial institutions, acting at the behest of the Americans, also approved increasingly generous loans and grants to Central America. It was notable in this context that aid was not dispensed proportionately but in effect linked to the existence of a favourable investment climate, buttressed in countries like Guatemala (as well as Brazil, Chile, the Dominican Republic and Uruguay) by military and police forces who ruled by means of repression, torture and assassination of members of the labour movement and the political opposition.

In a further effort to prevent a 'second Cuba' the Americans strongly encouraged the creation of the Central American Defense Council (CONDECA) by El Salvador, Guatemala, Honduras and Nicaragua in December 1963. Contrary to what its official title suggested, defence of the region against outside attack was never intended to be CONDECA's purpose. Rather, the centralization of military command structures and the standardization of organizational structures, training and equipment which took place under its auspices and under US supervision was intended from the beginning to 'pacify' the member countries themselves. The council served the local oligarchies as a powerful means of controlling their own peoples. Counterinsurgency tactics, that is, anti-guerrilla warfare, invariably dominated the joint manoeuvres of the regional armies. The practical relevance of the military community created by the integration of armed forces lay in the fact that one regime could now call on support from the others in its struggle against a liberation movement.

Table 8.2
US economic and military aid to Central America, 1953–79
(US$ million)

	1953–61	1962–69	1970–79	total
Costa Rica				
economic	71.5	115.7	118.0	305.2
military	0.1	1.7	5.1	6.9
El Salvador				
economic	14.3	115.1	89.0	218.4
military	0.1	6.5	10.2	16.8
Guatemala				
economic	134.7	170.8	220.5	526.0
military	1.5	18.3	22.1	41.9
Honduras				
economic	37.9	75.9	191.3	305.1
military	1.1	8.0	19.3	28.4
Nicaragua				
economic	46.2	116.2	183.4	345.8
military	1.9	10.4	20.3	32.6

Source: US Department of State

CONDECA — whose cohesion, incidentally, also suffered from the after-effects of the 'football war' — helped the Americans enormously because it allowed them to leave the fighting of civil wars to local substitutes. Instead of flexing its own military muscle and pursuing a gunboat diplomacy, as it was 'compelled' to do elsewhere, the regional power could rely on the local repressive apparatus for the protection of its interests. It also meant that from now on direct US interventions in Central America to suppress revolutionary movements would have to be regarded as admissions of failure, since the local sub-imperialist vassal had been found wanting. As long as the likes of Anastasio Somoza in Nicaragua fulfilled the roles of protectors of American interests, Washington could confidently turn its attention to other parts of the world. The Somoza regime gave direct support to the United States during the overthrow of the Arbenz government in Guatemala in 1954, the ill-fated Bay of Pigs invasion of Cuba in 1961 and the invasion of the Dominican Republic in 1965, sent soldiers to Vietnam in 1967 and El Salvador in 1971, supported the forces of reaction throughout Central America, and was the most active member of CONDECA. Hence Washington's vindictive reaction of the overthrow of its ally in the popular revolution in July 1979 which bought the Sandinista National Liberation Front (FSLN) to power.

From Carter to Reagan: the new cold war in the south

The inauguration of Jimmy Carter as president of the United States on 20 January 1977 heralded a turnabout in US Latin American policy similar to that effected by President Kennedy 16 years earlier. In much the same way as Kennedy had put the neglected southern neighbours back at centre stage, Carter now gave them an important place in his overall foreign-policy concept, which went far beyond the laissez-faire principles of his immediate predecessors.

Although the Nixon and Ford administrations had more or less surrendered Latin American policy to the whims of American economic interests, at least one of its luminaries had mapped out some activity. During his confirmation hearings in September 1973, the future secretary of state, Henry Kissinger, had declared his intention to give a high priority to US–Latin American relations. Soon after his appointment he began to woo the Latin Americans with the flattering offer of a 'new dialogue' and a commitment to regional co-operation in a spirit of equality. Although the 1975 Trade Act (with its specific exclusion of Venezuela and Ecuador from tariff concessions) put a stop to the dialogue even before it had begun, Kissinger nevertheless planned an extensive tour of the region, hoping in particular to improve relations with the rising economic power Brazil. He had to postpone the trip on several occasions because of other pressing commitments, but eventually visited six countries (Venezuela, Peru, Brazil, Colombia, Costa Rica and Guatemala) in eight hectic days in February 1976. During numerous meetings, receptions, and press conferences it became clear, however, that he was not rushing from capital to capital to express new-found sympathy for the Latin Americans but rather to anticipate difficulties for his country arising from the energy crisis and the shortage of raw materials.

In comparison, the Carter administration's Latin American policy seemed informed less by pragmatism and more by idealistic, even moralistic, considerations. Widely regarded as a significant new and hopeful departure, it reversed several key elements of earlier policies. Most importantly, the new administration promised to abandon the East–West straitjacket and to view international relations as a multipolar structure which included a North–South dimension, and to abandon the uniform Latin American policy in favour of a differentiated approach to each country which took into account specific national interests and concerns.

The philosophical position behind the new approach was called 'trilateralism'.

The 'enlightened' imperialists, the liberal and cosmopolitan east-coast establishment that controlled vast transnational economic empires, had realized well before Carter's inauguration that the United States' relative loss of power in the 1970s, both on the world political stage and in the world market, would compel it to relinquish its claim as the undisputed leading world power and move away from the bilateral confrontation of the two superpowers towards a 'partnership' with the emerging powers of Western Europe and Japan. Now that the 'American century' (the title of a book published in 1941 by Henry Luce, the owner of *Time* and *Life*) had come to an end, it was argued, the United States should seek to retain its position in the international system and regain lost positions in the Third World and in the communist world in concert with the other industrialized democracies.

The notion of trilateralism was first put forward in 1973 by the Trilateral Commission, a new think tank of business people and politicians chaired by David Rockefeller, director of the Chase Manhattan Bank. Trilateralists also dominated the influential Council on Foreign Relations, of which prominent figures like Kissinger, Cyrus Vance (Carter's first secretary of state) and George Bush (Reagan's vice-president and elected president in 1988) were members. Their slogan was, quite simply, 'capitalism first, America second'. Many of them gained positions of power in the Carter administration, and those who did not helped to develop a consistent overall plan for the new administration, including, among other elements, the integration of the South in the world economy, the creation of a new international economic order, and a new human-rights policy.

Two reports prepared by the independent Commission on US–Latin American Relations, known as the Linowitz reports, were particularly influential in shaping the new administration's Latin American policy. This 20-member commission (including six trilateralists) set up under the auspices of the Ford Foundation and chaired by Sol M. Linowitz, a lawyer and the US ambassador to the OAS under Johnson, set out its liberal prescriptions in 'The Americas in a Changing World', a report published in October 1974 and updated in the run-up to Carter's inauguration and published anew under the programmatic title 'The United States and Latin America: Next Steps' in December 1976. These reports recommended, in brief: avoiding paternalism or domination in relations with the Latin Americans; respecting the sovereignty of the Latin American countries; assigning fundamental importance to human rights; and linking the dispensation of military aid to a regime's human-rights record. Their specific proposals included more normal relations with Cuba, the renegotiation of the Panama Canal treaty and the investigation of human-rights violations in Chile. It was on these three issues that the Carter administration's Latin American policy would subsequently be put to the test.

The new morality reflected in these guidelines was less an expression of a guilty conscience than an indication of the profound crisis of US imperialism in the western hemisphere. Nor did this pragmatic reassessment arise from political naïvety. The ultimate aim of the trilateral strategy remained the protection of US interests. With regard to Latin America and the Caribbean the new foreign policy endeavoured to ensure stability for the benefit of US economic interests by making some essentially tactical concessions and by adapting tactics and policy instruments to changing realities. Substantive changes to US objectives were never seriously intended, and therefore the Carter administration's policy in essence did not differ from its ostensibly far more reactionary successor.

During the first two years of its term the Carter administration stuck to the proposed course. As President Carter declared in his inaugural address and reaffirmed in a speech to the OAS council on 14 April 1977, the commitment to human rights was 'a fundamental tenet of our foreign policy' and 'Our moral sense dictates a clear-cut preference for those societies which share with us an abiding respect for individual human rights'.[3] After the administration made clear its interest in a normalization of relations with Cuba, the two governments signed an agreement on fishing rights on 27 April and established interest sections in friendly embassies in each other's capitals on 1 September. And on 21 January 1978 the state department approved the exports of pharmaceutical products to Cuba, the first small breach in the US economic blockade. On the human rights front, the administration on 1 June 1977 signed the Inter-American Convention on Human Rights, which had been adopted in 1969 but which its predecessors had neglected to endorse, and it cut aid to the military regimes in Chile and Argentina because of their appalling human-rights records. It also passed the third test of its Latin American policy when, on 7 September 1977, President Carter and the Panamanian leader, General Omar Torrijos, signed, in the presence of the heads of government of almost all Latin American countries (only Cuba and Mexico were absent), two new treaties on the status and operation of the Panama Canal.

The canal treaties brought Panama considerable economic benefits, which, however, were more than balanced by a number of political concessions extracted by the Americans. The new arrangements in no real sense prejudiced US interests, for although formal ownership was relinquished the United States retained effective control over the canal. Right-wing groups nevertheless decried the treaties as a sell-out and fought a strong rearguard action against the treaties, which fuelled Latin American doubts on US policy in the long term. At the same time the region's more repressive military regimes, increasingly concerned for their survival in the face of a moralistic US policy, adopted a more aggressive stance. Using the argument that they would not tolerate further interference in their internal affairs, some (Chile, Uruguay, Argentina, Brazil, Guatemala, El Salvador and Nicaragua) even declined any further military aid from the United States, to the chagrin of the US arms manufacturers. The administration also made itself unpopular among many Latin Americans — by no means just the hard right — with its commitment to nuclear non-proliferation and restrictions on arms transfers. Under these and other pressures the new policy began to unravel. Despite all the good intentions, inter-American relations reached an almost unprecedented low in the course of 1977.

His Latin American strategy apparently in ruins, President Carter meekly gave in to right-wing pressure at home. The 'loss' of Nicaragua in July 1979, which traumatized Washington's political élite in much the same way as the 'loss' of China had 30 years earlier, sealed the return to an old-style policy. To erect a cordon sanitaire around Nicaragua, the Americans once again began to dispense generous military aid to the neighbouring countries, military advisers were sent to El Salvador, and the US southern military command (based in the Canal Zone) hurriedly devised plans to co-ordinate the activities of the Central American armies. Reports in September 1980 that 3,000 Soviet troops had 'arrived' in Cuba to challenge the US position in the hemisphere — they had in fact been stationed on the island for the last 17 years — provided the pretext to revert to the previous policy of isolating Cuba. The CIA's destabilization tactics which had proved so successful in Chile in the early 1970s were now used in Jamaica against the socialist government of the People's National Party (PNP) led by Michael Manley. US warships once again frequented the Caribbean in large numbers, carrying out extensive manoeuvres. Bilateral aid to compliant Caribbean countries was increased sharply, with the Dominican Republic and Haiti benefiting most from the about-face on the importance of human rights. (Aid to the region actually doubled between 1977 and 1980, not least because Washington was concerned to fill the strategic vacuum left by the British withdrawal from its former colonies, now newly independent island states.) In short, from late 1979 onwards, those Americans with interests in Latin America and the Caribbean could rest assured that it was 'business as usual' after the unsettling first two years of the Carter administration.

The change of policy, then, had been effected well before Ronald Reagan entered the White House on 20 January 1981. But the right-wing think tanks that would prove so influential over the next eight years — such as the Center for Strategic and International Studies (CSIS, to which the secretary of state, Alexander Haig, and the national security adviser, Richard Allen, contributed), the Hoover Institute (of which Reagan himself was an honorary fellow), the American Enterprise Institute (AEI) and the Heritage Foundation — wanted to go much further. The hard right had little difficulty in imposing its extremist line, for within the Reagan coalition comprising the traditional right, new right, neoconservatives and internationalists or trilateralists, the latter carried the least weight. (In a report entitled 'Governance in the Western Hemisphere', published under the auspices of the Aspen Institute for Humanistic Studies in June 1982, the trilateralists tried to revive, unsuccessfully, their argument that the United States should acknowledge the 'asymmetry of power' between the two Americas and that it should offer the Latins a partnership in foreign and economic issues.)

Ronald Reagan's personal political philosophy was of course far too crude to permit any nuances in foreign policy. When he accepted the presidential nomination at the Republican convention on 17 July 1980 he invoked 'manifest destiny' and divine providence. He saw the United States as a beacon of 'freedom' fighting a lonely battle against the totalitarian Soviet Union, the 'evil empire' — any run-of-the-mill western would supply the relevant ingredients. He owed his election to his appeal to the Americans' innate feeling of superiority, or rather to his confident reassertion that America and Americans were still 'the first and the best' in the wake of setbacks in Iran, Nicaragua and elsewhere. Many Americans longed for simple truths at a time of complex world-political changes and they wanted to see a 'strong' president at a time of perceived US weakness in foreign-policy matters. Onto a simple and self-righteous americanism — the missionary zeal which had inspired his nineteenth-century predecessors — Reagan grafted a rhetoric which was supposed to assure his compatriots that no one would ever dare push them around again.

In much the same way that the Linowitz reports had influenced the Carter administration, a report prepared by members of the rabidly anti-communist Council for Inter-American Security (CIAS) had a decisive influence on the Reagan administration's formulation of its Latin American policy. The following gives an indication of its import and tone:

> Containment of the Soviet Union is not enough. Détente is dead. Survival demands a new US foreign policy. America must seize the initiative or perish. For World War Three is almost over. America is everywhere in retreat … a worldwide counterprojection of America is in the offing. The hour of decision can no longer be postponed.[4]

Entitled 'A new inter-American policy for the 1980s', this confidential document argued, in essence, that Latin America was of vital importance to the United States within the context of the East–West struggle. What it called 'the projection of US global power' demanded a friendly Caribbean and a supportive South America. It accused the previous administration of having gambled away US power and influence in the region, particularly in the Caribbean, which, it warned, was turning into a 'Marxist-Leninist lake'.[5] To halt the communist onslaught, it even called for a 'liberation war against Castro'.[6]

The two men primarily responsible for the CIAS paper, Roger W. Fontaine and Gordon Sumner, both gained office and prestige in the administration: Fontaine was appointed the Latin American expert to the national security council, and Sumner, a retired general, was appointed special adviser to the assistant secretary for inter-American affairs, Thomas Enders.

Intent on disproving the traditional view that the Americans never paid enough attention to the countries south of the Rio Grande, the Reagan administration returned to the 'politics of strength' of the Eisenhower and above all the Truman administrations. It was no coincidence that the influential Fontaine, for instance, spoke of the need for 'nothing less than a Truman doctrine for the region', a Central American version of the 1947 doctrine (designed for Greece and Turkey) 'to help regimes in serious trouble who were friendly to the United States under attack from armed minorities that were aided and abetted by outside, hostile forces', then the Soviet Union, now the Soviet Union and Cuba.[7] The administration adopted this as a cornerstone of its Latin American policy, which received far greater priority than at any time since the early 1960s.

Putting America first and capitalism second, the Reagan administration launched an ideological crusade to regain lost positions and was even willing occasionally to subordinate the interests of big business to the cause. It summarily abandoned Carter's human-rights policy on the grounds that it impeded the realization of US objectives in the western hemisphere. Human rights, the argument went, were relative values of secondary importance to the national interest. (Not surprisingly, therefore, the regime of the Haitian dictator Jean-

Claude 'Baby Doc' Duvalier was not deemed repressive enough to warrant the withdrawal of US financial support.) Furthermore, on the basis of sophistry originated by Jeane Kirkpatrick, the US ambassador to the United Nations and an unreconstructed cold-war warrior, the administration developed a spurious distinction between 'authoritarian' and 'totalitarian' regimes in Latin America, with the right-wing military dictatorships falling into the less damnable former category and Cuba and Nicaragua falling into the latter. This shameless differentiation allowed it to justify, for instance, the resumption of loans by international financial institutions to the military regimes in Argentina, Chile, Paraguay and Uruguay while arguing for withholding loans to revolutionary Nicaragua.

Giving a high priority to Latin America was not enough in itself, as the administration discovered to its cost during the Falklands/Malvinas war between Argentina and Britain in April–June 1982. Haig completed a total of 32,965 air miles in twelve days of shuttle diplomacy between Washington, London and Buenos Aires to try to prevent a war between the United States' NATO ally and its Rio Pact ally over the god-forsaken but strategically important islands in the South Atlantic. When, on 30 April, Haig announced the failure of his mediation efforts and the administration's decision to side with Britain, it was clear that the Americans would lose, whatever the outcome of this senseless war. Argentina, hitherto a valued partner of the United States in the struggle against the communist revolutionaries in Latin America, now found itself cast as an enemy. Deeply angered, the reactionary military regime in Buenos Aires, which had fought a brutal dirty war against its own people in the late 1970s, most unusually began to express anti-US sentiments. At a conference of the Non-Aligned Movement in Havana in June 1982, the Argentine foreign minister, Nicanor Costa Méndez, found praise for those countries which had succeeded in breaking out of their dependence on the superpowers, even mentioning Cuba by name. ₁

After the United States had made this enormous strategic miscalculation in its relations with Latin America, President Reagan went on a tour of the region in early December to retrieve lost ground. But in his inimitable way he managed only to make matters worse. At the official banquet hosted by the president of Brazil he toasted Bolivia (a slip by an old man, but also indicative of Washington's scant regard for Latin America) and in Colombia he found himself at odds with his counterpart on Central American policy. At least he was in his element at the final stage of his trip, in Honduras — the main battleground of the struggle against communist subversion and the Moscow–Havana–Managua axis.

As noted earlier, Central America and the Caribbean took centre stage in the Reagan administration's foreign policy. Although developments in naval, aircraft and missile technology since 1945 probably considerably reduced the strategic importance of the Caribbean, it was still considered the springboard for US domination of all of Latin America and the gateway to the Atlantic, while the Panama Canal was still considered the United States' most important inland waterway. The bases at Guantánamo, San Juan and Roosevelt's Road (on Puerto Rico) and in the Canal Zone, as well as dozens of smaller air and naval bases in the region, were considered vital outposts for the protection of US national security. Shipping in the Caribbean and the South Atlantic could be controlled from Puerto Rico, and the Eastern Caribbean formed part of the US navy's undersea surveillance system, monitoring submarine movements in the Atlantic. Moreover, the Caribbean basin was the United States' most important source of raw materials within the hemisphere: Mexico was the major supplier of silver, zinc, gypsum, antimony, mercury, bismuth, selenium, barium, rhenium and lead; Venezuela supplied around a third of US imports of iron ore; Jamaica supplied nearly half of bauxite imports; and Caribbean refineries produced more than half of the oil products imported by the United States.

The Reagan administration's strategy to protect the concentrated US interests in the Caribbean differed in some respects from that of its predecessors. First, it tried to regionalize US policy by moving away from isolated interventions in particular countries towards an integrated concept to prevent the spread of liberation movements across national boundaries. Second, it tried to give US policy an inter-American guise, by: calling for a revival of the Rio Pact and the OAS; recommending the 'interamericanization' (add: while retaining US control) of the Panama Canal; reviving CONDECA and holding joint manoeuvres in Central America; and proposing to transform the School of the Americas — the 'school of coups' founded and run by the US army in the Canal Zone to train Latin America's military men in the art of counterinsurgency — into an inter-American institution (under the Panama Canal treaties, it would have had to close its doors as a purely US centre in 1984 in any case). And third, it stressed bilateralism, granting financial aid primarily on a country-by-country basis, which enabled it to protect US interests and demand concessions more effectively than was possible through the international financial institutions.(The above observations also applied to the United States' Latin American policy in general.)

The CBI constituted the one exception to the bilateralist line. When it was first mooted in early 1981, this multilateral aid package, described by the administration as a Marshall Plan for the region but by most others more sceptically as a 'mini Marshall Plan', was supposed to provide $1 billion for the region and involve, apart from the United States, Mexico, Canada, Brazil, Colombia, Venezuela and the European Community and Japan. But when President Reagan outlined a detailed proposal in a speech to the OAS on 24 February 1982 only Mexico, Canada and Venezuela remained as potential donor countries and the total package had shrunk to $350 million. Cuba, Grenada and Nicaragua would of course be excluded from the plan, which included direct aid as well as a range of trade preferences. Draft legislation for the CBI was submitted to Congress in March 1982 with a request for urgent adoption. Its slow progress prompted the president to upbraid the legislators, but to no avail. The second, miniature, edition of the Alliance for Progress was doomed. The CBI was effectively abandoned even before any funds were made available.

The war against Nicaragua

Organized in 1962 as a guerilla movement committed to the overthrow of the

Somoza regime, the FSLN developed a strategy of prolonged people's war in the 1970s and was able to build a strong base among peasants and workers as well as sections of the middle-class opposition in Nicaragua to the point where it posed a serious threat to the dictator. The Americans viewed the Sandinistas' advance with increasing concern, not least because Nicaragua had always had a special place in their imperialist designs — the US ambassador had written in 1890: 'The nation that controls Lake Nicaragua will control the destiny of the western hemisphere'.[8] No doubt Washington would have given a great deal to thwart the sons and daughters of the legendary Augusto Sandino. But on 21 July 1979 they entered Managua in triumph, and Somoza fled the country with the millions of dollars he had extorted from his people.

The Americans made a number of eleventh-hour attempts to prevent a Sandinista victory. In June 1979 they tried to secure passage of an OAS resolution calling for the creation of an inter-American military force to intervene in Nicaragua. But this transparent attempt to gain international legitimacy for US intervention failed, as did the plan to preserve the national guard — the notorious force the Americans had created in Nicaragua 40 years earlier to maintain order — and the proposal to replace Somoza with what was euphemistically called a 'moderate' government. Apparently the Americans envisaged a kind of 'Somocism' without Somoza. But the Nicaraguan people wanted to be rid of both, and they sent Washington's man in Managua packing. They were able to do so in no small measure because of two favourable geopolitical factors which dominated the 1970s — the relative weakness of the United States since the Vietnam war and East–West detente. From the beginning the Americans tried to undo the realities created by the new government in Managua. To wipe the 'second Cuba' off the political map, it was decided in the first instance to apply economic and financial pressure.

Plundered by Somoza, Nicaragua desperately needed financial aid for reconstruction. Physical damage from the war alone was estimated at $600 million, capital flight because of the war at another $500 million. Moreover, Somoza had left a mere $3.3 million in foreign reserves. The Sandinistas had no choice but to request massive foreign aid from the international financial institutions, the commercial banks and other governments, above all the government of the northern economic giant. In December 1979 Jaime Wheelock and other FSLN leaders undertook a 14-day goodwill tour of the United States to promote the Nicaraguan revolution and lobby for aid to rebuild their battered country.

But most doors in official Washington remained firmly closed. Congress spent months deliberating a loan of $75 million. In the course of the debates the House of Representatives twice went into secret session, for the first time since 1830, to discuss Cuban influence in Nicaragua. The loan was eventually authorized in June 1980, but with the conditions that most of it would go to the private business sector and that it would not be used in projects which involved Cuban personnel. (It should be noted here that the two sides in the debate on aid to Nicaragua were by no means as implacably opposed as might appear. The polemics of hardliners and softliners, hawks and doves, on Capitol Hill were little more than tactical skirmishes. Both sides agreed that control over Nicaragua should be reasserted at the earliest opportunity.)

The Sandinistas profited little from Washington's measly dollar donations, most of which in any case were tied to the purchase of US goods and would hardly have been made had it not been for the banks wanting to collect debts incurred under Somoza. One of President Reagan's first acts in office was to 'punish' Nicaragua, which he imagined right at the top of the Soviets' hitlist for Central America. On 23 January 1981 he announced the withholding of the remaining $15 million of the aid package on the grounds that Nicaragua was providing arms to the left-wing guerillas in El Salvador, a decision confirmed three months later.

The Reagan administration moved quickly beyond the credit squeeze and applied a whole array of measures to pressurize into submission the government of one of the United States' weakest neighbours because it did not fit into its one-dimensional worldview. The economic warfare included ploys which had been tested successfully by the CIA in Chile in the 1970s, such as: forging córdobas and dollars to produce bottlenecks in supplies and push up prices; buying up foodstuffs and essential goods to engineer shortages; attacking key economic infrastructure, such as bridges, the oil refinery and the cement factory; reducing the quota for sugar imports from 58,800 to a mere 6,000 tons; and blocking applications for credits and loans from the international financial institutions — so that at Washington's behest the IMF stopped lending money to Nicaragua after 1980, the World Bank reduced credits for Nicaragua from $52 million in 1980 to $16 million in 1982 and the Inter-American Development Bank (IDB) stopped loans to Nicaragua until September 1982. Private enterprise also contributed to the blackmail, with Standard Fruit reneging on a contract for the marketing of Nicaraguan bananas and the Sears stores moving their stocks to Costa Rica.

But it soon became apparent that these official reprisals and the pinpricks by the private sector were only the beginning. The most effective weapons in Washington's arsenal were political and military, namely the financing of right-wing opposition parties in Nicaragua and the financing and training of Nicaraguan exiles (mostly members of the disbanded national guard) into a guerilla force operating mainly from Honduras — the infamous counter-revolutionaries or 'contras'.

As a prelude, the state department on 23 February 1981 published what it described as incontrovertible proof of Nicaraguan and Cuban complicity in supplying arms to the Farabundo Martí National Liberation Front (FMLN) in El Salvador. The administration threatened both Nicaragua and Cuba with intervention and continued to do so long after the authenticity of the documentary evidence had been convincingly questioned. (Two years later a former CIA analyst, David MacMichael, revealed that there had been no confirmed reports of arms shipments from Nicaragua to El Salvador since April 1981.)

But the Americans' real aims were rather more ambitious than preventing the export of the Nicaraguan revolution to neighbouring countries. The Reagan administration wanted the overthrow of the Sandinistas at all costs. Planning for the war against Nicaragua began immediately after Reagan took office, with an assistant secretary of state, Thomas O. Enders, acting as co-ordinator. On 9

March 1981, President Reagan gave the CIA a free hand in the preparation of military operations. And on 1 December he authorized a directive prepared by the national security council (number 17) which called for a $19 million destabilizing programme of paramilitary, political and intelligence work in Nicaragua, including the arming of opposition groups. A special operations group at CIA headquarters codenamed 'Programa Nicaragua' co-ordinated the 'covert' war against Nicaragua.

But the assault on Nicaragua, which hawks in the Reagan administration vilified as an outpost of something called the 'terrorist international' established by Moscow and Havana, did not remain covert for very long. Already on 13 November 1981 Haig had let slip in a hearing of the House committee on foreign affairs that he would support right-wing forces intending to overthrow the Sandinistas. Three months later, on 14 February 1982, the *Washington Post* reported the existence of the national security council's secret plans. Although neither the CIA nor the White House denied the report, they sought to placate public opinion by duplicitously claiming that the intention was merely to pressure the Sandinistas, not to oust them.

The anti-Sandinista campaign, shamelessly publicized henceforth, became an almost frivolously executed attack on a sovereign Latin American country — a blatant violation of international law, a violation of the OAS charter, and in the end also unlawful under US law after the House of Representatives on 21 December 1982 adopted the so-called Boland Amendment prohibiting the executive from spending funds to overthrow the Sandinista government. But a Democratic-dominated House would not be able to deter the Republican administration from prosecuting its crusade against evil, and in any case the latter could rely on a solid majority for its policies in the Senate.

In the meantime the not-so-covert war against the Sandinistas was in full swing. With the $80 million of official US military and non-military aid they received between 1981 and 1984 the contras built up a massive operation comprising a political headquarters in Miami and ten training camps located both in Nicaragua and Honduras, where 10,000 former members of Somoza's national guard and 2,000 Miskito Indians received training from 50 CIA agents as well as dozens of former US soldiers and intelligence officers. Organized in two groups set up under the auspices of the CIA — the Nicaraguan Democratic Forces (FDN) operating from Honduras and the Revolutionary Democratic Alliance (ARDE) operating from Costa Rica — the contras launched their dirty war in northern Nicaragua. Despite their modern equipment they avoided direct confrontations with the Sandinista army. Instead they kidnapped peasants, raped women, massacred children and slaughtered teachers, civil servants and other representatives and supporters of the Sandinista system. They appeared to have no other ambition than to terrorize their people and to return their own country to its previous status as a US satellite.

When technical perfection was required, the CIA used its own people. On 11 October 1983 missiles launched from superfast Piranha boats exploded a fuel tank in the port of Corinto and in early 1984 commandos mined the Nicaraguan ports to paralyse shipping. (The Nicaraguan government subsequently brought a case to the International Court of Justice, which on 27 June 1986 convicted the United States of numerous violations of human rights and international law and called for the payment of compensation. Washington refused to recognize the jurisdiction of the court, and ignored the verdict.)

No matter how assiduously President Reagan and his propagandists tried to make out the contras to be 'freedom fighters', mentioning them in the same breath as the American founding fathers and the heroes of the French revolution, they were terrorists. And despite some half-hearted attempts initially to deny any direct involvement, it was clear that the Americans had recruited, organized, trained, led and supplied the contras from the beginning. The contras were their monstrous creation. By the end of 1985 the US-backed aggression had cost 11,000 Nicaraguan lives and caused economic damage calculated at $1.3 billion.

As evidence of the dirty war in Nicaragua mounted, the director of the CIA, William Casey, in January 1983 admitted to the intelligence committees of both houses of Congress that his organization had been involved in acts of sabotage committed by the contras. As ever, he pointed to the need to stop arms shipments from Nicaragua to the Salvadorean guerillas to justify the operations. The intelligence committee of the Democrat-controlled House of Representatives saw things differently, however. In a report issued on 14 May it criticized the methods adopted by the administration, the CIA's intelligence operations and that organization's link-up with the contras. The House on 28 July prohibited the funding of CIA operations against Nicaragua by 228 votes to 195 after a bitter three-day debate. But once again the Senate came to the administration's rescue. Its intelligence committee on 22 September voted to continue the CIA's covert actions against Nicaragua until what it called 'left-wing subversion' had been rooted out in Central America.

Washington's efforts to soften up the Sandinistas from within dovetailed with a strategy of containment, even encirclement, from without. On the basis of the domino theory, whose assumption that countries would fall to the communists in sequence had already been used to frighten a sceptical public during the Vietnam war, the Reagan administration decided at an early stage to mobilize Nicaragua's neighbours both against their own internal left-wing oppositions and against the Sandinistas. The stakes were high: the objective was to prevent Nicaragua, 'another Cuba', being followed by El Salvador as 'another Nicaragua', by Honduras as 'another El Salvador' and so on until, as Ronald Reagan declared with typical hyperbole during the 1980 election campaign, 'we're the last dom-ino'.[9]

In March 1981 the Reagan administration proposed, and Congress subsequently approved, quadrupling military aid to the junta in El Salvador from $5.9 million in 1980 to $35.4 million in 1981 and doubling the number of US military advisers in the country from 25 to 45, as well as doubling economic aid from $72.5 million to $148.4 million. In January 1982 the administration agreed to replace aircraft and helicopters knocked out by the guerillas, and allocated another $82 million in military and economic aid. The issue of respect for human rights was raised when Congress discussed new aid appropriations both in July 1982 and July 1983, and on both occasions the secretary of state, George Shultz, assured the legislators that the Salvadorean authorities had improved on their human-rights record. El Salvador, if one was to believe the administration, was at the forefront of the struggle for freedom, justice and democracy and against totalitarian oppression. The reality was rather different. The human-rights organization Amnesty International reported in 1982 that 'the Inter-American Commission on Human Rights [has] singled out El Salvador as one of the two countries where the commission considered that the most serious violations of the right to life took the form of summary executions' and in this context referred to 'state terrorism'.[10] The lives of peasants and workers counted for little in El Salvador, a country ruled by an oligarchy of 14 families which kept the masses at the margin of existence and where those even vaguely suspected of protesting against poverty and oppression were brutally murdered by paramilitary organizations or the army itself. Between 1979 and 1985, some 50,000 civilians were killed in the civil war.

A similar situation obtained in Guatemala, where left-wing guerilla movements opposing the successive military regimes greatly expanded their popular base in the 1970s and formed a united front, the Guatemalan National Revolutionary Unity (URNG), in February 1982. The rulers fought a war against their own people, particularly the Amerindian majority (which was also being marginalized by the expansion of cash-crop agriculture). Estimates put the number of civilian deaths attributable to state terror and unofficial death squads at between 30–70,000 for the period 1954–82, and at around 6,000 per year from 1983–86.

While the human-rights situation also worsened perceptibly in Honduras in the early 1980s, the political situation was slightly different in that country because of the presence of US troops and, no doubt related to this, the absence of a strong opposition. The Americans pumped massive military and development aid into Honduras with the intention of turning it into the main bulwark against 'communism' and the main base for the contras. By 1982 the Honduran army had become the largest in Central America. It benefited from the presence of 114 US military advisers and 1,000 US combat troops as well as frequent joint manoeuvres. The Americans' temporary presence became permanent from 1984 onwards, as they converted the country's airfields to military purposes and began to use them so extensively that Honduras became known as the United States' unsinkable aircraft carrier in Central America.

President Reagan raised the stakes dramatically on 1 July 1983 when he accused the Soviet Union, Cuba and Nicaragua, in even harsher tones than usual, of intending to enthral all of Central America. Words were followed by unequivocal deeds. US and Honduran troops held large-scale, joint land, sea and air manoeuvres (known as 'Big Pine II') in Honduras and off its Caribbean and Pacific coast from August until the following February. Military commanders and senior administration officials made great play of the potential offensive purposes of the simulated landings which formed a major element of the exercises. Moreover, as the US fleet set off for Central America, Jeane Kirkpatrick on 20 July openly urged the Nicaraguan people to remove the Sandinista government, and in November the defence secretary, Caspar Weinberger, the Republican leader in the Senate, Howard Baker, the special envoy to Central

America, Richard Stone, and the US ambassador in Costa Rica, Curtin Windsor, all went on record as saying that they could not exclude the possibility of military action against Nicaragua, including an invasion of the country. Amid growing concern that the administration might provoke a conflagration, two Democratic senators, Edward Kennedy and Gary Hart, introduced draft legislation to put a stop to the US-backed and -organized aggression, but to no avail. The administration could continue to play the military option for all it was worth.

All this was happening against a background of Latin American attempts to defuse the conflicts in Central America. To this end the governments of Colombia, Mexico, Panama and Venezuela on 9 January 1983 formed the Contadora group (named after the Panamanian island where the decision to launch the mediation effort was taken). On 17 July it proposed a ten-point draft peace plan for the region, whose key provisions included the creation of demilitarized zones, international supervision of borders, a ban on arms supplies to the region and the withdrawal of all extra-regional armed forces. In response, the Cuban government offered to withdraw its advisers from Nicaragua and suspend arms shipments, while the Nicaraguan government offered Honduras a non-aggression treaty and proposed a comprehensive ban on arms shipments to El Salvador. Washington's only concrete reaction, apart from paying lip-service to the plan, was the mobilization of US troops around Nicaragua. When Managua made several gestures of good will in the latter part of 1983 — such as relaxing press censorship and declaring an amnesty for political opponents — Washington did not respond. In fact for the next three years it did its utmost to undermine the Contadora mediation effort.

The political solutions which began to be discussed more widely in early 1984 appeared to reduce the likelihood of a direct US intervention in Nicaragua. But the Reagan administration's interest in or commitment to a settlement arose only out of short-term tactical considerations. The 1984 election campaign already cast its shadow, and this no doubt accounted for the more restrained tones emanating from Washington. The military option had by no means been discarded, as evidenced by the simultaneous broadening of the joint US–Honduran manoeuvres into a permanent US military presence in Honduras. The hypocrisy behind the Americans' attitude to Central America was also revealed by the work of a bipartisan commission on Central America set up by President Reagan and chaired by Kissinger. In its final report published on 11 January 1984, the 12-member commission linked further aid to El Salvador to an improvement in the human-rights situation there while at the same time effectively endorsing, although not unanimously, the removal of the Nicaraguan government by the contras. (Nothing was ever heard of the commission's main proposal, an injection of $24 billion in development aid over a five-year period to help the five countries overcome the worst of their problems.)

Having been re-elected in November 1984, President Reagan marked the return to the previous hardline policy with the proclamation on 1 May 1985 of a total trade embargo on Nicaragua. This escalation of the economic war — more of symbolic than practical value, since trade between the two countries had already declined considerably in the previous years — contravened US law, the

OAS charter (which explicitly prohibits the application of economic pressure by one state against another) and the free-trade arrangements under the General Agreement on Tariffs and Trade (GATT). On 4 December the UN general assembly denounced the embargo and reaffirmed the right of every sovereign country to determine its own development priorities and political organization by 84 votes to 4 (Gambia, Grenada, Israel and the United States) and 37 abstentions. The Americans of course took no notice.

Under George Bush, who was elected president in November 1988, US Central American policy was expected to be stripped of some of its more paranoid and apocalyptic elements. But as long as the Americans continue to view their back yard through the East–West prism and refuse to recognize that its problems are rooted in the North–South conflict, there can be little hope for a substantive policy change. The economic war continues under Bush, and Washington's contribution to the Central American peace process remains lacklustre. The simple truth is that countries which do not accept American values and dictates will be deemed 'bad' neighbours, with all the far-reaching consequences of such. That is unlikely to change in the foreseeable future.

Epilogue: Grenada 1983, the first in a new round of US interventions?

Grenada is a small island in the Caribbean between Venezuela and Trinidad, only 33 kilometers long and 19 kilometers wide, with a population of around 100,000, producing nutmeg, cocoa, sugar and rum. It was claimed for Spain by Columbus in 1498 — he nearly sailed straight past — and conquered by the British 250 years later. It became independent in 1974 as part of the Commonwealth. In the early 1980s it attracted the attention, briefly but fatefully, of the colossus of the north.

On 13 March 1979 the New Jewel Movement (NJM), led by Maurice Bishop, ousted Eric Gairy, the mentally somewhat confused dictator and a friend of the United States, in a bloodless coup while Gairy was at the United Nations urging research into unidentified flying objects. To the chagrin of the Americans, the NJM began to introduce socialist policies — Jewel being an acronym for Joint Endeavour for Welfare, Education and Liberation — based on a kind of direct democracy. This alarmed Washington not because of its economic interests in Grenada — which were minimal — but because of strategic considerations. It feared that the island, at the juncture of some of the Caribbean's major shipping lanes, which transported half of all US oil imports, might fall into communist hands. The victory of the Sandinistas in Nicaragua four months later transformed this specific fear into a near-panic about the future of the whole region.

A new airport at Point Salines which the Grenadians began constructing with the help of Cuban workers, but which also involved other foreign interests, notably British, provided a focus for the Americans' paranoia. The Reagan administration saw the airport as a future Soviet–Cuban base, a staging post for a Cuban air route to Africa, and a direct threat to US national security. In fact the Grenadians hoped to gain access to the international tourism trade, a potentially lucrative source of foreign exchange for the country. Hitherto visitors could only reach the island via Martinique or Barbados, with the final leg of the journey to be completed in small propeller planes and uncomfortable buses — not an ideal itinerary to promote mass tourism. On the principle that any publicity is good publicity, the Grenadians appeared not too concerned by the fuss made over the new airport: 'Now that the Americans have declared Point Salines to be a threat to their national security, we are building the best-known airport in the world', Bishop declared sarcastically.[11]

In mid-1983 conflicts and rivalries within the NJM came to the fore, which fuelled speculation in the United States that the Soviet Union and Cuba were deeply involved in the country's politics. The Americans claimed that Bishop, their new-found friend, was being pushed out by a radical left-wing group around the deputy prime minister, Bernard Coard, and the commander of the army, Hudson Austin. It was certainly true that the group around Coard secured a majority on the NJM's central committee, and then took control of the army and placed Bishop under house arrest on 13 October. Six days later, after strikes and demonstrations in support of the former leader, Bishop was murdered by Coard supporters (the exact details have never been established).

The Americans of course saw evidence of a Cuban plot, but it would have defied logic for the Cubans to participate in a coup with uncertain outcome and thereby to provide the Americans with an excuse to do what they had done for decades — send in the marines 'to protect the lives of US citizens'. President Fidel Castro did everything to avert this. He accused the Coard group of endangering the revolution and likened them to Pol Pot and the Khmer Rouge, rejected the new rulers' request to strengthen the Cuban presence on the island (at the time totalling 784 women and men, including 640 construction workers), and on 22 October he offered to enter into discussions with the Americans on ways to ensure the safety of Cuban and American citizens on the island.

On 24 October the White House spokesman still assured the public that none of the US citizens in Grenada — mainly around 1,000 students at Grenada's medical school — had been hurt or were in any danger. Nevertheless, on the following morning some 1,900 US marines, assisted by 600 troops from six Caribbean countries (Antigua and Barbuda, Barbados, Dominica, Jamaica, Saint Vincent and Saint Lucia), landed on the island without prior warning or a declaration of war. The pacification operation, known as 'Urgent Fury', eventually involved a total of 6,000 marines. (In the course of the invasion the US commander ordered shots to be fired at the Cuban construction workers — 90 minutes before Washington's negative answer on a joint effort to safeguard foreign citizens reached Havana.)

Questioned by a sceptical media, and to give the operation even a semblance of legitimacy, Washington had to fall back on references to 'intelligence reports' on the security situation on the island. Cuban officials calculated afterwards that in the desperate effort to justify the invasion to world public opinion the administration had lied on 19 occasions, including 13 directly involving the president himself. Attention focused particularly on the administration's claim that as events were unfolding it had been informed by the Barbadian government that the governor-general of Grenada, Sir Paul Scoon, had used a confidential channel to pass on a request for an intervention by the Organization of Eastern Caribbean States (OECS) to restore order on the island. The only problem with this account was that Scoon's request was made public only *after* the first troops had landed. This was not the only blemish on the ostensibly multinational enterprise. In its defence, secretary of state George Shultz repeatedly invoked the Rio Pact, whose article 3 he claimed justified collective action in the interests of regional security. He conveniently failed to mention that this article permits such action only in the event of an American state becoming the victim of aggression from *outside the hemisphere*. Should this not be the case, as it patently was not in Grenada, international obligations required a meeting of the OAS before any action could be taken.

The Reagan administration cared little for the niceties of international law when it wanted to use the big stick. The assault by the world's most powerful military power on one of its smallest countries did not constitute justice but the rule of the jungle. It was meant to set an example to those who where deemed to threaten the national security of the United States. There was ample evidence in early 1984 that the administration considered the invasion of Grenada a dry run for interventions in other Central America and Caribbean countries. The colossus of the north had changed little since the rise of American imperialism at the end of the last century.

Notes

1. Quoted in North American Congress on Latin America 1971 p. 11.
2. Jonas, 'An Overview: 50 Years of Revolution and Intervention in Central America', in Dixon and Jonas (eds.) 1983 p. 21.
3. Inaugural Address, 20 January 1977, quoted in *Keesing's Contemporary Archives*, p. 28245.
4. Committee of Santa Fé 1980 p. 1ff.
5. Ibid., p. 1.
6. Ibid., p. 32.
7. Interview in *Miami Herald*, 24 August 1980, quoted in Pearce 1981 p. 172.
8. Quoted in Crawley 1984 p. 34ff.
9. Quoted in Pearce, op. cit., p. 172.
10. Amnesty International, *Report 1982*, p. 138.
11. Address at public meeting in Santiago de Cuba, 27 July 1983, recorded by the author.

Appendix

1. US-Latin American trade 1825–1980
(US$ million)

year	exports from US	imports from Latin America	trade balance
1825	27	21	+6
1830	20	17	+3
1835	27	27	0
1840	24	24	0
1845	23	24	-1
1850	20	33	-13
1855	34	55	-21
1860	46	80	-34
1865	81	67	+14
1870	54	117	-63
1875	65	163	-98
1880	64	179	-115
1885	66	146	-80
1890	93	199	-106
1895	99	209	-110
1900	132	185	-53
1905	177	316	-139
1910	263	408	-145
1915	275	574	-299
1920	1,581	1,812	-231
1925	892	1,045	-153
1930	698	793	-95
1935	383	490	-107
1940	788	665	+123
1945	1,386	1,749	-363
1950	2,863	3,103	-240
1955	3,499	3,609	-110
1960	3,874	3,963	-89
1965	4,266	4,370	-104
1970	6,533	5,836	+697
1975	17,099	16,057	+1,042
1980	38,718	37,229	+1,489

Source: *Historical Statistics of the United States*

206 Â Hemisphere to Itself

2. Direct US investment in Latin America 1880–1980

(US$ million)

1880	100
1890	250
1897	300
1914	1,700
1919	2,400
1929	3,519
1936	2,847
1940	2,771
1950	4,445
1955	6,031
1960	7,481
1965	9,441
1970	12,252
1975	16,394
1980	20,037

Source: *Historical Statistics of the United States*

3. Inter-American conferences since 1826

conference	date	venue	outcome
Panama Congress	1826	Panama City	Formal plan for Latin American confederation (not followed up)
First Pan-American Conference	1889-90	Washington	Foundation of International Union of American Republics and Bureau of American Republics
Second Pan-American Conference	1901-2	Mexico City	Arbitration treaty on financial demands; acceptance of Hague Convention
Third Pan-American Conference	1906	Rio de Janeiro	Debt repayments issue referred to Hague Conference
Fourth Pan-American Conference	1910	Buenos Aires	Bureau reorganized into Pan American Union (PAU)
Fifth Pan-American	1923	Santiago	Agreement on Conference resolution of regional conflicts; chair of PAU made elected office
Sixth Pan-American Conference	1928	Havana	Convention on the Rights and Duties of States regarding civil wars
Seventh Pan-American	1933	Montevideo	Convention on the Rights

Conference			and Duties of States; principle of non-intervention
Inter-American Conference on the Maintenance of Peace	1936	Buenos Aires	Declaration on inter-American solidarity and co-operation; reaffirmation of non-intervention
Eighth Pan-American Conference	1938	Lima	Regular consultations of foreign ministers
Inter-American Conference on Problems of War and Peace	1945	Mexico City	Act of Chapultepec
Inter-American Conference on the Preservation of Hemispheric Peace and Security	1947	Rio de Janeiro	Rio Pact
Ninth Pan-American Conference	1948	Bogotá	Foundation of the Organization of American States (OAS/OEA)
Tenth Pan-American Conference	1954	Caracas	Declaration against communist aggression
First Extraordinary Inter-American Conference	1964	Washington	Requirements for admission of new OAS members
Second Extraordinary Inter-American Conference	1965	Rio de Janeiro	Broader scope for Inter-American Commission on Human Rights
Third Extraordinary Inter-American Conference	1967	Buenos Aires	Revision of OAS charter
Summit meeting of American heads of state	1967	Punta del Este	Action plan for strengthening the Alliance for Progress and the economic integration of Latin America
First Special OAS General Assembly	1970	Washington	Anti-terrorism resolution
Second Special OAS General Assembly	1970	Washington	Anti-terrorism resolution
Third Special OAS General Assembly	1971	Washington	Anti-terrorism resolution
First OAS General Assembly	1971	San José	Resolutions on control of arms expenditure, trade expansion; organizational changes

2–13 OAS General Assembly	1972–83	various	various
4–9 Special OAS General Assembly	1977–82	Washington	various

4. US government doctrines on inter-American affairs

date	name	content
1823	Monroe Doctrine	No transfer of former Spanish territories; America for the Americans; no interference by European powers in the hemisphere; opposition to foreign political ideologies
1845	Polk Corollary	No transfer of independent territories; affirmation of US interests in Caribbean
1889	Hayes Corollary	US control over future interoceanic canal
1895	Olney Declaration	US dominance in the hemisphere
1904	Roosevelt Corollary	US as international police power
1914	Lodge Corollary	No foreign bases in the hemisphere
1928	Clark Memorandum	Revision of Roosevelt Corollary
1944	Dulles Doctrine	Reaffirmation of opposition to foreign political ideologies (communism) in the hemisphere
1962	Kennedy Doctrine	Infiltration of foreign military powers in the hemisphere a danger to US national security
1965	Johnson Corollary	No 'second Cuba' in the hemisphere

5.   Chronology of major armed US interventions in Latin America since 1853

date	country and justification
1853, Mar	Nicaragua, 'to protect American lives and interests' during political disturbances
1854, Jul	Nicaragua, to avenge 'insult' to US ambassador: destruction of San Juan del Norte
1857, Apr-May and Nov-Dec	Nicaragua, in connection with the attempt by the American filibuster William Walker's attempt to gain control of the country
1860, Sep-Oct	Colombia, in Bay of Panama, 'to protect American interests during a revolution'
1866, Nov	Mexico, 'to protect American residents'
1894, Jul-Aug	Nicaragua, 'to protect American interests in Bluefields following a revolution'
1898, Apr-Jul	Cuba, 'to secure Cuban independence' during the Spanish-Cuban-American war
1903, Mar	Honduras, 'to protect the US consulate and steamship wharf in Puerto Cortés during a period of revolutionary activity'

1903, Mar-Apr	Dominican Republic, 'to protect American interests in Santo Domingo during revolutionary outbreak'
1903, Nov-Jan 1914	Panama, 'to protect American interests and American lives following Panama's secession from Colombia'
1906, Sep-Jan 1909	Cuba, 'to restore order, protect foreigners and establish a stable government after serious revolutionary unrest'
1912, Jun-Aug	Cuba, 'to protect American interests in Oriente province and in Havana'
1912, Aug-Aug 1925	Nicaragua, 'to protect American interests during an attempted revolution' in 1912; 'to promote peace and political stability' until 1925
1913, Sep	Mexico, to evacuate US citizens from Ciaris Estero
1914, Jan-Feb and Oct	Haiti, 'to protect US citizens during serious unrest'
1914, Apr-Nov	Mexico, to uphold US rights and secure redress of grievances: occupation of Vera Cruz
1914, Jun-Jul	Dominican Republic, to protect American interests during revolutionary unrest
1915, Jul-Aug 1934	Haiti, 'to maintain order'
1916, Mar-Feb 1917	Mexico, to pursue 'bandits' during revolutionary unrest
1916, May-Sep 1924	Dominican Republic, 'to maintain order'
1917, Nov-Feb 1922	Cuba, 'to protect American interests during an insurrection'
1918, Aug-Aug 1919	Mexico, to pursue 'bandits'
1925, Oct	Panama, 'to keep order and protect American interests' during strikes and revolutionary unrest
1926, May-Jun	Nicaragua, 'to protect American interests' during a coup
1926, Aug-Jan 1933	Nicaragua, 'to protect American interests' after a coup
1954, May-Jun	Guatemala, to overthrow Arbenz government (CIA operation)
1961, Apr	Cuba, to overthrow Castro government (CIA operation)
1965, Apr-May	Dominican Republic, 'to protect American lives' and 'to prevent a communist takeover' during the attempt to restore the elected government to power
1973, Sep	Chile, to overthrow the Allende government (CIA operation)
1981, Jan-	Nicaragua, to overthrow the Sandinista government (CIA operation)
1983, Oct	Grenada, 'to protect American citizens' and 'to restore order'

Selected bibliography

Abel, Elie (1966) *The Missile Crisis*. Philadelphia.

Adams, D. K. (1967) *America in the Twentieth Century*. Cambridge.

Agee, Philip (1981) *Whitepaper, Whitewash*. Ed. Warner Poelchan. New York.

Aguilar, Alonso (1968) *Pan-Americanism: From Monroe to the Present, A View from the Other Side*. New York and London.

Ahrens, Dieter (1965) *Der karibische Raum als Interessensphäre der Vereinigten Staaten*. Stuttgart.

Alexander, Robert J. (1962) 'New Directions: The United States and Latin America'. *Current History* 42, 246 (February): 65–70.

Alperovitz, Gar (1967) *Atomic Diplomacy*. New York.

Alvarez Díaz, José R. (ed.) (1965) *A Study on Cuba: The Colonial and Republican Periods and the Socialist Experiment*. Coral Gables.

Andino, Ricardo L., Doris Mies and Roland Schmidt (1982) *Revolution in Mittelamerika*. Frankfurt.

Armstrong, Robert C. (1981) 'Reagan Policy in Crisis: Will the Empire Strike Back?' *NACLA Report on the Americas* 15, 4 (July–August): 2–36.

Aspen Institute for Humanistic Studies (1982) *Governance in the Western Hemisphere*. Ed. Viron Vaky. New York.

Bailey, Norman A. (1965) *Latin America: Politics, Economics and Hemisphere Security*. New York.

Baldwin, David A. (1966) *Foreign Aid and American Foreign Policy: A Documentary Analysis*. New York.

Behrendt, Richard F. (1948) *Inter-American Economic Relations: Problems and Prospects*. New York.

Bemis, Samuel F. (1943) *The Latin American Policy of the United States: An Historical Interpretation*. New York.

____ (1949) *John Quincy Adams and the Foundations of American Foreign Policy*. New York.

____ (1955) *The United States as a World Power: A Diplomatic History 1900–1955*. New York.

Berle, Adolf A. (1962) *Latin America: Diplomacy and Reality*. New York and Evanston.

Bermúdez, Antonio J. (1963) *The Mexican National Petroleum Industry: A Case Study in Nationalization*. Stanford.

Bernstein, Marvin D. (ed.) (1963) *Foreign Investment in Latin America: Cases and Attitudes*. New York.

Bidwell, Percy W. (1945) 'Imports in the American Economy'. *Foreign Affairs*

24, 1 (October): 85–98.

Blasier, Cole (1971) 'The Elimination of United States Influence' in Carmelo Mesa-Largo (ed.) *Revolutionary Change in Cuba* pp43–80. Pittsburgh.

Boorstein, Edward (1968) *The Economic Transformation of Cuba*. New York and London.

Brock, Lothar (1975) *Entwicklungsnationalismus und Kompradorenpolitik: Die Gründung der OAS und die Entwicklung der Abhängigkeit Lateinamerikas von den USA*. Meisenheim.

Brown, Dee (1970) *Bury My Heart at Wounded Knee: An Indian History of the American West*. New York, Toronto and London.

Buchanan, Norman S. and Lutz, Friedrich A. (1947) *Rebuilding the World Economy: America's Role in Foreign Trade and Investment*. New York.

Burr, Robert N. (1973) 'United States Latin America Policy 1945–1972' in Schlesinger (ed.) pp. xix–li.

____ (1967) *Our Troubled Hemisphere: Perspectives on United States–Latin America Relations*. Washington.

Burr, Robert N. and Hussey, Roland D. (eds) (1955) *Documents on Inter-American Cooperation*. Philadelphia.

Castro, Fidel (1983) *Speeches* vol. 2. New York.

Cavalla Rojas, Antonio (1983) 'US Military Strategy in Central America: From Carter to Reagan' in Dixon and Jonas (eds) pp. 255–80.

Center for Inter-American Relations (1975) *The Americas in a Changing World*. Ed. Sol M. Linowitz. New York.

____ (1976) *The United States and Latin America: Next Steps*. Ed. Sol M. Linowitz. New York.

Chamber of Commerce of the United States (1919) *Foreign Trade*. Washington.

____ (1938) *South America's Trade*. Washington.

____ (1940) *Foreign Trade Trends in Items Affected by Trade Agreements*. Washington.

____ (1951) *The Interdependence of the Latin American and US Economies*. Washington.

Cohen-Orantes, Isaac (1971) 'The United States as a Regional Power in Central America'. *Annals of International Studies* 2: 39–48.

Commager, Henry S. (ed.) (1963) *Documents of American History*. New York.

Committee of Santa Fé (1980) *A New Inter-American Policy for the 1980s*. Santa Fé.

Connell-Smith, Gordon (1966) *The Inter-American System*. New York, Toronto and London.

Crawley, Eduardo (1984) *Nicaragua in Perspective*. New York.

Dangerfield, George (1952) *The Era of Good Feelings*. New York and London.

DeConde, Alexander (1951) *Herbert Hoover's Latin American Policy*. London and Stanford.

Dennis, Lawrence (1931) 'Revolution, Recognition and Intervention'. *Foreign Affairs* 9, 2 (January): 204–21.

Denny, Harold N. (1929) *Dollars for Bullets*. New York.

Dixon, Marlene and Jonas, Susanne (eds) (1983) *Revolution and Intervention in*

Central America. San Francisco.

Draper, Theodore (1962) *Castro's Revolution: Myths and Realities.* New York.

Dreier, John C. (1962) *The Organization of American States and the Hemisphere Crisis.* New York and Evanston.

Eisenhower, Dwight D. (1963) *The White House Years: Mandate for Change.* London.

Eisenhower, Milton S. (1959) *United States–Latin American Relations.* Department of State Inter-American Series 55. Washington.

Enders, Thomas O. (1981) 'Strategic Situation in Central America and the Caribbean'. *Current Policy* 352 (14 December).

Etzioni, Minerva (1970) *The Majority of One.* Beverly Hills.

Fabian, Horst (1981) *Der kubanische Entwicklungsweg: Ein Beitrag zum Konzept autozentrierter Entwicklung.* Opladen.

Fenwick, Charles G. (1963) *The Organization of American States: The Inter-American Regional System.* Washington.

Fishel, Murray I. (1963) *United States Military Assistance to Latin America 1951–1960.* Unpublished manuscript. Denver.

Foner, Philip S. (1972) *The Spanish–Cuban–American War and the Birth of American Imperialism.* New York and London.

Francis, Michael I. (1977) 'United States Policy Toward Latin America: An Immoderate Proposal'. *Orbis* 20, 4 (Winter): 991–1006.

Furtak, Robert F. (1967) *Kuba und der Welkommunismus.* Köln.

Galeano, Eduardo (1973) *Open Veins of Latin America.* Translated Cedric Belfrage. New York and London.

Gannon, Francis X. (1982) 'Globalism Versus Regionalism: US Policy and the OAS'. *Orbis* 26, 1 (Spring): 195–221.

Gantenbein, James W. (ed.) (1950) *The Evolution of Our Latin American Policy: A Documentary Record.* New York.

Gellman, Irwin F. (1979) *Good Neighbor Diplomacy: United States Policies in Latin America 1933–1945.* Baltimore and London.

Gerassi, John (1963) *The Great Fear: The Reconquest of Latin America by Latin Americans.* New York and London.

Gilhodes, Pierre (1980) 'Les relations entre les États-Unis et l'Amérique Latine 1960–1980'. *Relations Internationales* 23 (Autumn): 223–49.

Goldenberg, Boris (1965) *The Cuban Revolution and Latin America.* London.

Grabendorff, Wolfgang (1973) 'Aussenpolitische Emanzipation Lateinamerikas' in Wolfgang Grabendorff (ed.) *Lateinamerika: Kontinent in der Krise* pp. 340–78. Hamburg.

Green, David (1971) *The Containment of Latin America: A History of the Myths and Realities of the Good Neighbor Policy.* Chicago.

Guerra, Ramiro (1975) *La expansión territorial de los Estados Unidos a expensa de España y los países hispanoamericanos.* La Habana.

Guerra, Sergio and Prieto, Alberto (1978) *Estados Unidos contra América Latina: dos siglos de agresiones.* La Habana.

Healy, David F. (1963) *The United States in Cuba 1898–1902.* Madison.

Horowitz, David (1965) *The Free World Colossus. A Critique of American*

Foreign Policy in the Cold War. New York.

Horowitz, David (ed.) (1969) *Corporations and the Cold War*. New York.

Horowitz, Irving L. (1975) 'United States Policies and Latin American Realities: Neighborliness, Partnership and Paternalism'. *Latin American International Affairs Series* 1: 39–56.

Hoyt, Edwin C. (1966) 'Law and Politics in the Revision of Treaties ... Affecting the Panama Canal'. *Virginia Journal of International Law* 6, 2 (April): 289–310.

Huberman, Leo and Sweezy, Paul M. (1961) *Cuba: Anatomy of a Revolution*. New York.

Hull, Cordell (1934) *International Trade and Domestic Prosperity*. US Department of State Commercial Policy Series 33. Washington.

_____ (1949) *Memoirs*. New York.

Hutchinson, Lincoln (1906a) *Report on Trade Conditions in Argentina, Paraguay and Uruguay*. US Department of Commerce and Labor Special Agent Series 8. Washington.

_____ (1906b) *Report on Trade Conditions in Central America and on the West Coast of South America*. US Department of Commerce and Labor Special Agent Series 9. Washington.

Inman, Samuel G. (1957) 'The Rise and Fall of the Good Neighbor Policy'. *Current History* 32, 188 (April): 193–9.

_____ (1965) *Inter-American Conferences 1826–1954: History and Problems*. Washington.

Jonas, Susanne (1983a) 'An Overview: 50 Years of Revolution and Intervention in Central America' in Dixon and Jonas (eds) pp. 3–24.

_____ (1983b) 'The New Cold War and the Nicaraguan Revolution' in Dixon and Jonas (eds) pp. 219–36.

Katz, Friedrich (1981) *The Secret War in Mexico*. Chicago and London.

Kennan, George F. (1967) *Memoirs*. Boston.

Kennan, George F. ('X') (1947) 'Sources of Soviet Conduct'. *Foreign Affairs* 25, 4 (July): 566–82.

Kessler, Francis P. (1977) 'Kissinger's Legacy'. *Current History* 72, 424 (February): 76–88.

Kindleberger, Charles P. (1973) *The World in Depression 1929–1939*. London.

Kirk, John M. (1983) *José Martí: Mentor of the Cuban Nation*. Tampa.

Kissinger, Henry A. (1982) *Years of Upheaval*. Washington.

Kollmann, Eric C. (1963) 'Imperialismus und Anti-Imperialismus in der politischen Tradition Amerikas'. *Historische Zeitschrift* 196, 2 (April): 343–62.

Krakau, Knud (1967) *Missionsbewusstsein und Völkerrechtsdoktrin in den Vereinigten Staaten von Amerika*. Frankfurt.

_____ (1968) *Die kubanische Revolution und die Monroe-Doktrin: Eine Herausforderung der Aussenpolitik der Vereinigten Staaten*. Frankfurt and Berlin.

Krehm, William (1984) *Democracy and Tyrannies of the Caribbean*. Westport.

Kretzschmar, Winfried W. (1964) *Auslandshilfe als Mittel der Aussenwirtschafts und Aussenpolitik: Eine Studie über die amerikanische Auslandshilfe von 1945 bis 1956*. München.

Krippendorff, Ekkehart (1970) *Die amerikanische Strategie: Entscheidungsprozess und Instrumentarium der amerikanischen Aussenpolitik.* Frankfurt.

Küntzel, Ulrich (1968) *Der Dollar-Imperialismus.* Neuwied and Berlin.

____ (1974) *Der nordamerikanische Imperialismus: Zur Geschichte der US–Kapitalausfuhr.* Darmstadt and Neuwied.

LaFeber, Walter (1963) *The New Empire: An Interpretation of American Expansionism 1860–1898.* Ithaca.

____ (1978) *The Panama Canal: The Crisis in Historical Perspective.* New York.

____ (1983) *Inevitable Revolutions: The United States in Central America.* New York and London.

Langley, Lester D. (1968) *The Cuban Policy of the United States: A Brief History.* New York, London and Sydney.

Lawrezki, Josef (1981) *Simón Bolívar: Rebell gegen die spanische Krone, Befreier Südamerikas.* Köln.

Lechner, Norbert (1970) 'Sozialwissentschaftliches Krisenmanagement in Lateinamerika' in Danckwerts, Dankwart (ed.) *Die Sozialwissenschaften in der Strategie der Entwicklungspolitik* pp. 111–57. Frankfurt.

LeRiverend B., Julio (1967) *Economic History of Cuba.* Translated María Juana Cazabón and Homero León. Havana.

Lerner, Max (1958) *American Civilization.* London.

Levin, Aida Luisa (1974) *The OAS and the United Nations: Relations in the Peace and Security Field.* New York.

Lieuwen, Edwin (1961) *Arms and Politics in Latin America.* New York.

____ (1965) *US Policy in Latin America: A Short History.* New York, Washington and London.

Lipson, Charles H. (1976) 'Corporate Preferences and Public Policies: Foreign Aid Sanctions and Investment Protection'. *World Politics* 28, 3 (April): 296–421.

Lowenthal, Abraham F. (1969/70) 'The Dominican Intervention in Retrospect'. *Public Policy* 18 (Fall): 133–48.

____ (1978) 'Latin America: A Not-So-Special Relationship'. Foreign Policy 32 (Fall): 107–26.

Magdoff, Harry (1969) *The Age of Imperialism: The Economics of US Foreign Policy.* New York and London.

Manger, William (1961) *Pan America in Crisis: The Future of the OAS.* Washington.

Martí, José (1975) *Inside the Monster: Writings on the United States and American Imperialism.* Ed. Philip S. Foner. New York and London.

Mason, Daniel (1970) 'US Imperialism and Latin America: The Rockefeller Report'. *Political Affairs* 49, 7 (July): 2–14.

May, Ernest R. (1963) 'The Alliance for Progress in Historical Perspective'. *Foreign Affairs* 41, 4 (July): 757–74.

McEoin, Gary (1962) *Latin America: The Eleventh Hour.* New York.

Meek, George (1975) 'US Influence in the Organization of American States'. *Journal of Inter-American Studies and World Affairs* 17, 3 (August): 311–25.

Meneses, Enrique (1968) *Fidel Castro.* Translated J. Halcro Ferguson. London.

Merk, Frederick (1966) *The Monroe Doctrine and American Expansionism*. New York.

Merle, Robert (1965) *Moncada: Premier combat de Fidel Castro*. Paris.

Mesa-Lago, Carmelo (ed.) (1971) *Revolutionary Change in Cuba*. Pittsburgh.

Meyer, Lorenzo (1968) *México y Estados Unidos en el conflicto petrolero 1917–1942*. México.

Mikesell, Raymond F. (ed.) (1962) *US Private and Government Investment Abroad*. Eugene.

Miner, Dwight C. *The Fight for the Panama Route: The Story of the Spooner Act and the Hay–Herrán Treaty*. New York.

Molineu, Harold (1973) 'The Concept of the Caribbean in the Latin America Policy of the United States'. *Journal of Inter-American Studies and World Affairs* 15, 3 (August): 285–307.

Morales, Minerva (1963/4) 'Política económica de los Estados Unidos en la América Latina'. *Foro Internacional* 4, 13–16: 397–428.

Morris, Richard B. (ed.) (1976) *Encyclopedia of American History*. New York.

Morse, F. Bradford and Atkeson, Timothy B. (1967) 'United States Private Investment under the Alliance for Progress'. *Boston University Law Review*: 143–80.

Munro, Dana G. (1964) *Intervention and Dollar Diplomacy in the Caribbean 1900–1921*. Princeton.

National Planning Association (1939) *War and Our Latin American Trade Policy*. Planning Pamphlets 2. Washington.

Nearing, Scott S. and Freeman, Joseph (1925) *Dollar Diplomacy: A Study in American Imperialism*. New York.

Nelson, Lowry (1972) *Cuba: The Measure of a Revolution*. Minneapolis.

Niess, Frank (1972) 'Das Bild der kubanischen Revolution in der bürgerlichen Geschichts- und Sozialwissenschaft'. *Das Argument* 75, pp. 184–213.

____ (1978) 'Die Kontinuität der US–Aussenpolitik im 20. Jahrhundert: Praxis des Weltmarkts und One-World-Theorie'. *Gulliver: Deutsch–Englische Jahrbücher* 3: 44–58.

____ (1984) 'Zwischen kaltem und heissem Krieg in Mittelamerika: Reagan's Karibik-Politik'. *Blätter für deutsche und internationale Politik* 29, 5: 587–600.

Nixon, Richard M. (1969) *Action for Progress for the Americas*. US Department of State Inter-American Series 97. Washington.

North American Congress on Latin America (1970) *Subliminal Warfare*. New York.

____ (1971) *Yanqui Dollar: The Contribution of US Private Investment to Underdevelopment in Latin America*. New York and Berkeley.

____ (1973) 'US Strategies for Central America'. *Latin America Report* 7, 5 (May–Jun).

Notter, Harley (1937) *The Origins of the Foreign Policy of Woodrow Wilson*. Baltimore.

Omang, Joanne(1985) 'A Historical Background to the CIA's Nicaragua Manual' in Omang, Joanne and Neier, Aryeh (eds) *Psychological Operations in Guerrilla Warfare*. New York.

Organization of American States (1982) *The OAS and the Evolution of the Inter-American System*. Washington.

Payer, Cheryl (1974) *The Debt Trap: The International Monetary Fund and the Third World*. New York and London.

Pearce, Jenny (1981) *Under the Eagle: US Intervention in Central America and the Caribbean*. London.

Pepper, Charles M. (1906) *Report on Trade Conditions in Cuba*. US Department of Commerce and Labor Special Agent Series 6 and US Congress, 59th Congress, 1st session Senate Document 439. Washington.

Perkins, Dexter (1933) *The Monroe Doctrine 1867–1907*. Baltimore.

___ (1941) *A History of the Monroe Doctrine*. Boston and Toronto.

Petras, James F. and Morley, Morris H. (1975) *The United States and Chile: Imperialism and the Overthrow of the Allende Government*. New York and London.

___ (1983) 'Economic Expansion, Political Crisis and US Policy in Central America' in Dixon and Jonas (eds) pp. 189–218.

Pollock, David H. (1978) 'La actidud de los Estados Unidos hacia la CEPAL: Algunos cambios durante los últimos 30 años'. *Revista de la CEPAL* 2: 59–86.

Quintanilla, Luis (1970) 'From the Worst to the Best' in Ronning, C. Neale *Intervention in Latin America* pp. 63–9. New York.

Ratliff, William (1980) 'United States Policy Toward the Caribbean'. *Willamette Law Review* 17, 1 (Spring): 221–30.

The Report of the President's National Bipartisan Commission on Central America ('Kissinger Report') (1984) New York.

Robinson, William I. and Norsworthy, Kent (1987) *David and Goliath: Washington's War Against Nicaragua*. London.

Rockefeller, Nelson A. (1969) *The Rockefeller Report on the Americas*. Chicago.

Rosset, Peter and Vandermeer, John (eds) (1983) *The Nicaragua Reader: Documents of a Revolution under Fire*. New York.

Rubottom, Roy Richard (1960) *International Communism in Latin America*. Department of State Inter-American Series 60. Washington.

Sayre, Francis B. (1936) *Reciprocal Trade Agreements*. US Department of State Commercial Policy Series 28. Washington.

___ (1937) *The 'Good Neighbor' Policy and Trade Agreements*. US Department of State Commercial Policy Series 34. Washington.

___ (1939a) *Five Years of the Trade Agreements*. US Department of State Commercial Policy Series 59. Washington.

___ (1939b) *The Dependence of Domestic Markets upon Foreign Trade*. US Department of State Commercial Policy Series 61. Washington.

Schlesinger, Arthur M. (1965) *A Thousand Days: John F. Kennedy in the White House*. Boston.

Schlesinger, Arthur M. (ed.) (1973) *The Dynamics of World Power. A Documentary History of United States Foreign Policy 1945–1973*, vol. 3 (Latin America). New York.

Schlesinger, Stephen C. and Kinzer, Stephen ((1982) *Bitter Fruit: The Untold Story of the American Coup in Guatemala*. Garden City.

Schmitt, Karl M. (1974) *Mexico and the United States 1921–1973: Conflict and Coexistence*. New York.

Schneider, Ronald M. (1959) *Communism in Guatemala 1944–1954*. New York.

_____ (1965) 'The US in Latin America'. *Current History* 48, 281 (January): 1–18.

Schnelle, Kurt (1981) *José Martí: Apostel des freien Amerika*. Köln.

Schubert, Alex (1978) *Panama: Geschichte eines Landes und eines Kanals*. Berlin.

Scroggs, William O. (1932) 'The American Investment in Latin America'. *Foreign Affairs* 10 (April): 502–4.

Siegel, Lenny (1974) 'AFL–CIA'. *Pacific Research and World Empire Telegram* pp 5–14 (November–December).

Silva Herzog, Jesús (1962) *Hispanoamérica en lucha por su independencia*. México.

_____ (1971) *La Revolución Mexicana*. México.

Slater, Jerome (1967) *The OAS and United States Foreign Policy*. Columbus.

Smith, Robert F. (1962) *The United States and Cuba: Business and Diplomacy 1917–1960*. New York.

_____ (1963) *What Happened in Cuba?: A Documentary History*. New York.

Sprout, Harold and Margaret (1944) *The Rise of American Naval Power 1776–1918*. Princeton.

Stark, Harry (1961) *Social and Economic Frontiers in Latin America*. Dubuque.

Stephansky, Ben S. (1975) '"New Dialogue" on Latin America: The Cost of Policy Neglect'. *Latin American International Affairs Series* 1: 153–66.

Stimson, Henry L. and Bundy, McGeorge (1947) *On Active Service in Peace and War*. New York.

Strong, Josiah *Our Country*. Cambridge, Mass. Reprinted 1963.

Tannenbaum, Frank (1961) 'The United States and Latin America: The Sins of the Fathers'. *Political Science Quarterly* 76, 2 (June): 161–80.

_____ (1966) *Ten Keys to Latin America*. New York.

Taylor, Philip B. (1956) 'The Guatemalan Affair: A Critique of United States Foreign Policy'. *American Political Science Review* 50, 3 (September): 787–806.

Trask, David F. (1981) *The War with Spain in 1898*. New York and London.

Truman, Harry S. (1955) *Memoirs*. New York.

Tulchin, Joseph S. (1966) 'Latin America: Focus for US Aid'. *Current History* 51, 299 (July): 28–34.

US Congress (1804) *Debates in the House of Representatives on the Bills for ... the Louisiana Treaty*. 8th Congress, 1st session. Philadelphia.

_____ (1837) *Boundary United States and Mexico*. 25th Congress, 1st session, House of Representatives Executive Document 42. Washington.

_____ (1852) *Island of Cuba*. 32nd Congress, 1st session, House of Representatives Executive Document 121. Washington.

_____ (1859) *Acquisition of Cuba* ('Slidell Report'). 35th Congress, 2nd session, Senate Report 351. Washington.

_____ (1886) *Report of the Commission [on trade with Latin America]*. 48th Congress, 2nd session, House of Representatives Executive Document 226. Washington.

____ (1890) *International American Conference: Reports of Committees and Discussions Thereon*. 51st Congress, 1st session, Senate Executive Document 232. Washington.

____ (1906) *Address by Elihu Root before the Trans-Mississippi Commercial Congress*. 59th Congress, 2nd session, Senate Document 211. Washington.

____ (1909) *Papers on Free Trade in Cuba*. 61st Congress, 1st session, Senate Document 17. Washington.

____ (1914) *Addresses Before the Southern Commercial Congress*. 63rd Congress, 2nd session, Senate Document 440. Washington.

____ (1915) *Latin American Trade*. 63rd Congress, 3rd session, Senate Document 714. Washington.

____ (1928a) *Operation of the Naval Service in Nicaragua*. 70th Congress, 1st session, Senate Document 86. Washington.

____ (1928b) *Use of the United States Navy in Nicaragua*. 70th Congress, 1st session, Hearings before Senate Committee on Foreign Relations. Washington.

____ (1929) *Policies of United States in Haiti*. 71st Congress, 2nd session, House of Representatives Document Report 52. Washington.

____ (1931) *United States Marines in Nicaragua*. 71st Congress, 3rd session, Senate Document 288. Washington.

____ (1943) *Extension of Reciprocal Trade Agreement Act*. 78th Congress, 1st session, Hearings before House of Representatives Committee on Ways and Means. Washington.

____ (1950) *A Decade of American Foreign Policy 1941–1949*. 81st Congress, 1st session, Senate Document 123. Washington.

____ (1951) *Report on Mutual Security Program*. 82nd Congress, 1st session, House Report 872. Washington.

____ (1959) *Report on United States Relations with Latin America* ('Selden Report'). 86th Congress, 1st session, House of Representatives Report 354. Washington.

____ (1960) *United States–Latin American Relations: US and Latin American Policies Affecting their Economic Relations*. 86th Congress, 1st session, Committee Print. Washington.

____ (1962a) *Latin America and United States Policy* ('Mansfield Report'). 87th Congress, 2nd session, Senate Document 82. Washington.

____ (1962b) *Special Report on Latin America* ('McClellan Report'). 87th Congress, 2nd session, Senate Document 80. Washington.

____ (1962c) *Study Mission to South America* ('McGee Report'). 87th Congress, 2nd session, Senate Document 91. Washington.

____ (1969) *Inaugural Addresses of the Presidents*. 91st Congress, 1st session, House of Representatives Document 142. Washington.

____ (1970) *United States Foreign Policy for the 1970s*. 91st Congress, 2nd session, House of Representatives Document 258. Washington.

____ (1976) *Final Report of the Select Committee to Study Governmental Operations with Respect to Intelligence Activity ('Church Report')*. 94th Congress, 2nd session, Senate Report 755. Washington.

___ (1977) *Background Documents Relating to the Panama Canal*. 95th Congress, 1st session, Committee Print. Washington.
US Department of State (1928) *A Brief History of Relations between the United States and Nicaragua 1909–1928*. Washington.
___ (1930) *Report of the President's Commission [on Haiti]*. Latin American Series 2. Washington.
___ (1943) *The Reciprocal Trade Agreement Program in War and Peace*. Commercial Policy Series 73. Washington.
___ (1946) *Building a New World Economy*. Commercial Policy Series 94. Washington.
___ (1954) *Our Southern Partners*. Inter-American Series 49. Washington.
___ (1961) *Cuba*. Inter-American Series 66. Washington.
Van Alstyne, Richard W. (1960) *The Rising American Empire*. Oxford.
Varga, Eugen (1947) 'Anglo-American Rivalry and Partnership: A Marxist View'. *Foreign Affairs* 25, 4 (July): 583–95.
Wehler, Hans-Ulrich (1971) 'Der amerikanische Imperialismus vor 1914' in Mommsen, Wolfgang J. (ed.) *Der moderne Imperialismus* pp. 172–92. Stuttgart.
___ (1974) *Der Aufstieg des amerikanischen Imperialismus: Studien zur Entwicklung des Imperium Americanum*. Göttingen.
Welles, Sumner (1934) *The Trade Agreements Program*. US Department of State Commercial Policy Series 2. Washington.
___ (1935a) *Inter-American Relations*. US Department of State Latin American Series 8. Washington.
___ (1935b) *Pan American Cooperation*. US Department of State Latin American Series 10. Washington.
___ (1935c) *Two Years of the 'Good Neighbor' Policy*. US Department of State Latin American Series 11. Washington.
___ (1941) *Post-War Commercial Policy*. US Department of State Commercial Policy Series 71. Washington.
___ (1944) *The Time for Decision*. New York and London.
Whitaker, Arthur P. (1954) *The Western Hemisphere Idea: Its Rise and Decline*. Ithaca.
Williams, Edward J. (1978) 'Oil in Mexican–US Relations: Analysis and Bargaining Scenario'. *Orbis* 22: 201–16.
Williams, William A. (1955) 'The Frontier and American Foreign Policy'. *Pacific Historical Review* 24, 4 (November): 379–95.
___ (1959) *The Tragedy of American Diplomacy*. New York and London.
___ (1969) 'The Large Corporations and American Foreign Policy' in Horowitz (ed.) pp. 71–104.
Wise, David and Ross, Thomas B. (1964) *The Invisible Government*. New York.
Wood, Bryce (1961) *The Making of the Good Neighbor Policy*. New York and London.
Wythe, George (1964) *The United States and Inter-American Relations: A Contemporary Appraisal*. Gainesville.
Zorrilla, Luis G. (1977) *Historia de las relaciones entre México y los Estados Unidos 1800–1954*. México.

Index